# Capabilities, Innovation and Economic Growth

The question of whether we can foster growth and innovation while promoting individual freedoms poses a challenge for everyone studying and working on innovation and development policies. Whilst innovation literature is largely dominated by a focus on efficiency, development literature tends to focus on equality and pays less attention to mechanisms fostering economic and social change. This book aims to move beyond these barriers and to identify development policies that foster both efficiency *and* equality, exploring the connection between innovation policies and the improvement of individual freedoms.

*Capabilities, Innovation and Economic Growth* argues that we can answer these questions by focusing on the relation between Amartya Sen's human development approach and the Neo-Schumpeterian analysis of innovation systems. After considering the connections between the two schools of thought and the way they enrich each other's perspectives, chapters go on to show how policy can support virtuous circles in which innovation, human development and economic growth interact and mutually reinforce each other. This is undertaken through the descriptive analysis and the empirical testing of a sample of nations and European regions. The volume concludes with an exploration of the contribution that the capabilities approach can give to the design of innovation policy, and with the analysis of macroeconomic policies favorable to innovation and human development.

This will be essential reading for: students and academic economists interested in development, growth and innovation; policy makers and officers in charge of defining development and innovation plans at national and regional level; and consultants and managers in development agencies implementing innovation and development projects.

**Michele Capriati** is professor of economic policy at the University of Bari, Italy.

# Routledge Studies in Development Economics

For a complete list of titles in this series, please visit www.routledge.com/series/ SE0266

# Capabilities, Innovation and Economic Growth

## Policymaking for Freedom and Efficiency

**Michele Capriati**
Translated by Helen Bekele Lemma

LONDON AND NEW YORK

First published 2018 by Routledge

2 Park Square, Milton Park, Abingdon, Oxfordshire OX14 4RN

52 Vanderbilt Avenue, New York, NY 10017

*Routledge is an imprint of the Taylor & Francis Group, an informa business*

First issued in paperback 2019

*British Library Cataloguing-in-Publication Data*
A catalogue record for this book is available from the British Library

*Library of Congress Cataloging-in-Publication Data*
A catalog record for this book has been requested

ISBN: 978-1-138-85781-0 (hbk)
ISBN: 978-0-367-87243-4 (pbk)

Typeset in Bembo
by Apex CoVantage, LLC

To Giulio and Marinella

# Contents

# Figures

# Tables

# Maps

# 1 Introduction

## Capabilities, innovation and economic growth

This book is born out of a doubt and a dissatisfaction. The doubt comes from the existing interpretations of the efficiency/equity nexus. The prevailing opinions consider these two goals in terms of trade-off and prioritise efficiency over equity. Many believe that a better distribution of resources and opportunities among people may reduce efficiency. At the same time, many advocate that a concerted focus on efficiency will bring about the necessary resources for equity. What if the opposite were true? I suspect (along with many other authors, as we shall see) that this isn't a one-way relationship and that efficiency can also benefit from equity.

My dissatisfaction arises from having seen, in recent decades, governments (advised by economists) operate following the previous idea that puts efficiency at the top of the political and economic agenda. For many years, the issue of equity was not part of the vocabulary and concrete actions of those who govern and those who provide ideas to govern. This long epoch has led many economies to deepen inequalities among their citizens and at the same time, appears to have been unable to make the best use of all available resources. In fact, many economies are struggling to find a path to long-lasting and sustainable growth. Many resources are used for financial speculation, unnecessary expenditure and consumption, while only a few are directed to productive activities and collective needs. The choice to ignore a fair distribution of the opportunities to live a life worth living seems to have led many countries on the path of a slow decline, and the global economy towards a state of perpetual instability and uncertainty.

This doubt and dissatisfaction led me to investigate the interconnections between two major schools of economic thought: the innovation economy and the capability approach.

These two schools of thought follow different intellectual and practical paths. The first focused mainly on the operation of the most advanced economies, the second, since its inception, on developing countries. Both nevertheless have a common starting point, i.e., the dissatisfaction with the neo-classical paradigm and with the idea that, as noted by Hirschman (1981), there is only one economy (just as there is one physics) and that in a market economy the benefits are proportionally distributed among all the participants in the economic activities as per their contribution.

The overall guiding objectives of the two approaches, however, are different. The capability approach has as its objective the expansion of the achievements and freedoms of individuals, and therefore, the ensuing normative apparatus has *equity* at its core; the studies on innovation, on the other hand, have focused on increasing the *efficiency* of companies and of the whole economy. However, it is precisely because of this complementarity, as we shall see, that the two approaches have a strong potential for integration. Thus, comparing these two schools of economic thought on the common grounds of growth and development strategies seemed to me a way of satisfying my curiosity and ease my discomfort.

This book can be seen as an attempt to respond to the following questions.

1   Can the process of innovation benefit from a more general expansion of the capabilities of individuals?
2   Can the process of innovation contribute to human development?
3   How are processes of innovation, expansion of human development and economic growth linked together?
4   Is there any empirical evidence at the national and regional levels that confirms the importance of these interrelations?
5   How can innovation policies be redirected to benefit capabilities?
6   How can macroeconomic and welfare policies be redirected to benefit capabilities and innovation?

The book is divided into three parts. In the first (Chapters 2 and 3), I attempt to answer the first two questions and explore the ideas and concepts related to the two schools of thought that this book focuses on: innovation and human development. In the second (Chapters 4, 5, 6), I attempt to answer the next two questions, analysing data from two data sets, a national and a regional one. In the third (Chapters 7, 8, 9), I address the subject of policies in order to answer the last two questions. Here is a more detailed overview of the book chapters.

In Chapter 2, I summarise the core concepts developed by the literature on innovation systems and the main characteristics of the capability approach. Given the vastness of these two strands of the economic literature, I focus on concepts that I consider important for my analysis and useful for my 'toolbox'.

In Chapter 3, I build on the ideas introduced in the previous chapter with the aim of identifying similarities and links between innovation and capabilities. The chapter addresses issues that affect technologies and inclusive innovation, learning and human capabilities, inequality, social capital, democracy and social security. In my view, these issues constitute an interesting ground for an integrated approach. The chapter ends with a graph illustrating the interconnection between the three dimensions of innovation, human development and economic growth, as an attempt to summarise the discussion.

Chapter 4 focuses on the main analyses and models that examined the relationships between innovation and growth, growth and human development, and innovation and human development. While the literature is particularly exhaustive on the first of the three relationships, it is less so on the other two.

Early empirical evidence confirms the links between these processes. In particular, within the relationship between economic growth and human development, it is important to distinguish short-term links, which appear to be weak, from the long-term links, which instead seem to be more significant.

In Chapters 5 and 6, I try to collect empirical evidence around these three relationships through an analysis based on two datasets, a national and a regional one. In Chapter 5, I focus on growth, human development and innovation indicators trying to verify whether there are any regularities in their respective levels and variations, and whether it is possible to identify groups of countries/regions with similar behaviour. In Chapter 6, the focus shifts to the links between the three dimensions mentioned above, exploring the degree of correlation and interdependence between them. In particular, the tests aim at verifying the existence of simultaneous relationships between innovation, growth and human development, both at the level of nations and region. Within the regional analysis, I take into consideration the role of geographical proximity.

The last part of the book is devoted to policies. In Chapter 7, I address the basic ideas that justify current public decision making, highlighting how the concepts of market and system failures are not sufficient to motivate innovation policies. Innovation policies assume economic growth as an implicit objective and tend to ignore the ethical dimension of the public choices in this field.

In Chapter 8, I propose a different approach to the formulation of innovation policies that takes into account people's freedoms and capabilities. I will focus, in particular, on how a more inclusive and democratic approach can direct policy instruments for innovation at the level of individual projects and large mission-oriented programmes, and for the evaluation and forecasting of long-term impacts of technologies.

Chapter 9 focuses on macroeconomic issues. I begin by discussing the centrality of employment in the three processes of innovation, growth and human development. I then address the policies of cycle stabilisation and their importance for employment and innovation processes. The final part of the chapter is devoted to expenditure policies that, I believe, are consistent with the expansion of individuals' freedom, and to some proposals encouraging greater equity in tax collection.

Chapter 10 draws the final conclusions.

In his latest book, Atkinson (2015) observes 'When President George W. Bush announced in 2006 the American Competitiveness Initiative, doubling US spending on innovation-enabling research, the policy paper stated that "research pays off our economy". But did any journalist ask him "for-whom?"' (p. 120). And to this question, we may add, "For what?"

Questions like these would help people to form a more complete opinion on their rulers' political choices. And this may prompt the rulers to pay more attention to the views of citizens. But usually this does not happen. Why? Because, probably, it is believed that research, technology and innovation have a life and an autonomy of their own, that they belong to a system difficult to understand by the 'non-experts'. Yet, much of innovation and change observed in our lives over the last decades depended on the resources the state invested in research

(Mazzucato, 2013) and thus, on public money. It is therefore completely legitimate to hope that a higher and more widespread awareness is achieved, allowing every citizen to ask with persistence and conviction these two simple and insidious questions, "For whom?" and "For what?"

This work is essentially an exploration of ideas, issues, data and proposals. As such, it is exposed to some risk of inaccuracy and incompleteness. The fuzziness finds a partial justification in an observation made by Sen, that 'it is better to be vaguely right than precisely wrong'. Obviously I hope that, despite its vagueness, the proposed reasoning has some elements of good sense. It is up to the reader to establish it. The incompleteness has its justification in the vastness of the addressed topics that can only be discussed by making some choices, which always leads to some simplifications.

To reduce these risks, some colleagues and friends lent their hand by critically reading preliminary parts of the work. Special thanks are extended to Franco Botta, for his insightful contribution of ideas, to Marialuisa Divella, who helped me in the preparation of the empirical part of the book, and to Marinella Capriati and Lloyd Chapman, for their careful revision of the text. Suggestions also came from Nicola Coniglio, Francesco Prota, Marco Sanfilippo, Gianfranco Viesti and other researchers who participated in internal seminars at the Department of Political Science of the University of Bari, where some chapters of this book were presented. Preliminary works on some issues addressed in this book were presented at the XXX Italian Conference of Regional Science (Florence, 2009), at the Human Development and Capability Association Conference (The Hague, 2011), the European Association for Evolutionary Political Economy Conference (Vienna, 2011), the Geography of Innovation Conference (Utrecht University, 2014). I want to thank the discussants and the participants at the presentation sessions for their useful suggestions. Naturally, the inaccuracies and mistakes that could still be present in the book are to be attributed entirely to me.

## References

Atkinson, A.B. 2015. *Inequality: What Can Be Done?* Cambridge MA; London, UK, Harvard University Press.

Hirschman, A.O. 1981. *Essays in Trespassing: Economics to Politics and Beyond*, Cambridge, Cambridge University Press.

Mazzucato, M. 2013. *The Entrepreneurial State: Debunking the Public vs. Private Myth in Risk and Innovation*, London, Anthem.

# Part 1

# Ideas

# 2 The toolbox

In concluding her book "The Economics of Imperfect Competition", Joan Robinson (1969) apologised to her readers for the excessive abstractness of the discussion, hoping that *the economist, who is prepared to work stage by stage towards the still far-distant ideal of constructing an analysis which will be capable of solving the problems presented by the real world, may perhaps find in this tool-box some implements which will serve his turn*" (p. 327).

I find it very inspiring to think of the work of each economist as a tool-box from which we may draw in order to further knowledge and tackle real-world problems. This allows us to conceive of economic science as a constantly evolving collective effort to which scholars contribute by recombining existing insights as well as by adding something new.

In this chapter I focus on some of the concepts and ideas presented in the innovation literature and the human development literature. To continue with Robinson's metaphor, I will take out from each of the two boxes only the instruments that are most helpful for my purpose. I present these tools in this chapter. These concepts will be then further explored in Chapter 3, with the aim of highlighting the relations between these two literatures.

## 2.1 Innovation, growth and development

### a. Innovation and structural change

Innovation is the introduction of new activities related to the production and exchange of products and processes. It is relevant to all human activity, at all stages of development. Interpreted this way, it is not only restricted to the business of highly advanced economies but also constitutes the driving force behind the growth of less-developed countries (Fagerberg and Godinho, 2005).

The concept of innovation is understood by some authors in a very narrow sense, namely as "*new to the world*" innovations (Furman et al., 2002; Furman and Hayes, 2004), which restricts the boundaries of the innovation phenomenon to "*a first world activity*" (Fagerberg et al., 2010a, 2010b).[1] It follows that this approach disregards innovations that may represent a change for the market in which they have been launched or for the individual firm by which they have been introduced or adopted, thus neglecting the notion of innovation as put forward by Schumpeter (1939). Indeed, according to the Austrian economist and political scientist, the concept of innovation should include the introduction of new products, the changes in technology to produce products already launched in the market, the opening of new markets or of new sources of supply, new forms of work organisation, or a better use of input materials, and the start-up of new commercial organisations. In sum, Schumpeter thinks of innovation as "'doing things differently' in the realm of economic life" (Schumpeter, 1939, p. 84).

The study of innovation started from analysis of the most developed countries, as scholars aimed to understand the mechanisms underlying the multiple changes experienced by these countries. In this respect, a contribution of paramount importance was made by the so-called *evolutionary framework*. This approach draws not only on Schumpeter's work, but also on the Darwinian tradition of biological change, borrowing some of its most important notions,[2] in particular the idea of *"natural selection"*, which refers to market forces determining survival and growth (Nelson and Winter, 1982; Laurent and Nightingale, 2001).

The idea of change put forward by this stream of literature emanates from a deep criticism of the *neo-classical (orthodox) model*, both for its static foundation (Schumpeter, 1936) and its inability to grasp capitalism's ever-changing nature (Nelson and Winter, 1974, 1982). The orthodox approach holds that it is possible to obtain a static general equilibrium, and it implicitly assumes perfect information, rational behaviour of economic agents, zero profits and diminishing returns. However, this contrasts with the empirical and historical evidence showing that firms operate in markets in perpetual disequilibrium, have to face widespread asymmetry of information among agents, and search for activities yielding increasing returns to scale and differential profits. In contrast with the neo-classical model, the evolutionary interpretation of economics relies on these more realistic assumptions (Nelson and Winter, 1982), puts emphasis on the ever-changing nature of markets and puts innovation at the centre of these dynamics of change.

According to Schumpeter, innovation is at the core of capitalism and affects both its capacity to expand and its tendency to incur cyclical crises.

> *Nothing can be more plain or even more trite common sense than proposition that innovation, as conceived by us, is at the center of practically all the phenomena, difficulties, and problems of economic life in capitalist society and that they, as well as the extreme sensitiveness of capitalism to disturbance, would be absent if productive resources flowed – either in unvarying or continuously increasing quantities – every year through substantially the same goals, or were prevented from doing so only by external influences.*
>
> *(Schumpeter, 1939, p. 87)*

Therefore, innovation is simultaneously a fundamental cause of discontinuity in the short run and an essential factor of growth in the long run. Increases in productivity and crises coexist in the capitalist system, and both stem from the way technologies are adopted and spread in economic and social contexts.

Increases in productivity in the long run depend on the introduction and diffusion of specific constellations of *"general purpose technologies"* (Rosenberg and Trajtenberg, 2001) or of new *"technological paradigms"* (Dosi, 1982) and wider *"techno-economic paradigms"* (Freeman and Perez, 1988; Perez, 2002) such as those which emerged since the industrial revolution in areas like steam and railways; steel, electricity and heavy engineering; oil, automobile and mass production; information and telecommunications.

Every technological revolution brings some important changes: the growth of productivity and innovation in industries where the goods typical of the new paradigm are directly embedded; a continuous flow of incremental and complementary innovations; the growth of related industries which use these innovations as inputs; and changes in infrastructure designed to favour their diffusion. In historical experience, this process has required five to six decades (Schumpeter, 1939; Perez, 2002; Reinert, 2007) during which the economy has passed through different phases: a first one characterised by the introduction and diffusion of new technologies; a second one of crisis and subsequent adjustment; a third phase of maximum deployment of the benefits of change; and a fourth one marked by a slow decline and progressive replacement by another paradigm (Perez, 2002).

In the initial period during which new technologies are introduced, economy and society go through significant, pervasive changes as new economic activities replace old ones; the opening of new markets substitutes the slowly declining previous ones; the areas in which these activities are located grow more rapidly than others; workers are required to wield new skills, thereby undermining earlier expertise accumulated over the years; new social groups gain space and break up consolidated balances; and institutions are modified in order to adapt to and direct the changes occurring in the economy as well as the society (Freeman and Perez, 1988; Perez, 2002; Reinert, 2007; Perez, 2010a).

Furthermore, these changes are characterised by disequilibria and divergences that generate a climate of excitement to which the financial sector is not alien. The financial sector plays a crucial role in pushing forward the developments described above: first, it feeds the growth of the innovative sectors, providing the necessary means for their expansion, and in doing so, deepens the disparities between successful and declining firms as well as between actors with high and low income levels (Perez, 2009). The deepening of these gaps, in turn, widens two relevant disequilibria: that between the demand and supply of new goods and services (demand does not properly follow supply due to the unequal distribution of incomes) and that between the nominal and the real value of the innovative activities. Indeed, frantic and sometimes irrational investment in highly promising sectors gives rise to speculative bubbles that can explode, dragging the economy into a recession and sometimes even into a phase of deep depression (Perez, 2009; Perez, 2010b).

The economic and social consequences of crisis increase political pressure for a more equal distribution of the benefits flowing from innovation as well as for greater market regulation. The crisis is thus followed by a turning point during which institutions play a crucial role: they have to acknowledge the profound transformations that have occurred and devise a set of rules adapted to address these transformations as well as limit their negative social and economic effects. Hence, this is the phase in which public choices may or may not bring the economy and the society out of crisis and give rise to a more equal distribution of the resources and benefits of change.

Once an adequate institutional framework is in place, the general social welfare of a society may be expanded and new persons, groups and territories included as recipients of the benefits of new technologies: "*This crucial re-composition happens at the turning point which leaves behind the turbulent times of installation and paradigm transition to enter the 'golden age' that can follow, depending on the institutional and social choices made*" (Perez, 2002, p. 43).

Seen from a historical perspective then, the changes induced by technological revolutions and related innovation processes are truly profound. They go beyond the technological dimension, touching the financial, social and institutional realms. It is thus a structural change in a broad sense, which can only roughly be measured by the generally used indicators such as per capita GDP and labour productivity. Moreover, it is only in the long run that we may fully grasp the depth of the changes in society and the modifications of lifestyle which have been driven by innovation.

### b. Innovation systems

Starting from the idea that innovation prompts change due to "*the network of institutions in the public and private sectors whose activities and interactions initiate, import and diffuse new technologies*" (Freeman, 1987, p. 1), some authors have introduced the concept of "*National Innovation Systems*" (NIS) (Freeman, 1987; Lundvall, 1992, 2007a; Nelson, 1993; Edquist, 2005; Soete et al., 2010; Lundvall et al., 2009).[3] The basic (very stylised) idea is that if the process of innovation is characterised by the interaction of many agents, only systemic analysis will allow us to grasp the way in which individual actions result in global change.

Lundvall defines the concept of NIS in the following broad sense:

> The National System of Innovation is a social system. A central activity in the system of innovation is learning, and learning is a social activity, which involves interactions between people. It is also a dynamic system, characterized both by positive feedback and by reproduction. Often, the elements of the system of innovation either reinforce each other in promoting process of learning and innovation or, conversely, combine into constellations blocking such processes. Cumulative causation, and virtuous circles, are characteristics of systems and sub-systems of innovation.
>
> (Lundvall, 1992, p. 2)

This broad concept of innovation has been criticised by some scholars for being too broad (Vertova, 2014; Hartmann, 2013; Edquist, 2005). Therefore, in order to better identify the borders of the Innovation System (IS), Lundvall (2007a) has also introduced a distinction between the "*core*" and the "*wider setting*". The "core" includes firms and their interactions with each other (networking, cooperation, and competition) as well as with knowledge institutions and organisations (universities, public research labs and R&D departments belonging to larger firms). The "wider setting" encompasses the education system, labour markets, financial markets, systems of intellectual property rights, the regulation of market competition and welfare systems. In essence, it refers to the formal institutional setting in which the "core" of the system is embedded and with which it interacts.

The concept of innovation adopted by those following the NIS approach is also characterised by greater attention given to the process of innovation rather than simply to its results. As already mentioned, Schumpeter's classic definition of innovation refers to "*any 'way of doing things differently' in the economy*" and the initial introduction of new combinations. Under the innovation systems approach, it is also important to consider the processes of diffusion and the way "novelties" are employed. Indeed, in this framework, the actual use of the new products and processes introduced, as well as the resulting interactions between producers and users are not less important than their launch in the market. Therefore, the wider approach adopted here (Lundvall, 1992) puts greater emphasis on non-formalised modes of innovation diffusion and on social and cultural aspects affecting agent behaviour.

Thus, as we have seen, scholars tend to adopt either a broad or narrow definition of innovation. In the narrow sense, they look above all at "new to the world" innovations, mostly based on STI (science, technology and innovation) activities whose intensity is generally measured by R&D investments (expenditure, staff) and number of patents, and which are mainly carried out by major institutions of public and private research. In a broader sense, however, the innovation process flows from capabilities to adapt and absorb new technologies, and therefore, refers to activities of *learning by doing*, *learning by using* and *learning by interacting* (DUI: Doing, Using and Interacting). These capabilities foster the learning of individuals, firms and markets where they have been introduced (Asheim and Parrilli, 2012); they require continuous efforts to improve the learning capacities of individuals and organisations, as well as social rules and institutions (Jensen et al., 2007; Lundvall, 2007b).[4]

The fact that these paths of innovation and growth are the result of complex relationships between individuals, institutions, business and social contexts, suggests that these interactions can develop in different ways and that each national system is the historical result of these interactions. Therefore, it must also be taken into account that various different approaches to development can be tried by each system. In other words, there is no one single path – such as the one indicated by the country leader – but numerous paths exploiting knowledge, as well as social and institutional relationships, that are country and history-specific (Freeman, 2002).

### c. Learning and innovation

Although the evolutionary approach is mainly interested in structural changes occurring within firms (the main actor), it also emphasises relationships between individual learning and innovation. Indeed, as Nelson and Winter (1982) have stated in their seminal work:

> *Although our theory is concerned with the behavior of business firms and other organizations, we find it useful to begin the analysis with a discussion of some aspects of individual behavior. An obvious reason for doing so is that the behavior of an organization is, in a limited but important sense, reducible to the behavior of the individuals who are members of that organization. Regularities of individual behavior must therefore be expected to have consequences, if not counterparts, at the organizational level.*
>
> (p. 72)

Their approach, however, looks at individuals and their capabilities in direct relation to specific operative functions and sees them as the outcome of regularities in behaviour:

> *By a 'skill' we mean a capability for a smooth sequence of coordinated behavior that is ordinarily effective relative to its objectives, given the context in which it normally occurs. Thus, the ability to serve a tennis ball well is a skill, as is the ability to engage in competent carpentry, drive a car, operate a computer, set up and solve a linear programming model, or judge which job candidate to hire.*
>
> (p. 73)

This way of thinking about the role of individuals in relation to their economic activities is closely linked to the widely used concept of *human capital* (Burton-Jones and Spender, 2011), understood as the set of individual capabilities and knowledge applied to economic activities.

While the work of Dulum et al. (1992) shares the evolutionary conception of the economy as a historically changing system, it puts emphasis not only on skills, but also on the learning and interaction processes by which they are generated. It also offers a less deterministic understanding of the relationship between individuals and economic processes than the evolutionary approach, which is based on insights from biological science. Indeed, "*it is crucially important to take into account that, in social evolution, human beings are creating and shaping own conditions in a way which has no immediate counterpart in biological evolution*" (p. 301). In particular, the authors highlight that human intelligence, notwithstanding the influence of the social context, cannot be considered to be completely dependent on external events because intelligence has the power, exercised both individually and collectively, to change the environment in which it operates.

> *Learning – both intra-cultural and cross-cultural, to which there is no counterpart in biological evolution- is the main characteristic of social and economic evolution and*

*learning can be affected by policy making and, deliberately, institutionalized in more or less efficient way.*

(Dulum et al., 1992, p. 299)

Hence, to sum up, the "broad" approach to the study of IS pays greater attention to individuals' capabilities and processes of learning and interaction, not only at the economic level, but also at social and institutional ones. This characteristic, as we shall see, makes this approach particularly suitable for direct comparison with the capability approach and to identifying development policies with a greater focus on people. By contrast, the "narrow" approach puts more emphasis on change understood as improvements in efficiency and increased competitiveness for large firms. In sharp contrast to the NIS approach, scholars working within the 'narrow' framework consider the factors that influence individual capabilities to be invariant elements specific to each cultural and political context.

### d. Proximity

Innovation cannot be fully understood without considering the central role of spatial proximity and the interaction between different agents in this process. A growing number of studies show that in an era of global competition when success increasingly depends on the ability to produce new and better products and processes, tacit knowledge (i.e., person-embodied knowledge, the diffusion of which is strongly influenced by distance and language) is the most important resource for the generation of innovation (Pavitt, 2002). This is because the widespread availability of ICTs (information and communication technologies) has rendered access to explicit/codified knowledge (in databases, blueprints, operating instructions, etc.) quite simple now. It follows that the creation of distinctive capabilities and competitive products increasingly depends on the production and use of tacit knowledge (Asheim and Gertler, 2005; Asheim and Parrilli, 2012).

Tacit knowledge is difficult to transfer over long distances because it is heavily dependent on the social and institutional context in which it is produced. Analysis that underlines the centrality of learning processes in activating change (Lundvall, 1992; Lundvall and Johnson, 1994) has shown how tacit knowledge is the result of complex social interaction. This interaction includes the flow of various types of knowledge between companies (i.e., clients, suppliers and competitors), research organisations (i.e., universities, public and private research centres) and public agencies (i.e., centres of technological transfer, development agencies, company incubators). The quality of interaction between these actors greatly (although not exclusively) depends on their ability to transfer non-codified knowledge through relationships based on proximity (Robertson et al., 2009).

Hence, the *spatial dimension* becomes highly relevant to the production and diffusion of tacit knowledge for two reasons. First, tacit knowledge cannot be exchanged beyond a certain distance, as it is shaped by meanings specific to the social and institutional context where it is generated; this dependence on the context makes it a spatially determined factor. Second, since innovation is increasingly a process based on interaction between firms, research organisations and public agencies generating knowledge through processes of *"learning by interacting"* (Lundvall, Johnson, 1994), these relationships mostly require *"face-to-face"* contacts between agents sharing the same language, principles, social and technical norms, mutual trust and professional credit. Therefore, the competences necessary for the functioning of the learning and innovation processes, as well as for the related knowledge transfer, are highly *time and space specific*.

As long as spatial proximity is decisive for the transfer and diffusion of the tacit component of knowledge, the spatial agglomeration of firms (Porter, 2000), industrial districts (Becattini et al., 2009) and regions (Cooke, 2001; Braczyk et al., 1998) remain critical dimensions for analysis of the innovation process. In other words, if an important part of learning takes place at the territorial level, "learning regions" are an important field of analysis.

The concept of *Regional Innovation Systems* (RIS) directly refers to the National Innovation Systems. We have seen that the NIS framework is directly concerned with the processes and resources necessary for initiating and maintaining an innovation process. RIS analysis is based on similar interpretations of the innovation phenomena, but pays greater attention to their territorial dimension. Within this framework, 'region' can be understood as a level of governance between the national level and the individual firm or cluster of firms. Regional governance can be in the hands of both private (individuals or associated firms, chambers of commerce and trade unions) and public actors (local governments, universities and development agencies). These actors are linked by relationships of exchange as well as by a certain degree of interdependency and share a "regional culture" based on sets of common attitudes, values, norms, routines and expectations. This regional culture, as we have seen, influences the way agents (individuals, firms and organisations) interact with each other in a given territory.

Regions and territories are home to localised capabilities and intangible assets directly linked to the cultural and social context in which firms are located. These assets change slowly, showing a high tendency towards *path dependency*. Cultural background, social relationships and past institutional contexts affect agents' current choices and the intensity of their knowledge exchanges. If a firm, a cluster or a territorial area is the first to embark upon a certain innovation path, it has the advantage of being "the first mover", but it also runs a risk of being locked into that specific route due to reliance on the established modus operandi from the specialisation of production and the underlying knowledge base. If this firm (cluster or territory) were to come across another successful innovative path, possibly embarked upon by another firm (cluster or territory), switching to this alternative route would be difficult and expensive, because of its reliance on the established modus operandi. This could trigger a possible gradual decline.

## e. Innovation, institutions and social capital

The prevailing neoclassical approach presents an idealised world of economic relationships existing in an institutional vacuum, the market of course being the one exception. In this world, rational agents interact to exchange; preferences of customers on the one hand and supply by producers on the other determine the conditions for the best possible use of resources and for the best possible conditions of public welfare. It follows that there is no need for institutions because the rational behaviour of agents makes them useless. Nevertheless, if we understand the economy as a cumulative process of knowledge and innovation rather than as a system in equilibrium fully determined in time and space, then institutions and institutional change come to play a crucial role (North, 1990, 2005).

> *Institutions are sets of habits, routines, rules, norms and laws, which regulate the relations between people and shape human interaction. By reducing uncertainty and, thus, the amount of information needed for individual and collective action, institutions are fundamental building block in all societies.*
>
> (Johnson, 1992, p. 26)

According to North (1990), institutions are the rules of the game of a society. Thus, their change affects the evolution of a society over time and is the key factor in understanding history. In particular, institutions play a critical role in decreasing uncertainty in relationships between agents by establishing regularity and a stable structure of shared rules. When certain habits and routines (Nelson and Winter, 1982) stabilise and are generally accepted by groups and communities, they create regularities of social behaviour such as norms, rules, laws and traditions. These may be *formal and explicit*, like state laws, but in many cases also *informal and implicit*, like moral norms and everyday habits. What is common to the huge variety of institutions is that they regulate social and economic behaviour and reduce uncertainty in individual and group relationships. The existence of habits and routines makes it so that every activity needs not be started up from scratch or as if it had never been carried out before. Instead, certain activities and relationships are consistently realised using existing norms, rules and habits in their specific contexts, thereby making the activities more predictable. We see, then, that institutions ensure the stability necessary for the functioning of society. This implies that there are limits to institutional change and that *inertia* is an essential feature of institutions. However, this does not mean that the latter do not change at all over time; indeed, institutions evolve with changes in practice, moral codes, laws and conventions, although their transformations are slower than those pertaining to the economy.

Other authors refer to a broader definition of institutions, which in addition to the 'rules of the game' of a society includes also non-market institutions (Cimoli et al, 2009). With this understanding, institutions define incentives and place limits while also shaping and organising individuals' behaviour. In this sense, the smooth functioning of the economic system is critically dependent on the presence of institutions performing a variety of roles: universities and public labs producing new knowledge; antitrust and intellectual property institutions regulating innovative practices through policy and legislation; business and labour associations affecting the distribution of resources; public administrations driving firms' choices through the provision of financial and fiscal incentives.

> *Far from the fury of market fundamentalism, our basic view is that non-market institutions (ranging from public agencies to professional associations, from trade union to community structures) are at the core of the very constitution of whole socio-economic fabric.*
>
> (Cimoli et al, 2009, p. 340)

Clearly, within the evolutionary framework, institutions do matter, and the market is just one of the many institutions functioning in economy and society. While it is of great importance, it is not the only one. Indeed, "*believing in 'market omnipotence' entails misleading policy conclusions: it disregards the importance of non-market institutions and, moreover, it neglects the complementarities between market and non-market mechanisms of economic performance*" (Cimoli et al., 2009, p. 339).

Of course, institutions are not the only drivers of innovation. The literature is clear that *social capital* also plays a major role in the processes of innovation. Two dominant understandings of social capital are relevant to our analysis here. The first emphasises social capital as a cultural phenomenon and refers to the civic engagement of a society's members, the existence of social norms promoting collective actions, and the level of trust in public institutions (Putnam, 1993). In this interpretation, social capital has the properties of a public good and is the basis of the functioning of democracy and of the control of institutions (see below on this). The second interpretation of social capital (Bourdieu, 1986) refers to investments in social networks carried out by individuals. Thus, social capital here is a private good which allows individuals to benefit in terms of status and "symbolic capital". In this understanding, positive economic externalities can be gained in the form of collective action facilitation.

In both interpretations, social capital facilitates changes occurring in the economic sphere and particularly in the innovation processes. Civic participation allows for more thorough control and greater supervision of institutional operations. It encourages the creation of formal rules and contributes to greater accountability on the part of the government. Participatory policy choices and more closely controlled institutions make it possible to design innovation strategies corresponding to the real needs of citizens[5] (Streeten, 2002). Interpersonal networks based on trust can facilitate economic transactions between individuals, reducing transaction costs and easing the spread of information. As argued by many scholars, networks of trust play a crucial role in the spread of knowledge and in fuelling the innovation process:

> *We will argue that the production and efficient use of intellectual capital is fundamentally depending upon social capital. In a successful learning economy rooted in social cohesion and trust, it is easier to engage in interactive and apprenticeship*

*learning resulting in the passing on of elements of tacit knowledge from individual to individual and from generation to generation. This is more difficult in a context without trust and with long distance among professions and in hierarchies. Thus, undermining trust and social capital undermines the reproduction and use of intellectual capital. A development strategy that focuses only on production capital and intellectual capital is not sustainable.*

(Lundvall et al., 2009, p. 30)

### f. Developing countries and inclusive innovations

According to the definition elaborated at the beginning of this chapter, processes of innovation are to be found in all economies, regardless of their stage of development. Nevertheless, only in recent years has there been increased attention to the link between IS and development of less industrialised countries (Lundvall et al., 2009; Fagerberg et al., 2010a, 2010b).

In developing countries, growth is rarely the outcome of an autonomous process of innovation. Rather, it is the result of financial, technological and competence transfers from more developed countries. In this respect, the availability of new technologies is a good opportunity to initiate, through their use and modification, a process of learning which may lead to innovation, diffusion and the accumulation of specific knowledge (Lundvall, 2007b). However, this depends greatly on the actual ability of these countries to build institutional, technological and educational systems able to use these technologies efficiently, modify them and produce them autonomously (Lundvall et al., 2009; STEPS Centre, 2010; Leach and Scoones, 2006; UNDP, 2001). The political and institutional limits characterising most developing countries severely inhibit the spontaneous development of these processes.

The questions we are faced with then are as follows: How can one build institutions and relationships between companies so as to enhance innovation and growth? What degree of innovation and participation of citizens is necessary in order to select and plan innovation paths? Must we wait for the evolution and maturation of an economy and society to run its course and for the spontaneous creation of "innovation systems" and "social capabilities" necessary to take advantage of available technological potentials? Or is it possible to imagine ways of creating and fostering these conditions?

An important insight into the relationship between innovation and inclusion in developing countries comes from Arocena and Sutz (2012). They claim that "*the direct attack of all types of poverty problems becomes a legitimate part of what research and innovation policies have to deal with. If that is so, the emergence of 'inclusive' innovation systems, notwithstanding its difficulties, becomes possible*" (p. 150). This point of view expands the possible interactions between innovation and inclusion, going well beyond the simple role of "technology artefacts".

The authors highlight that by combining efforts to generate knowledge and innovation on the one hand, and the various aspects of social exclusion on the other, it is possible to trigger the emergence of "Inclusive Innovation Systems", necessary for a development strategy (see below).

The issue of *inclusive innovation* has recently risen to prominence in certain international organisations (OECD, 2013; World Bank, 2013) and also in a recent study published in two special editions of the journal "Innovation and Development", close to the Globelics association (Global Network for Economics of Learning, Innovation and Competence Building Systems).

But what exactly is meant by "inclusive innovation"? "*The inclusion, within some aspects of innovation, of groups who are currently marginalized*" (Heek et al., 2014, p. 177). In different societies, this might include different groups, such as women, youth, disabled, ethnic minorities, informal sector entrepreneur and the poor.

Renewed interest in these issues is closely linked to the observation that, although some large countries have achieved both growth and a related real decrease in the percentage of the population living below the poverty line over the last two decades, many developing countries continue to experience extreme poverty conditions, malnutrition, high rates of infant mortality and stagnant or declining life expectancies. At the same time, most developed countries suffer from massive problems of inequality and different levels of social exclusion.

Some studies show that innovation generated by formal structures and organisations dealing with research, technology and production is seldom undertaken so as to meet the consumption and work needs of the poorest. The expected redistributive "trickle-down" stemming from this kind of innovation has turned out to be neither automatic nor immediate.

Undoubtedly, one factor responsible for the coexistence of a period of growth with the persistence of high levels of poverty is the specific typology of the innovation process in place. Characterised by high capital intensity, significant economies of scale, the wide use of skilled labour and high infrastructural quality, it is largely geared to the production and sale of high-quality products targeted mainly at high-income customers (and countries). However, this further marginalises the poor, both as consumers and producers (Chataway et al., 2014).

Hence, this strand of literature argues that innovation arising in informal contexts can improve life conditions and prompt more inclusive and sustainable development. Innovation is therefore conceived as a means to expand the opportunities available to all groups of people and thus, share benefits and increase participation in decisions about the strategies of development to be pursued (Santiago, 2014).

The basic idea of innovation systems may be applied to contexts where individuals, organisations and groups try to solve a problem in a creative way. Indeed, viewing innovation activities as problem-solving activities allows us to place more easily informal contexts within the traditional theoretical frameworks on innovation systems. In such informal contexts, novelties will be incremental rather than radical, and highly context-dependent (Heeks et al., 2014).

The central question of this literature is thus simple and challenging at the same time: "can innovation contribute to building a more inclusive development process?" Scholars find that it can, and have identified types of inclusive innovations as follows:

> ***Reverse innovations.*** These are innovations generally driven by multinational firms aiming at entering markets catering to those located at the

bottom of the pyramid (BOP), in particular through redesigning production processes in order to create new, more affordable products for low-income customers.

**Pro-poor innovations**. Distinct from BOP innovations, which are undertaken by private firms, these refer to public programmes of research and technology focused on creating innovations aimed at utilising the labour of the poor and drawing them into the production process. These projects are, however, characterised by a top-down approach to innovation and research.

**Appropriate technology** (or "innovation from below"). Inspired by the ideas of Owen and Ghandi, as well as by the thoughts of Schumacher (1973), this kind of innovation is based on the idea of promoting small-scale and labour-intensive technologies, as they are better suited to contexts characterised by a large labour force. By contrast, the prevailing typologies of innovation tend to exclude the poor from the processes of invention and production of technologies.

**Grassroots innovations**. These types of innovations are similar to those mentioned above, although they are more intensively based on indigenous, traditional or local knowledge. This kind of bottom-up innovation has been strongly influenced by the experience of innovations based on the central role of local communities.[6]

On the whole, these experiences this far do not represent a well-defined area of investigation, mainly because they have yet to be placed in an overall unifying framework and above all, because the guidelines that would allow us to define an agenda for policy have not been spelled out. However, their existence at least lends support to the idea that, although so far global innovation trends have been highly discriminating towards the poorest populations, it is possible to foresee alternative paths of innovation and growth (Altenburg, 2009; Chataway et al., 2014).

## 2.2 Human development and the capability approach

### a. From income to capabilities

Since the beginning of the 1990s, in part resulting from the publication of the Human Development Reports sponsored by UNDP (United Nation Development Programme), there has been a growing interest in the concept of *human development*. The authors of the first report, right from the first lines, explain the essential traits characterising this new understanding of development.

> *This Report is about people – and about how development enlarges their choices. It is about more than GNP growth, more than income and wealth and more than producing commodities and accumulating capital. A person's access to income may be one of the choices, but it is not the sum of total human endeavours. Human development is a process of enlarging people's choices. The most critical of these wide-ranging choices are to live a long and healthy life, to be educated and to have access*

*to resources needed for a decent standard of living. Additional choices include political*
*freedom, guaranteed human rights and personal self-respect.*

(UNDP, 1990, p. 1)

Behind this new understanding of development lie the contributions of some of the world's leading economists, such as Streteen, Stewart, Ranis, ul Haq and Sen. The idea of human welfare put forward by these scholars is an alternative to the welfarist paradigm, which has been dominant in economics. The latter relies on the *"space of utilities"*, which means that it bases the evaluation of human choices on the level of generated utility, and thus on income or consumption as indicators of individual's welfare. Sen criticises the foundations of this approach (Sen, 1984) and questions both the idea of using "utility" as a metric of human well-being and also the assumption that an individual's utilities can be aggregated using forms of quantitative measures. On the contrary, he argues that the overall condition of individuals should be related to other important information well beyond the simple satisfaction stemming from possession or consumption of tangible goods. Therefore, according to Sen, the evaluation of such information has to be moved to the *"space of capabilities"*.

> *The capability approach is a broad normative framework for the evaluation and assessment of individual well-being and social arrangements, the design of policies, and proposals about social change in society (. . .). The core characteristic of the capability approach is its focus on what people are effectively able to do and to be; that is, on their capabilities.*
>
> (Robeyns, 2005, p. 94)

Within the capability approach (CA), tangible and intangible goods are considered *instruments* (means) facilitating access to specific *capabilities* (i.e., effective freedom to do and to be) and *functionings* (i.e., achievements, such as being able to have good health, to be adequately nourished or to have adequate shelter). As shown by Figure 2.1 below (adapted from Robeyns, 2005, p. 94), an individual's choices depend on the opportunities allowed by both the socio-economic system and the availability of means.

Hence, within this framework, what really matters for the assessment of individuals' welfare is the nature of the life they actually live. Indeed, life standards are based on the actual quality of life and not on the mere possession of material goods.

### b. Capabilities and functionings

In the CA, an important distinction is made between *functionings* and *capabilities*, that is *"between the realized and the effectively possible; in other words, between achievements on the one hand, and freedoms or valuable options from which one can choose on the other"* (Robeyns, 2005, p. 94).

Hence, human welfare should not be evaluated in terms of goods that one can possess and consume, but rather in terms of what people are or want to be

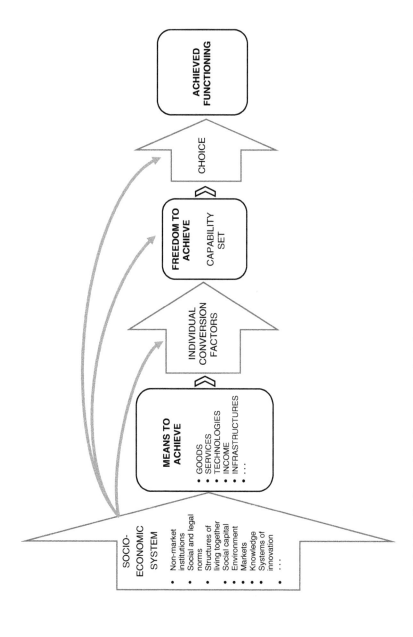

*Figure 2.1* A stylised non-dynamic representation of a person's capability set and his/her socio-economic system

in terms of health, knowledge and participation in the life of their community. Therefore, life is seen as composed of a set of functionings, encompassing various states of being and doing. Valuable functionings can refer to basic things, such as adequate nourishment or good health, as well as to more complex acquisitions, like being happy or having self-respect (Chiappero-Martinetti, 2000).

Closely linked to the concept of functionings, the notion of capabilities represents the various combinations of functionings (beings and doings) that a person can achieve. Therefore, capabilities reflect a person's freedom to choose between one type of life and another. As stated by Sen, "*Just as the so-called 'budget set' in the commodity space represent a person's freedom to buy commodity bundles, the 'capability set' in the functioning space reflects the person's freedom to choose from possible livings*" (Sen, 1992, p. 40).

Certain capabilities have an intrinsic ethical value, such as the capabilities of being adequately nourished, having access to clean water, being healthy, having a certain level of education, participating in one's political community and so on. These capabilities are at the core of Sen's idea of *human development*. Accordingly, the CA holds that social arrangements must be shaped to ensure that everyone has access to adequate levels of these capabilities.

It must be stressed, however, that not all the capabilities have this intrinsic ethical value. If many of them actually allow the achievement of a better way of being and doing, many others are irrelevant or even harmful for human development. For example, the availability of various brands of detergents, varying according to their aesthetic details and (only presumed) performance, does not extend the capabilities of users; also, the ability to use weapons for personal defence certainly does not represent either the most appropriate response from an ethical viewpoint or the least harmful to third parties. As we shall see, these differentiations are relevant to the use of technologies, and it is crucial to analyse if their contribution is, in each case, instrumental, relevant, desirable and not harmful to the expansion of the capabilities with ethical value.

### c. Objective and subjective well-being

According to the CA approach, human well-being is *objective, plural and incomplete*. First of all, this implies that the assessment of human welfare conditions is composed of *objective elements*, i.e., well-being is not dependent on individuals' preferences. Subjective preferences could even be against individuals' well-being, because as in the case of people deprived or oppressed, *adaptive preferences* often reinforce systems of oppression and thus, they cannot be considered to reflect genuine choice. For example, in an authoritarian society, people may internalise the idea of eschewing pluralism of information and political representation because they consider them unnecessary or even dangerous for the achievement of welfare in that society. Given the adaptive nature of individuals' preferences, it is clear that they are only a very limited guide for the assessment of human well-being. Within the CA, the values of freedom of information and political representation are objective, rather than subjective and dependent on individuals' evaluation of welfare. This approach thus puts forth an objective theory of human welfare, i.e., a theory of what is a "good life" for people, regardless of their individual preferences.

Second, although the CA assumes an objective nature of welfare, it does not aspire to a comprehensive definition of the concept. Indeed, as Sen argues, *"the evaluation of capabilities need not to be based on one particular comprehensive doctrine that orders the achievements and the lifestyles"* (Sen, 1992, p. 83). He thus avoids identifying which capabilities are worth promoting and holds instead that the CA should merely identify the space within which what a person may value doing or being is assessed. In this view, each society has its own set of valued capabilities, varying according to cultural, environmental and social conditions.

Third, the CA, besides being pluralist, is also *incomplete*. This means that even though it is open to different specifications depending on environmental and cultural contexts, it is also characterised by extreme vagueness in the definition of well-being. This is unavoidable and definitely inconsistent with the search for a complete and exhaustive order of capabilities by which human welfare can be promoted, leading to a fundamentally incomplete definition. However, this does not prevent us from trying to identify what human well-being is: indeed, *"if an underlying idea has an essential ambiguity, a precise formulation of that idea must try to capture that ambiguity, rather than lose it"* (Sen, 1992, p. 48). In other words, even though the CA cannot provide a precise and exhaustive definition of what is meant by "quality of life", it is still effective in determining what should be included in the evaluation of individuals' welfare.

Hence, in Sen's view, the identification of capabilities more conducive to human welfare should be the outcome of an *"evaluative exercise"* carried out by individuals in their own society or community. The aim of this exercise would be to develop an appropriately weighted system reflecting the opinions of people in a society or community about the capabilities they consider valuable for both individual and collective welfare. Clearly, this implies social evaluation and thus also some forms of rational approval requiring public discussion and democratic consensus.

This great reliance on public discussion, as well as on the opportunity to identify (case by case, context by context, territory by territory) the set of freedoms that individuals choose to live with and fight for, puts some distance between Sen's perspective and that put forward by Martha Nussbaum, another scholar who has greatly contributed to the definition of the CA. In particular, her idea of well-being is based on the ethics of Aristotle and on the idea that what is good for humans lies in performing well all the activities that are typical of a human being. Hence, she asks herself what is necessary for a life worthy of human dignity and thus identifies ten crucial capabilities that allow people to live a dignified and prosperous existence[7] (Nussbaum, 2011). All the capabilities in this list are considered essential in order to assure a good quality of life, implying that the loss of even one of them prevents individuals from leading a decent life.

On the one hand, this contribution seems to overcome the vagueness that some have identified in the definitions of specific capabilities provided by Sen. On the other hand, it has also been criticised, especially for its paternalism and lack of scientific methodology in the identification of the ten capabilities (Stewart and Deneulin, 2002). The first criticism refers to the claim of there being universal objectives that hold regardless of cultural and contextual variations; the second is related to the unclear procedure followed by the author in identifying the ten key capabilities included in the list. It is not clear, for instance, if consultation with citizens and communities was undertaken, how many people were involved, how the synthesis was arrived at, and how those capabilities were actually chosen.

### d. Inequality according to the capability approach

Following Sen, in order to analyse and evaluate inequality, "*equality of what?*" becomes a key question. The relevance of this question comes from the diversity characterising human beings. Indeed, the principle of equality can be applied to different dimensions, leading to very different results. As Sen has put it, "*Human diversity is no secondary complication (to be ignored, or to be introduced "later on"); it is a fundamental aspect of our interest in equality*" *(Sen, 1992, p. xi)*. Hence, within this framework, equality is assessed by comparing some traits or aspects of a person (income, wealth, happiness, rights) with the corresponding traits or aspects of another person. It follows that the outcome depends on the choice of the specific traits or aspects upon which the measurement of inequality is based.

> *Equality in terms of one variable may not coincide with equality in the scale to another. For example, equal opportunities can lead to very unequal incomes. Equal incomes can go with significant differences in wealth. Equal wealth can coexist with very unequal happiness. Equal happiness can go with widely divergent fulfilment of needs. Equal fulfilment of needs can be associated with very different freedoms of choice. And so on.*
>
> (Sen, 1992, p. 2)

Sen's approach uses an original conceptual apparatus in assessing economic inequality and particularly the conditions of poverty. As claimed by the Indian economist, "*If poverty is seen as the deprivation of some minimum fulfilment of elementary capabilities, it becomes easier to understand why poverty has both an absolute and a relative aspect*" (Sen, 1992, p. 9). This allows us to analyse poverty in whatever country, even in those most economically advanced, such as the United States and Europe.

Of course, according to this perspective, it is incorrect to analyse inequality based only on income levels. Indeed, an unequal distribution of incomes does not necessarily imply actual inequality between people; what we can do or acquire depends not only on our available income, but also on the variety of our physical and social characteristics, which affect our lives and make us who we are. This leads us to the crucial distinction between *actual acquisitions* (i.e., what we actually manage to achieve) and the *freedom to acquire* (i.e., the real opportunity to achieve what we value). These do not necessarily coincide, but they can both be characterised by inequality.

Moreover, the possibility that the means available to individuals (tangible or intangible goods, and technologies) will boost access to certain functionings depends on three sets of *conversion factors*. The first set refers to individuals'"personal" characteristics, such as health, gender and skills. These affect the extent to which people can actually transform available means into functionings. For example, a disabled person or one who simply does not know how to ride a bicycle is not able to use the bicycle to activate the functioning of mobility. The second and the third sets of conversion factors are related to the *social context* (public policies, social norms, relationships among groups of power, etc.) and the *environment* in which people live (climate, geographical location). For instance, if there are no roads or they are not easy to follow because they are located in a mountainous area, or if cycling around is considered inappropriate for women because of existing social norms, a female individual (although able to go cycling) cannot activate her functioning of mobility.

> *The capability approach thus takes account of human diversity in two ways: by its focus on the plurality of functionings and capabilities as the evaluative space, and by the explicit focus on personal and socio-environmental conversion factors of commodities into functionings, and on the whole social and institutional context that affects the conversion factors and also the capability set directly.*
>
> (Robeyns, 2005. p. 99)

All this leads us to two important remarks. First, traditional economic studies tend to follow the restrictive practice of treating income symmetrically, i.e., they disregard the difficulty that some may have in translating economic income into real well-being and freedom. The material resources and primary goods that a person owns are likely to be very imperfect indicators of the freedom to do or to be. Second, the rhetoric of equality ("all men are created equals") pays little attention to the actual differences between individuals, which might originate in personal reasons (gender, age, state of health, mental and physical abilities) or have exogenous causes (the economic and social environment, family membership, etc.). Achieving meaningful equality for all may require very unequal treatment in favour of those in a position of disadvantage.

### e. Efficiency and equality

A crucial issue for the thesis of this book concerns the conflict between *efficiency and equality*. Sen groups the main critiques on equality, advanced by the supporters of efficiency, around two main arguments: one focusing on *incentives* and the other on *operational asymmetries*.

The first line of criticism by those critical of the promotion of equality emphasises the need for incentives. Adherents believe that people must be given the right incentives to direct their behaviour towards achieving goals of personal growth. In this perspective, a certain degree of inequality can play a positive role, encouraging hard work, entrepreneurship, innovation and investment.

Following this, the pursuit of equality may even hamper social and economic improvements.

The second line of critique holds that a trade-off between efficiency and equality is rooted in the operational asymmetry, necessary to promote economic and social efficiency. This asymmetry arises from the presence of different skills and specialisations among individuals and implies that a degree of concentration of power and incomes amongst the most skilled and talented people is useful. While such concentration will generate a certain level of inequality, it will also result in improved functioning of economy and society by allowing the most talented people to use the best available resources. This, in turn, could benefit the entire community.

Promoting inequality as a means of creating incentives does not seem objectionable when individuals' differential performances have their basis in differences in commitment and other motivational factors. However, the argument for incentivization loses its appeal when inequality in acquisitions and freedom do not arise from differences related to individuals' decisions. "*For example, to the extent that gender or age is responsible for inequality of capabilities, the policy response may take the form of providing special help to members of the more deprived gender or age categories. Since it is impossible to change one's age rapidly, and particularly hard to change one's sex, the special treatments may not generate incentive problems of the standard kind*" (Sen, 1992, p. 142). These inequalities in capabilities often limit individuals' access to work activities in the first place, thereby rendering income differentials redundant in their role as stimuli to commitment. Allocating community resources to eliminate or reduce such inequality of capabilities between individuals would allow the mechanism of incentives to work better.

Turning now to the second functional justification of inequality, namely the promotion of *operational asymmetry*, a capability approach would require the verification of the (presumed) highest capabilities of each individual in a society as well as particular attention to mechanisms aimed at maximising people's professional capacities. Clearly, a greater number of people able to fulfil their tasks with competence can only benefit overall efficiency. However, even in this case, acting on the lack of freedom (to access adequate education, satisfactory standards of health, services and support in dealing with studies, effective professional training programs, etc.) would be the best way to broaden the pool of skilled and competent people who could make the best use of available resources. This would, in turn, increase the well-being of the entire society.

### f. Agency

Another fundamental concept within the CA is that of *agency*. In the discussion so far, we have referred to the freedom of people to achieve valuable functionings relevant to their individual well-being. A person, however, may have other objectives in his or her life beyond personal well-being. Hence, agency acquisition refers to the achievement of goals and values that a person has reasons to pursue and which may not be correlated with personal well-being. For instance, if people believe that the social and economic progress of their community is important, their agency achievements will imply an assessment of the state of things in terms of these objectives and not just in terms of personal well-being. Therefore, the pursuit by individuals of personal well-being and of broader objectives (related to the aims of the entire group, community or society in which they are included) are both relevant.

However, freedom of agency and individual welfare are not completely independent; indeed, they may mutually reinforce or contradict each other. For instance, not achieving agency objectives, such as greater political freedom, can lead to frustration and thus to a loss of individual well-being; similarly, an increase in the capacity to promote individual objectives of agency (via, for example, a totalising political commitment) can lead to a reduction in personal well-being.

Hence, on the relevance of human agency, Sen underlines that:

> In terms of the medieval distinction between 'the patient' and 'the agent', this freedom-centred understanding of economics and of the process of development is very much an agent-oriented view. With adequate social opportunities, individuals can effectively shape their own destiny and help each other. They need not be seen primarily as passive recipients of benefits of cunning development programs. There is indeed a strong rationale for recognizing the positive role of free and sustainable agency – and even of constructive impatience.
>
> (Sen, 1999, p. 11)

### g. Structures of living together

Individual agency is influenced by the context where people live. On this, a relevant strand of analysis within the CA refers to the relationship between *individual choices* and *social structures*. In essence, individual choices cannot be conceived of as simple outcomes of neutral personal inclinations – they are also deeply affected by social structures. In this respect, a concept that helps us place social relations in wider perspective is that of *structures of living together*.

In particular, some values cannot be understood outside a context of social practices and meanings. The shared meanings that we give to words, institutional norms, aesthetics, beliefs, ethnic, cultural and political practices are all irreducible social goods. These meanings are reinforced by individuals, although their existence is not dependent on them. A structure of living thus belongs to particular, historically determined communities and guarantees the conditions in which the lives of individuals can thrive (Deneulin, 2006; Stewart and Deneulin, 2002).

The structures of living together are historically, socially and culturally determined. It should be stressed that they are not always oriented towards collective welfare. In fact, certain structures of living together are characterised by unbalanced power relationships and thus by rules of submission and limitation of freedom, as, for example, in societies where religious norms are imposed on citizens who do not share the same religious beliefs. Nevertheless, since these structures of living together affect human flourishing, they need to be included in an analysis of development strategies (Deneulin, 2006, Stewart and Deneulin, 2002). In this respect, it is especially important to identify the structures that favour and promote the expansion of human capabilities, and to distinguish them from others which instead limit and contrast such development.

### h. Instrumental freedoms

The freedom of individuals is a central concern for Sen. In his analysis, effective development must remove all the lacks of freedom that prevent people from making choices (Sen, 1999). Therefore, in the capability approach the expansion of freedom is viewed as both the *primary end* and also the *principal means* of development.

> *They can be called respectively the 'constitutive role' and the 'instrumental role' of freedom in development. The constitutive role of freedom relates to the importance of substantive freedom in enriching human life (...). The instrumental role of freedom concerns the way different kinds of rights, opportunities, and entitlements contribute to the expansion of human freedom in general, and thus to promoting development.*
> (Sen, 1999, pp. 36–37)

Therefore, another important aspect characterising the stream of analyses within the CA concerns *instrumental freedoms*: namely, the set of rights, opportunities and entitlements, all of which are means for the promotion of human development.

In "Development as Freedom" (1999, Chapter 2), Sen identifies five families of *instrumental freedoms*.

1   **Political freedoms**. Broadly speaking, these are not only tied to the formal rights of electing political representatives, but also to a more general civic participation, the ability to criticise and keep an eye on representatives and the possibility for open debates.
2   **Economic facilities**. Sen understands these as the opportunities given to individuals to use economic resources for the purposes of consumption, production and exchange. Important here is the quantity of income as well as its distribution, the structure of markets, the presence of high entry barriers and the ability to access credit.
3   **Social opportunities**. This refers to the arrangements that a society makes regarding schools and healthcare which tangibly influence the freedom to live better (in good health, without contracting avoidable diseases or dying before one's time) and to actively and effectively participate in economic, social and political activities.
4   **Transparency guarantees**. Society can only work if a certain level of trust is established. Guarantees of transparency are essential to achieve this trust. Private and public actors play an important role in guaranteeing the right to information. These guarantees clearly serve to avoid corruption, financial irresponsibility and under-the-table negotiations. The opposite

of transparency can be found in the negative relationship networks that generate a shadow economy, criminality and poor transparency in public administration.

5   **Protective security**. This refers to protection of the most vulnerable groups or victims of serious deprivation. This deprivation or vulnerability is the result of material transformations which have had a negative effect on their lives. To safeguard against such social malaise, networks of social protection are necessary. This is the sphere of intervention in social protection that has to do with social safety nets, the pension system, social welfare, accident insurance, families and children.

Instrumental freedoms are highly interrelated and interdependent. This implies that the advancement of one type of freedom can also promote the advancement of other types of freedom, with mutually beneficial effect.

Sen highlights the fact that *"each of these distinct types of rights and opportunities helps to advance the general capabilities of a person. They may also serve to complement each other. Public policy to foster human capabilities and substantive freedoms in general can work through the promotion of these distinct but interrelated instrumental freedoms"* (Sen, 1999 p. 10).

Each instrumental freedom, while being connected to the others, is directly dependent on those institutions (first the political ones) which allocate resources to economic and social goals (Sen, 1999).

### i. Democracy and deliberative decision making

As Sen (1999) argues, there are three reasons to think that *political freedoms* should be a priority when making collective choices: their *direct importance*, their *instrumental capacity* and their *constructive role*.

*Direct importance* stems from the characteristic of being one of the *basic capabilities*. Indeed, freedom of expression, collective action and social organisation are themselves important as building blocks of a full life, valued by individuals. Similarly, the conscious formation of opinions by individuals requires free discussion and the full capacity to have their opinions known, without limits and constraints. This makes the role of political freedom central to the learning process of each citizen as well as to the formation of shared values.

Next, political freedoms have also an *instrumental capacity*, because the possibility to express freely and choose representatives creates a system of political incentives for power groups and governments that influence their decisions. *Control by the free electorate* means that politicians are forced, if they want votes and support, to be attentive to the criticism and demands of voters. This mechanism may also help in solving problems directly affecting the well-being of citizens.

Finally, political freedoms also play a *constructive role*, since the existence of civil rights and freedom of discussion offers a unique opportunity to *understand the concept of well-being*. Discussing, debating animatedly and openly and disagreeing, all favour the formation of informed and conscious choices about the values and the priorities that should be the basis of the political choices.

These choices have less value if they are imposed from above and thus transcend the public exchange of ideas. Indeed, public discussion plays a key role not only for the identification of the priorities and objectives of political choices, but also in enhancing the effectiveness of their realisation or implementation.

However, political freedoms are not everything. Their effective exercise depends on *democratic practice*. According to Dreze and Sen (2002), it is useful to distinguish between different causes limiting democratic practice.

First, democratic institutions *may work in a distorted way*. This happens when public services are not well organised or undergo distortions typical of corruption. A second limitation of democracy comes from the use of inadequate democratic institutions, *due to the lack of motivation or understanding of the mechanisms of participation*, as in the case of low participation in elections or of the complex mechanisms of judicial processes. The third reason for the failure of the democratic practice relates to *inequality*. Indeed, even when institutions are working properly, as in the case of free and fair elections, not only can effective participation be distorted by the pressure of economic power groups on citizens that participate, but access to justice can be strongly influenced by inequality (as is demonstrated, for example, by the capacity of the rich to hire the best and thus more expensive lawyers, even in the absence of corruption).

> *The foundation of democratic practice may be described as facility (functional democratic institutions), involvement (informed public engagement with these institutions), and equity (a fair distribution of power). The central relevance of equity arises from the fact that a fair distribution of power is a basic – indeed fundamental- requirement of democracy. A government 'by the people' must ultimately include all the people in a symmetric way, and this is essential also to enable the government to become 'of the people and for the people.*
>
> (Drèze and Sen, 2002, p. 354)

The latter limitation of democracy results from unequal distribution of economic and political power that, as we shall see in Section 3.4, severely limits the proper functioning of modern democracies.

We can differentiate between two forms of participation in democratic life: *democratic decision making* and *participatory decision making*.

In the first case, the practice of democracy is realised by conferring, through the vote, the representation of citizens' interests. This is an indirect form of representation in which decisions are made through representatives in legislative assemblies. In the case of participatory decision-making, citizens are instead directly involved in the decision-making process led by various interest groups formed around work, environmental, and social concerns, etc. Hence, in democratic decision-making, participation involves permanent political structures (electoral system, political parties, press, etc.), whereas participatory decision-making is independent of such traditional structures and is instead characterised by specific and direct forms of discussion and delegation.

The democratic process is itself characterised by certain ambiguities; indeed, the requests made through democracy are not always oriented to improve the well-being of citizens. For instance, in situations of perceived external threat, there is often greater investment in the military field instead of in health, education and social services; similarly, established democratic practice can "democratically" lead to situations characterised by a lack of respect of individual freedoms, as in the case of racism, gender or religious discrimination or economic or social marginalisation.

In addition, the process leading to democratic choices is not always linear and transparent. In fact, individuals' opinions are usually filtered and influenced by political parties, which, in turn, are often influenced by financial and industrial powers pursuing interests not always favourable to the overall community. Moreover, individuals' choices in the process of democratic decision can also be affected by religious or ethnic membership, implicit norms and social classes, which also follow special interests and thus make it difficult, and in some cases impossible, to reach a shared consensus.

This implies that, on the whole, simple democratic procedure may not be enough to ensure the development of a human community. One way to overcome these contradictions, typical to all democracies (even the more consolidated ones), lies in the definition and practical implementation of the rights enshrined in the Constitutions; these should serve as legal limits within which the democratic process takes place and include the necessary control mechanisms and institutional balances to ensure its effective functioning.

## Notes

1 As we shall see, beyond this idea of innovation, which we refer to as "restricted", there is a broader idea that includes more complex processes and typologies of change rather than simply the radical breakthroughs occurring in high-tech industries.
2 As the progressive development through the inheritance of certain traits and change is induced by the response to adversities, "organisational genetics" is referred to those organisational characteristics of a firm which can be transferred over time – genotypes, routines, etc.
3 These contributions also contain references to other specifications of the Innovation Systems approach related to sectorial and technological systems not discussed here for the sake of brevity.
4 We will recall and further deepen these topics, addressing the issue of the learning capabilities.
5 These aspects will be further explored in Chapter 3 and when discussing policies in Chapter 7.
6 The idea of "inclusive innovation" has been particularly influenced by the experience of the Honeybee Network in India (Gupta et al. 2011), namely a group of people and organisations that, although spread over more than seventy locations, share a common philosophy of recovery, valorisation and diffusion of traditional knowledge and grassroots innovations.
7 Life; bodily health; bodily integrity; senses, imagination and thought; emotions; practical reason; affiliation; other species; play; control over one's environment (Nussbaum, 2011, p. 33–34).

## References

Altenburg, T. 2009. Building Inclusive Innovation Systems in Developing Countries: Challenges for IS Research. In: Lundvall et al., 2009, 33–57.

Arocena, R. and Sutz, J. 2012. Research and Innovation Policies for Social Inclusion: An Opportunity for Developing Countries, *Innovation and Development*, 2(1), 147–158.

Asheim, B.T. and Gertler, M.S. 2005. The Geography of Innovation-Regional Innovation Systems. In: Fagerberg et al. 2005.

Asheim, B.T. and Parrilli, M.D. (eds.) 2012. *Interactive Learning for Innovation: A Key Driver Within Clusters and Innovation Systems*, Basingstoke, UK; New York, Palgrave Macmillan.

Becattini, G., Bellandi, M. and De Propris, L. (eds.) 2009. *A Handbook of Industrial Districts*. Cheltenham, UK; Northampton, MA, Edward Elgar.

Bourdieu, P. 1986. The Form of Capital. In: J. Richardson (ed.), *Handbook of Theory and Research for Sociology of Education*, Westport, Greenwood Press.

Braczyk, H., Cooke, P. and Heidenreich, M. (eds.) 1998. *Regional Innovation Systems*, London, UCL Press.

Burton-Jones A. and Spender J.C. (eds) 2011. *The Oxford Handbook of Human Capital*, Oxford, Oxford University Press.

Chataway, J., Hanlin, R. and Kaplinsky, R. 2014. Inclusive Innovation: An Architecture for Policy Development, *Innovation and Development*, 4(1), 33–54.

Chiappero-Martinetti, E. 2000. A multidimensional assessment of well-being based on Sen's functioning approach, "Rivista Internazionale di Scienze Sociali", n. 2, pp. 207-239.

Cimoli, M., Dosi, G., Nelson, R.R. and Stiglitz, J.E. 2009a. Institutions and Policies in Developing Economies. In: Lundvall et al. 2009, 337–359.

Cooke, Ph. 2001. Regional Innovation Systems, Cluster, and the Knowledge Economy, *Industrial and Corporate Change*, 10(4), 945–974.

Dalum, B., Johnson, B. and Lundvall, B.A.1992. Public Policy in the Learning Society. In: Lundvall 1992, 294–351.

Deneulin S. 2006. *The Capability Approach and the Praxis of Development*, Basingstoke, UK; New York, USA Palgrave Macmillan.

Dosi, G. 1982. Technological Paradigms and Technological Trajectories: A Suggested Interpretation of the Determinants and Directions of Technical Change, *Research Policy*, 11(3), 147–162.

Drèze, J. and Sen, A. 2002. *India: Development and Participation*, Oxford, Oxford University Press.

Edquist, C. 2005. Systems of Innovation – Perspectives and Challenges, In: Fagerberg, J., Mowery, D.C. and Nelson, R.R. (eds.), *The Oxford Handbook of Innovation*, Oxford, Oxford University Press, 181–208.

Fagerberg, J. and Godinho, M.M. 2005. Innovation and Catching-Up. In: Fagerberg, J., Mowery, D.C. and Nelson, R.R. (eds.), *The Oxford Handbook of Innovation*, Oxford, Oxford University Press, 514–542.

Fagerberg, J., Srholec, M. and Verspagen, B. 2010a. Innovation and Economic Development. In: Hall, B. and Rosenberg, N. (eds.), *Handbook of Economics of Innovation*, Amsterdam, Elsevier, 833–872.

Fagerberg, J., Srholec, M. and Verspagen, B. 2010b. The Role of Innovation in Development, *Review of Economics and Institutions*, 1(2), 1–29.

Freeman, C. 1987. *Technology Policy and Economic Performance: Lessons From Japan*, London, Pinter Publishers.

Freeman, C. 2002. Continental, National and Sub-National Innovation Systems-Complementary and Economic Growth, *Research Policy*, 31, 191–211.

Freeman, C. and Perez, C. 1988. Structural Crises of Adjustment, Business Cycles and Investment Behaviour. In: G. Dosi, Freeman, C., Nelson, R., Silverberg, G. and Soete, L. (eds.), *Technical Change and Economic Theory*, London: Francis Pinter, 38–66.

Furman, J.L. and Hayes, R. 2004. Caching Up or Standing Still? National Innovative Productivity Among "Follower' Countries", *Research Policy*, 33, 1329–1354.

Furman, J.L., Porter, M.E. and Scott, S. 2002. The Determinants of National Innovative Capacity, *Research Policy*, 31, 899–933.

Gupta, P., Kochhar, K. and Panth, S. 2011. *Bank Ownership and the Effects of Financial Liberalization: Evidence from India.* Working Paper 11/50, International Monetary Fund, Washington, DC.

Hartmann, D. 2013. *Economic Complexity and Human Development: How Economic Diversification and Social Networks Affect Human Agency and Welfare* Oxford, New York, Routledge.

Heeks, R., Foster, C. and Nugroho, Y. 2014. New Models of Inclusive Innovation for Development, *Innovation and Development*, 4(2), 175–185.

Jensen, M.B., Johnson, B., Lorenz, E. and Lundvall, B.A. 2007. Forms of Knowledge and Modes of Innovation, *Research Policy*, 36, 680–693.

Johnson, B. 1992. Institutional Learning. In: Lundvall 1992, 23–45.

Laurent, J. and Nightingale, J. 2001. *Darwinism and Evolutionary Economics.* Cheltenham, UK; Northampton, MA, Edward Elgar.

Leach, M. and Scoones, I. 2006. *The Slow Race: Making Technology Work for the Poor*, www.demos.co.uk.

Lundvall, B.A. 2007a. National Innovation Systems: Analytical Concept and Development Tool, *Industry and Innovation*, 14(1), 95–119.

Lundvall, B.A. 2007b. *Innovation System Research: Where It Came From and Where It Might Go*, Globelics Working Paper, No. 2007–01.

Lundvall, B.A. (ed.) 1992. *National System of Innovation: Towards a Theory of Innovation and Interactive Learning*, London, Pinter Publishers.

Lundvall, B.A. and Johnson, B. 1994. The Learning Economy, *Journal of Industry Studies*, 1, 23–42.

Lundvall, B.A., Joseph, K.J., Chaminade C. and Vang J. 2009. *Handbook of Innovation System and Developing Countries: Building Domestic Capabilities in a Global Setting*, Cheltenham, UK; Northampton USA, Edward Elgar Publishing Ltd.

Nelson, N.N. and Winter, S.G. 1974. Neoclassical vs Evolutionary Theories of Economic Growth: Critique and Prospectus, *The Economic Journal*, 84(336), 886–905.

Nelson, R.R. and Winter, S.G. 1982. *An Evolutionary Theory of Economic Change*, Cambridge, MA; London, UK, The Belknap Press of Harvard University Press.

Nelson, R.R. (ed.) 1993. *National Systems of Innovation: A Comparative Study*, Oxford University Press, Oxford.

North, D.C. 1990. *Institutions, Institutional Change, and Economic Performance*, Cambridge, Cambridge University Press.

North, D.C. 2005. *Understanding the Process of Economic Change*, Princeton, NJ, Princeton University Press.

Nussbaum, Martha C. 2011. *Creating Capabilities: The Human Development Approach*, Cambridge, MA; London, UK, Harvard University Press.

OECD (Organisation for Economic and Co-operation and Development) 2013. Innovation and Inclusive Development, Conference discussion report.

Pavitt, K. 2002. *Knowledge About Knowledge Since Nelson and Winter: A Mixed Record*, Electronic Working Paper Series, Paper No. 83, SPRU, University of Sussex.

Perez, C. 2002. *Technological Revolutions and Financial Capital: The Dynamics of Bubbles and Golden Ages.* London, Elgar.

Perez, C. 2009. The Double Bubble at the Turn of the Century: Technological Roots and Structural Implications, *Cambridge Journal of Economics*, 33, 779–805.

Perez, C. 2010a. Technological Revolutions and Techno-Economic Paradigms, *Cambridge Journal of Economics*, 34, 185–202.

Perez, C. 2010b. *The Financial Crisis and the Future of Innovation: A View of Technical Change With the Aid of History*, Working Papers in Technology Governance and Economic Dynamics no. 28.

Porter, M. 2000. Location, Competition, and Economic Development: Local Clusters in a Global Economy, *Economic Development Quarterly*, 14(1), 15–34.

Putnam, R.D. 1993. *Making Democracy Work: Civic Traditions in Modern Italy*, Princeton, NJ, Princeton University Press.

Reinert, E.S. 2007. *How Rich Countries Got Rich . . . and Why Poor Countries Stay Poor*, London, Constable.

Robertson, P.L., Jacobson, D. and Langlois, R.N. 2009. Innovation Processes and Industrial Districts. In: Becattini et al. 2009, 269–281.

Robeyns, I. 2005. The Capability Approach: A Theoretical Survey, *Journal of Human Development*, 6(1), 93–114.

Robinson, J. 1969. *The Economics of Imperfect Competition*, 2nd edition, London, Palgrave Macmillan, St Martin's Press.

Rosenberg, N. and Trajtenberg, M. 2001. *A General Purpose Technology at Work: The Corliss Steam Engine in the Late 19th Century US*. NBER Working Papers 8485, National Bureau of Economic Research, Inc.

Santiago, F. 2014. Innovation for Inclusive Development, *Innovation and Development*, 4(2), 1–4.

Schumacher, E.F. 1973. *Small Is Beautiful: Economics as If People Mattered*, London, Blond and Briggs.

Schumpeter, J.A. 1936. *The Theory of Economic Development: An Inquiry Into Profits, Capital, Credit, Interest, and the Business Cycle*, Cambridge, MA, Harvard University Press.

Schumpeter, J.A. 1939. *Business Cycles: A Theoretical, Historical and Statistical Analysis of the Capitalism Process*, New York, McGraw-Hill.

Sen A. 1992. *Inequality Reexamined*, Oxford, Oxford University Press.

Sen, A. 1984. *Resources, Values and Development*, Oxford, Basil Blackwell.

Sen, A. 1999. *Development as Freedom*, Oxford, Oxford University Press.

Soete, L., Verspagen, B. and Ter Weel, B. 2010. System of Innovation. In: Hall, H. and Rosenberg, N. (eds.), *Economics of Innovation*, vol. 2, Amsterdam, Elsevier, 1159–1180.

STEPS Centre 2010. *Innovation, Sustainability, Development: A New Manifesto*, Brighton, University of Sussex.

Stewart, F. and Deneulin, S. 2002. Amartya Sen's Contribution to Development Thinking Studies, *Comparative International Development*, 37(2), 61–70.

Streeten, P. 2002. Reflections on Social and Antisocial Capital, *Journal of Human Development*, 3(1), 7–22.

UNDP (United Nations Development Programme) 1990. *Human Development Report 1990*, Oxford, Oxford University Press.

UNDP (United Nations Development Programme) 2001. *Human Development Report 2001, Making New Technologies Work for Human Development*, Oxford, Oxford University Press.

Vertova, G. 2014. *The State and National Systems of Innovation: A Sympathetic Critique*, Levy Economics Institute Working Paper Collection No. 823.

WB (World Bank) 2013. *China: Inclusive Innovation for Sustainable Inclusive Growth*, Washington, DC, World Bank Group.

# 3 The interconnections between freedom and innovation

As we have seen, the central objective of the capability approach (CA) is to expand the freedom that the deprived people have to enjoy different ways of being and doing; this goal leads us to regard the expansion of the material well-being as a means of development rather than an end.

> It should be clear that we tend to assess development by the expansion of substantive human freedoms – not just by economic growth (for example, of the gross national product), technical progress, or social modernisation. This is not to deny, in any way, that advances in the latter fields can be very important, depending on circumstances, as 'instruments' for the enhancement of human freedom. However, they have to be appraised precisely in that light – in terms of their actual effectiveness in enriching the lives and liberties of people – rather than taking them to be valuable in themselves.
>
> (Drèze and Sen, 2002, p. 3)

The CA, therefore, considers the progress in the economic, technological and social fields as simple means for the attainment of the ultimate goal of human development. It is characterised by being a powerful normative tool for *outcome* evaluation; but it gives little emphasis to the *processes* that lead to a greater economic growth, technical progress and social modernisation.

Conversely, the Innovative System (IS) theory mostly focuses on *processes*. The idea of change that is implicit in the analysis of IS holds innovation is strongly dependent on cultural and historical contexts (path dependence), the role of institutions, political choices, the ability individuals and companies have to interact and learn, as well as mutual trust (social capital). These factors are not exogenous to the innovation systems but are a constitutive part of these (Lundvall, 1992; Lundvall et al., 2009), and their quality influences in a decisive manner the direction of change. Symmetrically, this attention to the process overshadows the assessment on innovation *outcomes*. Not all innovation is good. The outcomes of the innovation process, i.e., more productivity, more efficiency, more competitiveness, do not always translate into an improved well-being of people or a good distribution of the benefits and costs involved.

This chapter centres on the idea that the human development theory could offer a normative approach that can direct, in the most virtuous way, the processes of change and that the IS theory, with its focus on individual and collective learning processes, could, at the same time, represent an approach to growth consistent with the expansion of capabilities (see also Capriati, 2013). The intent is to make a modest contribution to the interrelation between two areas of economic analysis that have not always converged: the *efficiency* of production and exchange, and the *fair* distribution of resources and opportunities. In fact, as recalled by one of the fathers of development economics,

> *Traditionally economic theory, more explicitly from John Stuart Mill on, had made a distinction between two types of problems: those of production (including exchange) and those of distribution. As I had already shown during my "theoretical" period, this distinction is illogical for the purposes for which it was used, as production and distribution are interrelated within the same macro-system.*
>
> *Moreover, from Mill onward, the distinction had been used by economist as a means to escape from the problems of distribution by concentrating on those of production, usually with only a general reservation in regard to distribution and then thinking about distribution as a simply matter of money incomes. This reflected a bias on economic theory which is still with us, not least in research on underdeveloped countries, implying the view that egalitarian reforms are necessarily costly in terms of economic growth, and very definitely not productive. This view has continually been argued on speculative grounds. Even in regard to developed countries, very little empirical evidence has been provided, even for such simple "economic" interrelationships as the effects of a change in income distribution on savings, labor output, and efficiency.*
>
> (*Myrdal, 1973*, p. 10)

Myrdal also notes that focusing on issues of equality requires giving due consideration to a set of non-economic factors affecting the political and social relations, the economic structure, institutions, attitudes and all interpersonal relationships, echoing, in this way, the multidimensional concept of equality, as advanced by Sen (see above Chapter 2).

Myrdal's observation allows us to grasp more clearly the importance to reconnect the problems of distribution and equality (not intended as a *simple matter of money incomes*) with those of production and innovation, capturing thus their links and interrelations.

Below I will analyse the interconnections between CA and the IS theory. The theme is defined around five areas of particular interest, based on the review of the previous chapter. I will begin with an analysis on *the technologies and processes of inclusive innovation*, by focusing on the contributions they can make to the expansion of capabilities, on the one hand, and on the evaluation issues and democratic control, on the other. I will then proceed to the role of *learning* that is both a fundamental capability and the basic process of the operation of innovation systems. The third section will be dedicated to *equality* and innovation; we will try to explore more deeply the connection between the two, as mentioned already when referencing Myrdal. The fourth section will be dedicated to the performance of the *institutions and democratic processes*, and I will address questions such as: can we conceive of an innovative process in a context in which the most important democratic freedoms are denied? What is the contribution of well-functioning institutions to the innovation processes? In the fifth section, I analyse the importance of *the structure of living together, the social capital and the social protection systems* for the two approaches, to see how these networks can lead to achieving better living conditions for individuals while ensuring optimum conditions for growth and innovation. I will conclude this chapter with a section with a paragraph in which I will bring together in a simple circular causation diagram the analysed interconnections.

## 3.1 Technologies, inclusive innovation and capabilities

### Key ideas

CA sees technology as *a means* (among others) to achieve the objectives of well-being that people consider important. Recent reflections, however, have shown the importance of the relationship between technology and capabilities. Technologies, in fact, can decisively contribute to the expansion of capabilities (section a.). Also, evaluating the technologies based on the capabilities approach can help change the nature of the innovation process and technologies produced, bringing them closer to the needs of individuals and communities. This results from the importance that CA gives to a series of elements: the difference between the individual and social conversion factors that can increase or reduce the impact of technology; the protection of the individual diversity; the importance of freedom and of agency and consequently, the role of individuals and communities to take action through *public discussion* on the design and purpose of technology and innovation (section b.). The CA can foster a more advanced relationship between technology and people where the latter are not just passive recipients of interventions and artefacts designed and manufactured elsewhere, but active agents of change that influence the shape, results and capacity *to include* of the innovation processes (section c.).

### a. Technology and capabilities

Technology has important repercussions on the individuals' freedom of being and doing. It should therefore have an equally strong position in the capabilities approach. But this is not the case.[1] Indirectly, Sen has repeatedly mentioned the role of technology in his examples. When referring to a bike (as a means of transport), a gun or a mobile phone (Sen, 2010), he wanted to highlight the fact that technologies can improve people's freedom but they can also be used to produce negative effects. For example, a gun held by an individual can easily restrict someone else's freedom. Also, the technologies for producing hydrogen as a source of energy may be used for civilian purposes or to produce weapons of mass destruction. These considerations are based on the idea that technology is *a means* to achieve a certain opportunity to improve one's life. Below I will analyse some of the issues that arise from the intersection of CA, technology and development; we will also see how, as a result of this relationship, it is possible to give technology a more prominent role than that of being merely a means.

The first important contribution to the analysis of the technology/human development nexus came from the HDR (Human Development Report) 2001 (UNDP, 2001). According to the authors of this report, many people fear that new technologies may be of little use in developing countries; or that they could expand the already extreme inequalities between North and South and between the rich and the poor. These views assume a direct link between access to technological innovation and the level of income: the wealthier one is, the more technologies one can have. However, the inverse relationship is also true: a greater availability of technologies and training provides people with more tools to improve their standard of living. The Report outlines how technology is a tool, not just a result of growth and development, and how technologies, if well targeted to the real needs of the community, have a multiplier effect and create a virtuous circle: they increase people's health, knowledge and productivity, thereby augmenting people's income and by improving human development, creating future innovative capacities.

The 2001 report is rich in information used to analyse the relationship between technology and human development; among these, two are of particular interest for the section below.

The first concerns the relationship between technology and poverty. Typically, technology is generated in response to pressures stemming from the market mechanisms; poor countries, which by definition have low incomes, are not very attractive to the most innovative companies. This means that widely used technologies seldom meet the needs of poor countries. Without specific interventions, these technologies become a source of exclusion, rather than an instrument of progress. The needs of poor people could remain neglected, and new global risks may remain unaddressed. According to the HDR 2001, it is important to reflect on appropriateness of development interventions to ensure that the positive impacts of technologies are more meaningful than their risks.[2]

The second issue concerns the relationship between Internet and democracy. New technologies are creating opportunities to ensure improved health and nutrition, the expansion of knowledge, stimulation of economic growth as well as the expansion of opportunities for people's participation in their communities. 'The ultimate significance of the network age is that it can empower people by enabling them to use and contribute to the world's collective knowledge. And the great challenge of the new century is to ensure that the entire human race is so empowered–not just a lucky few' (UNDP, 2001, p. 23). Therefore, the widening of the democratic spaces and ensuring open access for all are major challenges that new information technologies pose to the global community.

Recently, some scholars (Oosterlaken, 2015, 2011; Kleine, 2013; Oosterlaken and Van den Hoven, 2012), especially philosophers of science, have taken up these issues and have found that it is critical to consider technology as an important determinant of human capabilities, for two main reasons.

First, as it has already been pointed out, technology is an important factor of expansion of human capabilities. Prefabricated homes rapidly ensure access to adequate shelter in areas lacking decent housing; means of transport such as cars, bicycles and public transportation allow individuals to move freely from place to place; the means of communication such as telephones, internet connections, etc., allow people to be involved in various forms of social interaction; and so on (Oosterlaken, 2011). Second, because the CA provides a useful tool for evaluating the impact of technologies introduced by development projects, such as evaluating ICT projects or assessing healthcare technologies or biotechnologies (Oosterlaken, 2011; Coeckelberg, 2011).

In these contributions, the emphasis is on technology as 'a set of material artefacts or systems of such artefacts' (Oosterlaken, 2011, p. 426), and the main goal is understanding the relationship between technology and social and individual change. In this regard, an important contribution of this school of thought is the critical assessment of technology transfer processes, which highlights that 'many of the past cases of failed technology transfer to developing countries are a perfect illustration of the fact that technologies do not expand human capabilities without the required interdependencies with people, social structures and other artefacts being present in the recipient country' (Oosterlaken, 2011, p. 431).

For the capability approach, the objective of technological advancement is not to create new gadgets but to be sure that people are enabled to live a life they have reason to believe is worth living. As I have briefly pointed out when discussing the HDR 2001, an interesting area of analysis concerns the inputs that ICTs can make to the advancement of developing countries (Johnstone, 2007; Zheng, 2009; Heeks, 2010). In recent years, this relationship has attracted significant attention mainly for two reasons. Over the last 10 to 15 years, ICTs have become a useful tool to fight poverty as well as a symbol of redemption. For example, farmers from remote rural areas use mobile phones to negotiate the price of their products and get higher profit margins by skipping the middle link of big traders as mediators (Hellsten, 2007).

The second reason lies in the pervasive nature of the ICTs and in their ability to potentially impact almost all sectors (healthcare, manufacturing, education. . .). This contributes to the expansion of capabilities in various dimensions enabling the poor to access services previously intended only for the most privileged. Given this characteristic of the ICTs (multi-purpose and multi-choice) and their ability to increase individuals' choices, they fit particularly well with the approach of capabilities.

A more careful consideration of the use of ICTs also offers us the opportunity to reflect on the technology as an 'artefact' and on the processes that lead to its creation and its dissemination. In fact, the use of a tool does not always translate into an effective increase in the capabilities of individuals because of differences in terms of conversion factors (see Chapter 2). The most economically advantaged may benefit more because they possess greater individual and social conversion factors (better environmental conditions, better health, social contexts and infrastructure more favourable to the use of technologies, good education systems, etc.), compared to those who are totally or partially deprived. Such differences should be duly taken into consideration in development projects that aim at spreading ICTs as an instrument of emancipation. Often, though, the opposite occurs: traditional development projects perceive beneficiaries as passive recipients of technologies. In this regard, the CA may provide a more appropriate framework for the intervention since it emphasises the importance of individuals' choices and their involvement in the early planning stages of the technological solutions (Johnstone, 2007; Zheng, 2009).

Development projects that rely on the use of ICTs are built on the idea of allocating technological resources to specific *activities*; consequently, their focus is directed at purely quantitative indicators such as the number of connected individuals, service users, coverage areas and so on. For the capability approach, however, the assessment of a technology transfer project should be undertaken by trying to understand *which areas of being and doing of individuals are actually expanded (or restricted)*. This criterion does not usually envisage the prediction of clear results but is based on the interactions between the parties involved and on subsequent adaptations of project objectives depending on the context and conditions of individuals[3] (Kleine, 2011). This problem is, as we shall see,[4] common to most of the development interventions that are based on the application of technologies and introduction of innovations (Stewart, 1977; Hirschmann, 1967) and has significant consequences in terms of innovation policies.

Agency, i.e., the ability to pursue goals that go beyond the personal well-being, plays a central role in the capability approach. Within the context analysed here, it allows us to understand how promoting the needs and aspirations of people and communities requires that they can exercise an active and critical capacity towards technologies. Focusing on the effective freedom of people rather than on the passive acceptance of technology is pivotal, especially in situations where technologies are generated in developed countries and transferred to the developing nations. Increasing users' involvement and awareness has two consequences: the first concerns *the need for a public discussion*, in the adoption and diffusion of innovation processes; the second affects *the assessment of technologies* to be adopted, shifting the emphasis to users' needs and expectations, away from the speed of diffusion, economic performance and programmers' intentions (Zheng and Stahl, 2012). I will examine below the first consequence, while the second will be further explained in the chapter on innovation policies (Chapter 8).

### b. Design and deliberative democracy

An emerging issue for both ICTs and technologies overall is the degree of democratic control over the processes of adoption and diffusion of innovations.

Technologies are not always inherently good. They are part of the environment that involves power distribution and in some cases, become an instrument of marginalisation of the weakest sectors of the population (Zheng and Stahl, 2011; Biggeri and Ferrannini, 2014). Democratic and participatory processes are therefore crucial for facilitating public debate, enabling groups and communities to assume primary responsibility for independently resolving issues of public interest (Crocker, 2008).[5] In order to be effective, this collective control must extend *not only to the use but also to the design* of technological solutions.

Related experiences can be observed in the works of many designers. The development phase must give attention to the capabilities of citizens and thus co-create their future and the world in which they live. It is equally important that designers pay great attention to human diversity. Some design and development frameworks reflect this orientation – for instance, *the universal/inclusive design movement* which, in particular, is applied in urban planning (Toboso, 2011; Oosterlaken, 2012, Chapter 13). Such interventions place at their core the participation of people who are directly affected by urban renewal projects. They take into account and accommodate the needs of individuals and groups of users, such as people with disabilities, children and elders, so as to enhance the capabilities of these actors, when planning buildings, for example, in order to facilitate wheelchair access and provide premises suitable to the needs of children and the elderly.

A key factor in the implementation of these interventions is that human development, rather than technology, are placed at the core of the projects. The building block of the capability approach is the human being, who designs manufacturing projects, urban spaces and infrastructure to improve his living conditions. In order to expand human capabilities and agency, it is therefore important to start from the needs of people and communities, plan interventions addressing their needs, including the selection of appropriate technologies, and understand the impact on the quality of people's lives, that result from these. This implies that the relationship between the involved individuals and communities becomes a learning process and not a passive acceptance of artefacts designed for contexts and goals not always compatible with the well-being of the individuals. Democratic control certainly gives rise to a number of problems: issues regarding the ownership of technologies, evaluation modalities and the type of democratic structures that should exercise control over them. These are some of the emerging questions that will be discussed further.[6]

To conclude this section on democratic design, it is helpful to summarise the important contribution made by the *Critical Theory school*. Critical Theory, particularly as advanced by Zheng and Stahl (2012), brings together the various strands of critical philosophy on technology and the CA. One of the outcomes of this approach is the definition of four principles, which a 'critical capability approach to technology' must aspire to; these can help us summarise what has been discussed in this chapter so far:

1   *Human-centred technological development.* Technology is a means, never an end in itself, and thus not desirable as such. Human dignity and human rights should motivate the design of technology, rather than, as it usually is, market forces or the satisfaction of individuals' needs for 'happiness'. 'Desires' therefore, cannot be considered as a rational basis for the choice of technologies. The critical approach promotes the expansion of capabilities and social emancipation as a criterion for a desirable design process.

2   *Human diversity*. Diversity may depend on different factors, such as individual characteristics, environmental conditions, prevailing culture, social and economic structures. As we have seen, human diversity is at the core of Sen's reflections on inequality. Human diversity allows us to reflect on the problem of conversion factors for the use of specific technologies. The same technology used by different individuals (because of personal characteristics or context) offers different opportunities to improve their conditions. 'The principle of human diversity will render invalid any assumptions or claims about universal benefits of technology' (Zheng and Stahl, 2012, p. 65). On this basis, the uncritical use of ICTs as an undifferentiated development tool is questionable.

3   *Protecting human agency*. It's important to avoid that technology or any other political and social structures limit the autonomy of human beings to choose their own life goals. Individuals must always retain power, as autonomous beings and masters of themselves. This concept is strongly linked to that of emancipation – that is, the elimination of the causes of alienation and oppression of individuals. A form of oppression is also evident in the reification of technology, the perception of it, as a material artefact with *objective* characteristics that are independent of social and economic decisions. 'Reification can limit agency, freedom and emancipation by obfuscating choices that users could have' (Zheng and Stahl, 2012, p. 65).

4   *Democratic discourse*. The democratic control over technologies becomes a crucial point for their good use. Despite the wide pervasiveness of technologies in our daily lives, they are not subject to any form of democratic scrutiny, but only to market mechanisms. Given their pervasiveness and importance for the quality of life of the entire society, many are wondering if this is right.

### c. Inclusive innovation and capabilities

Innovation issues are, by their nature, strongly linked to those of development (Fagerberg and Srholec, 2009; Fagerberg et al., 2010; Verspagen, 2005). Recently, this bond has been further consolidated both by two strands of literature: one analysing the contribution that *innovation systems* can make to the growth of the most disadvantaged areas of the planet (Lundvall et al., 2009);[7] the other, focusing on *inclusive innovation*, a process aiming at broadening the range of subjects that can benefit from the fruits of technological change (Altenburg, 2009; Cozzens and Sutz, 2014; Chataway et al., 2014; Heeks et al., 2014; WB, 2013; OECD, 2013).

This latter strand of literature has a lot in common with the issues addressed this far and as we have seen, with the interest shown by philosophers of technology in the capabilities/technology nexus (Oosterlaken, 2015). However, paradoxically, in the observations on inclusive innovation, the capabilities paradigm is not organically taken as a normative basis for the analysis of interventions and the consequent political proposal.

Indeed, for Papaioannou (2014) the idea of considering innovations as a means and not as an end is a limitation of the capabilities approach. This leads the CA to focus more on fair development than on fair innovation. For this scholar, Sen's interest is to understand whether innovations can be connected to the capabilities people have reason to believe valuable. Innovations of frugal, grassroots or pro-poor type (see Chapter 2), which can achieve results within certain contexts in developing countries, can sometimes be developed in conditions of totalitarianism and lack of individuals' freedom. For the CA, in those cases the innovations have little or no value. While acknowledging that 'the capabilities approach is a strong normative candidate for evaluating new models of innovation in terms of inclusiveness' (p. 191), Papaioannou argues that it has a major limitation: it employs liberal cosmopolitan politics and structures as a background framework. However, 'cosmopolitanism as a theory of global justice politically fails to promote inclusiveness on the ground' (p. 191). This is because it tends to view politics in terms of the formation of a common consciousness about issues of global inequality, and entrusts the solution to these problems to the agreements and negotiations of the cosmopolitan forums and top-down institutions, such as the World Trade Organisation, the World Bank and the UN. This, Papaioannou argues, is a mistake, since believes 'equity and participation are egalitarian principles which cannot be pursued and achieved through consensus at top-down political institutions' (p. 192).

The approach that Papaioannou considers as most appropriate to evaluate the emerging models of innovation in low and middle income countries is that of *basic needs*. He believes that the biggest advantage of this approach derives from its highly pragmatic nature and the fact that the expansion of the capacity presupposes the fulfilment of basic needs. According to Papaioannou the satisfaction of basic needs frees individuals from natural and social constraints; in addition, the choice of basic needs is done through democratic participation: through a bottom-up process 'that is different from the top-down process of cosmopolitan politics. The latter is centralised, global and consensus politics while the former is decentralised, local and conflict politics' (p. 193).

Indeed, these criticisms seem rather uncharitable towards the richness of the reflections made over the years, especially on the issue of democracy (see below in this chapter) within the capabilities approach. First of all, consider Sen's work on India (Dreze and Sen, 2002), as well as chapters on democracy in his 'Development as Freedom' (Sen, 1999). In these and other contributions, he clearly articulates his view on the democratic participation as being participatory and bottom-up. Indeed an insistence on democracy and the great trust placed in it by Sen have drawn criticism from some scholars, who called upon Sen to give greater attention to conflict-based politics over the distribution of resources at the national and global levels (Deneulin, 2006). Papaioannou's claim that the basic needs approach provides a superior normative framework does not take into account Sen's discussion of conversion factors and in failing to do so, leaves open the possibility that an equal distribution of a certain set of basic needs will translate in de facto inequalities (Deneulin and Stewart, 2002).

A key concept in this context is that of *inclusion/exclusion*, which refers to access/lack of access to capabilities that allow individuals to live lives worthy of their dignity. This concept is therefore strongly interrelated with social equity, opportunities and democratic participation. Can inclusive innovations expand opportunities for the inclusion of citizens?

To answer this question, we need to offer a definition of the concept of inclusion. In this regard, it is important to highlight the contribution of Joseph (2014) who, building on the work of Sen (2000), reflects on the different types of exclusion that may be encountered in real life. *Constitutive exclusions* occur when individuals are excluded for reasons inherent to their condition (e.g., disability, not knowing how to read and write). *Instrumental exclusions* are exclusions which are not important per se but can cause other types of exclusion (e.g., access to credit, which in itself does not cause severe limitations, but may indirectly cause important constraints in people's lives) ; *active exclusion* is an intentional exclusion of particular groups of people (e.g., by governments of particular groups of citizens); *passive exclusion* is the exclusion that is observed not because of intentional actions but because of existing limitations that are not addressed (in the fields of knowledge, health, etc.).

To these interesting types of exclusion, Joseph (2014) adds some forms of inclusion: *subordinate inclusion*, which occurs when the inclusion is uneven, resulting in lower returns for some individuals than others; *illusive inclusion*, which occurs when formal inclusion does not lead to real benefits, resulting in de facto exclusion. Going back to the concept of exclusion, Joseph also identifies *transient exclusion*, which can be caused by unequal development strategies à la Hirschman (1958), or by structural changes induced by innovation processes that, in the short term, favour certain sectors and exclude others; if the exclusion persists for a long period, it can then be labelled as *sustained exclusion*.

The acquisition of an innovation (frugal, grassroots, BRI)[8] has a limited impact on human development if it occurs in a context of political unfreedom and/or is the result of a decision taken by those external to the context of application, and thus, not based on the free choice of citizens who apply it. If the different types of exclusion mentioned above are not addressed, the change produced by inclusive innovation is weakened. In fact, like other forms of innovation, inclusive innovation may result in exclusion and generate costs in terms of unfavourable and dangerous working conditions, increased automation-induced unemployment, environmental degradation, the effects of 'creative destruction' and the consequent marginalisation of obsolete sectors. These costs are incurred by the communities, rather than the entrepreneurs who introduce innovations. The impact of innovations, including those classified as inclusive, must be assessed not only in terms of the income they are able to generate, but through a broader multi-dimensional approach, in order to understand the changes introduced in people's lives. In this context, as we shall see later (Chapters 7–9), the state has a central role to play in the distribution of benefits and costs of innovation, as well as in the regulation of relations between businesses, groups and individuals (Voeten and Naudé, 2014).

These considerations highlight how the Capabilities Approach is an appropriate tool for a multidisciplinary evaluation of the inclusiveness of innovations. In this regard, it is interesting to examine the following classification, which arranges innovations incrementally on the basis of the extent to which they include individuals and groups (Heeks et al., 2014).

> Level 1 – Intention: an innovation is inclusive if the intention of that inno-
> vation is to address the needs, wants or problems of excluded groups [. . .]
> Level 2 – Consumption: an innovation is inclusive if it is adopted and used
> by the excluded groups [. . .]
> Level 3 – Impact: an innovation is inclusive if it has a positive impact on the
> livelihoods of the excluded groups [. . .]
> Level 4 – Process: an innovation is inclusive if the excluded groups are
> involved in the development of the innovation [. . .]
> Level 5 – Structure: an innovation is inclusive if it is created within a struc-
> ture that is itself inclusive [. . .]
> Level 6 – Post-structure: an innovation is inclusive if it is created within a
> frame of knowledge and discourse that is itself inclusive (p. 177–178).

In this approach, the level of inclusion increases as we advance from level 1 to level 6. This scale is especially useful in combination with a capabilities-based critical approach, and it leads us to raise some questions: what is the purpose of inclusion? Within the context in which an innovative technology is introduced, is the introduction of such technology (for example, a laptop) inclusive if it is built and adapted for persons previously excluded and is used to bet on football matches? . . . (Levels 1–2). Does the inclusiveness of innovation result only from the increased number of users, or does it also extend to the use that they make of it to expand their opportunities to live well?

Importantly, all levels of inclusion overlook the pivotal question: included to access *what*? In particular, levels 1–3 implicitly assume a positive opinion on the possibility to access a greater quantity of goods, a superior quality of goods and services, or goods that intend to address the needs of the excluded popula-tion. Yet it fails to ask: which needs? On the other hand, levels 4–6 assume a more active role of the marginalised population, but similarly, the objectives of the innovation are not clear: which skills are necessary in order to participate in the process of innovation? Which learning processes? Which roles are to be played? Which weight is to be given to decisions? An inclusive structure (or a post-structure) is ensured if it is set up for the purpose of improving the liv-ing conditions of individuals: who designs such innovative structure? For what purpose? Are these structures aimed solely at income growth?

The usefulness of the CA and inclusive innovation nexus can be highlighted using the simple classification that we saw in the previous section, derived from the 'critical capability approach of technology'. It allows us to emphasise key issues, typically of an ethical nature but with strong practical implications. Below are some questions that may arise from applying this framework:

1   *Human-centred inclusive innovation.* Does the innovation enable individuals to live a life that they consider more valuable and increase their freedoms? If yes, which ones?

2   *Human diversity.* Does the innovation take into account human diversity? Does it restrict discrimination between individuals? Are there any actions planned to allow all potential users to access innovation results?
3   *Protecting human agency.* Does the innovation improve the ability of individuals to make conscious choices? Does it improve the free choice of individuals, or is it imposed by some private or public organisation?
4   *Democratic discourse.* Does the innovation process require a free and democratic debate on the needs and objectives of innovation? Has all the relevant information been transmitted appropriately to allow an informed choice? Have all stakeholders in the innovation process been involved? Which democratic structures are involved?

These and other questions should be at the core of assessments of innovative choices that are intended to increase inclusion, i.e., improve access to capabilities that allow individuals to live a life worth living.[9] In this sense, the concept of inclusion is strongly interrelated to social equity, opportunities and democratic participation. The opportunities, as we have seen, can be either reduced or increased by the process of innovation. Choices are affected by different levels of participation in the processes of change and the identification of the social goals. The impact of innovation initiatives on inclusion is likely to be compromised if not subjected to a normative evaluation of the above type through the questions listed.

## 3.2 Human capabilities and learning capabilities

### Key ideas

Learning is a topic of considerable convergence between the innovation systems and the capabilities approach literatures. The first focuses on the contribution that, through learning, people make to innovation processes and social and institutional change; the second distinguishes between the *direct* and indirect value of learning. Learning has a direct value in so far as it broadens the freedom to live a life worth living and an *indirect* value in so far as it affects access to material resources in the form of income and consumption. The concept of learning capabilities is, however, wider than that of *human capital*, which addresses only the functional knowledge and skills in the economic process (section a.).

An increase in learning and in the stock of knowledge does not always seem to be associated with an expansion of individual and community freedoms. In some countries, the advancement of learning coexists with exclusion, based on gender, religion, social groups and political ideals. This probably depends on the fact that *the expansion of the learning processes in itself does not solve some of the limitations to the individual and collective freedoms*. Institutions and social capital may be seriously affected by such forms of discrimination and may ultimately limit the innovation system's capacity to grow. Giving wider attention to individual freedoms and the democratic control of the institutions, as claimed by the CA, may be a more promising way forward for development and innovation (section b.).

### a. Human capabilities, learning capabilities and human capital

Perhaps the most immediate sphere of cross fertilisation between the CA and the IS theory is the relationship between human capabilities and learning capabilities. As stressed by Lundvall et al. (2009):

> *We see great potential in linking Sen's analysis of individual 'capabilities' to the analysis of innovation systems. In our view the most important of all capabilities is the capability to learn. This capability is fundamental for all the other capabilities and it is the one that will shape the dynamics of welfare. To put it crudely economic development is about enhancing capability and opportunity to learn at all levels. Technological learning is fundamentally important but so is the social and political learning that is necessary to build institutions and policy strategies that support competence-building.*
>
> *(p. 18–19)*

For Lundvall and Johnson (1994), the learning process is largely interactive and socially embedded, and it cannot be understood without taking into account its broader institutional and cultural context. On this point, this school of thought meets Sen's approach, presenting the learning process as a tool to 'free' individuals from limitations and make them actors of change.

> *Innovations introduce technical and organizational knowledge into the economy. We can think of them as "learning results" contributing to the removal of 'unfreedoms' like ignorance, lack of learning opportunities and lack of economic opportunities and we can think of them as contributing to the enhancement of substantive freedoms like the capability to work, communicate, learn and to participate democratically in political processes. They are important means in the process of development.*
>
> *(Lundvall, 2007a, p. 114)*

The core interest of Lundvall et al. is the contribution that the expansion of individual capabilities can make to the broader process of social and institutional learning. As we have seen, however, the CA assumes a different point of view: it goes beyond the instrumental role of human capabilities, recognising that their expansion is the ultimate goal of development policies. The area of learning processes therefore constitutes an important, even if largely still unexplored, common ground between the two schools of thought.

A notion widely used in the economic literature (Burton-Jones and Spender, 2011), conceptually close to the ideas of human capabilities and learning capabilities, is certainly that of *human capital* (Chiappero-Martinetti and Sabadash, 2014). It is precisely because of this proximity between these concepts that it is useful to understand some of the differences among them. Sen does exactly that (1999, p. 292–295), by devoting a paragraph in his 'Development as Freedom' (Sen, 1999) to the link between human capital and human capabilities. The two concepts have a profoundly different focus. In the first case, the emphasis is placed on the active role of individuals in the expansion of production possibilities through learning, education and acquisition of specific skills (thus, close to the definition of skills as put forth by Nelson and Winter seen earlier in par. 2.1.c). In the case of human capabilities, on the other hand, the focus is shifted to the freedom to live the life that individuals value, and the possibility to expand the real choices they have to pursue this life.

> *Given her personal characteristics, social background, economic circumstances, etc., a person has the ability to do (or be) certain things that she has reason to value. The reason for valuation can be direct (the functioning involved may directly enrich her life, such as being well-nourished or being healthy), or indirect (the functioning involved may contribute to further production, or command a price in the market).*
>
> *(Sen, 1997, p. 195)*

Human capital thus pertains to abilities that are indirectly valuable, and it is thus a concept that relates specifically to production and trade. The capabilities approach, on the other hand, assumes a more inclusive perspective on learning and covers both directly and indirectly valuable human abilities.

According to IS theory, learning,[10] i.e., the process that helps increase the knowledge of individuals,[11] has an impact both on productive efficiency and income (what Sen calls the 'indirect value') and on the broader capacity to know one's social, political and cultural contexts, on one's ability to choose and participate in community life. In this sense, learning is not only a valuable capability in itself but also instrumental to other valuable capabilities.

> *The learning capability is thus one of the most important of the human capabilities and it is conditioned by national institutions and forms of work organization. It does not only have an instrumental role in development but also, under certain conditions, substantive value. When learning takes place in such a way that it enhances the capability of individuals and collectives to utilize and co-exist with their environ-ment, it contributes directly to human well-being. Furthermore, to be able to par-ticipate in learning and innovation at the work place may be seen as 'a good thing' contributing to a feeling of belonging and significance.*
>
> *(Lundvall, 2007b, p. 36)*

Therefore, in Lundval's approach *the concept of learning capabilities is much broader than that of human capital*, because learning not only has economic consequences but also social ones and is useful to create a sense of belonging among individu-als who interact in this process. However, as mentioned earlier, for CA learning is just one aspect of a broader skill set that allows individuals to live a decent life, thus *differing from human capabilities*.

### b. Learning, inclusion and freedom

Learning is, in principle, essential to the strengthening of individual and collec-tive agency and thus crucial to improve public debate and the effective func-tioning of democracy. It contributes to the full social and economic integration of potentially marginalised groups such as women, ethnic and religious minorities, etc., and ultimately, improves the well-being of the people.

As demonstrated by the growth of some Asian countries such as China (Liu, 2009), it is possible to reconcile a substantial increase in an economy's stock of knowledge with limited democratic participation and restricted fundamental freedoms. In some countries, economic growth has failed to include women and, in most cases, has led to an increase in income inequality and increased poverty[12] (Atkinson, 2015). Recent history has thus shown that a greater diffusion of knowledge does not *in itself* lead to a greater freedom of choice, and it can go hand in hand with a greater expansion of unfreedom.

These differences demonstrate that it is possible to expand the learning processes and the stock of knowledge, and even to build innovation systems, while restricting individual freedoms or depriving groups of citizens of their fundamental rights. Therefore, while the stock of knowledge and the learning process that fuels it are crucial to ensure growth, they do not exhaust the range of capabilities necessary to increase individual freedom. They are a necessary, but not a sufficient, condition for human development.

Taking part in the process of economic expansion is hard for groups facing barriers created by an unfavourable social environment, such as discrimination based on gender, race or social background. These barriers exclude part of the population from economic participation as well as from the enjoyment of fundamental citizenship rights. Indeed,

> The acknowledgment of the role of human qualities in promoting and sustaining economic growth-momentous as it is-tells us nothing about why economic growth is sought in the first place. If, instead, the focus is, ultimately, on the expansion of human freedom to live the kind of lives that people have reason to value, then the role of economic growth in expanding these opportunities has to be integrated into that more foundational understanding of the process of development as the expansion of human capability to lead more worthwhile and more free lives.
>
> (Sen, 1999, p. 295)

Literature on IS mainly focuses on learning processes, but this emphasis is not sufficient to describe the way those systems operate in reality. Institutions and social capital are important components of IS. The proper functioning of institutions depends on the decision-making processes and the actual level of participation of people; while the contribution of the structures of living together (and of the social capital) is important to support the cohesion needed in the process of change. In these and other cases, the expansion of freedoms and the effective participation of citizens, not just individual and collective learning, are prerequisites for the proper functioning of innovation processes.

Finally, the fruits of economic growth driven by knowledge do not automatically translate into interventions that aim to overcome exclusion and inequality. As we saw in Chapter 2 when dealing with the relationship between innovation and structural change, innovation generates costs and benefits, whose

distribution does not follow natural laws but rather depends on political decisions and on the proper functioning of the democratic system.[13]

## 3.3 Innovation, capabilities and inequality

*Key ideas*

The last four decades have seen a rise in income and wealth inequality in developed countries, mainly caused by budgetary policies and a slowdown in population and income growth. These dynamics are likely to entrench a state of
economic and social immobility and reduce the innovation potential of economies (section a.). Innovation and the excessive volatility of the economy can
lead to a net loss of jobs, cause a reduction of the levels of tacit knowledge of
businesses and workers and deepen inequalities (section b.). The CA understands
inequality as a 'multi-dimensional' phenomenon. Assuming this point of view,
inequality will never foster efficiency because those who are excluded from the
valorisation process based on gender, age or territory will never be in a condition
to engage and to best use their expertise to contribute to growth (section c.).

### a. Inequality and long-term change

The third issue which we will focus on covers inequality and its relationship
with innovation and growth. We will start from the most recent research on the
subject which, because of tradition and availability of data, addresses the issue
of inequality in terms of 'what one owns' (income, consumption, wealth) rather
than 'freedom to be and do'. As we have seen in the analysis of capabilities, the
income dimension of inequality is important but not exhaustive. There are
indeed other 'spaces' (variables) in which the differences between individuals
can be much greater than those reported by income alone. Nevertheless, the
recent contribution of important authors to the discourse on inequalities, their
long-term effects and policies seeking to reduce their burden,[14] seems to be a
good starting point for our discussion.

In recent years, important contributions have been made on the subject of
inequality (Franzini and Pianta, 2016; Atkinson, 2015; Piketty, 2014; Deaton,
2013; Stiglitz, 2012, 2015; Bowles, 2012). These studies have explored, from
different points of view, the problem of excessive divergence of material well-
being (income and wealth) between an increasingly smaller group of those who
have more and more and a larger group of those who have less and less.

According to Piketty (2014), over the last forty years developed countries
have witnessed an enormous concentration of material well-being in the higher
income brackets. Using original sources collected over the last fifteen years of
research, this author has constructed a long-term series (typically from the late
nineteenth century to the present) to show that:

- Income concentration in the US (the share of the top decile on the total
  income) has decreased from 40% to 50% between 1910 and 1920 to less
  than 35% in the post-war period before rising to 45% to 50% in 2010.

- The capital/income ratio in Europe decreased from 6 to 7 between the late nineteenth century and 1910 to 2 to 3 in 1950 before increasing again to 4.6 in 2010.

According to the author, the rise in inequality was caused primarily by two mechanisms: the uncontrolled increase in higher pay and the process of wealth accumulation and concentration. The first resulted, since the eighties, mainly from the budgetary policies implemented by most of the industrialised countries; the second from the fact that return on capital was higher than income growth (divergence $r > g$). For Piketty, this phenomenon can, in the long-term, be even more destabilising than the first and can generate growing imbalances in the distribution of wealth. In fact, developed countries are experiencing a low population and income growth. On the one hand, this increases the weight of the capital accumulated by previous generations and on the other, it causes the return of capital to significantly exceed the general growth rate of the economy. The occurrence of these two trends results in persistent inequality in the distribution of wealth.

These processes directly affect innovation as well as social and economic change. When growth is very weak, assets are handed down from generation to generation without major changes: endowment, business and professions are simply transferred from father to son. The competitive pressure from new entrants is low or non-existent, and the assets, are not divided among a higher number of heirs due to a low population growth. On the contrary, with a sustained growth of even only 1% to 1.5% per year, each new generation creates new businesses, new technologies and new social and economic conditions. With growth, new subjects claim their place in society by creating new products and new companies, and change stimulates the generation of new knowledge and new professional skills. This possible increase in the social and economic mobility does not in itself guarantee greater income equality, but it allows the disruption of old equilibria reinforced by a static economy and may favour over time, with adequate policies, the reduction in capital and income inequalities.

Another important element to reflect upon regarding the relationship between equality and long-term changes concerns the role of knowledge. According to Piketty, 'The main forces for convergence are the diffusion of knowledge and investment in training and skills' (Piketty, 2014, p. 21). And again, 'In the long run, the best way to reduce inequalities with respect to labour as well as to increase the average productivity of the labour force and the overall growth of the economy is surely to invest in education' (Piketty, 2014, p. 469). The dissemination of knowledge will allow both productivity growth (and therefore the expansion of resources potentially available to every individual) and the reduction of inequalities between individuals and between countries.

The IS approach (the "broad" version) is in line with these reflections. In fact, Lundvall (2011) emphasises that

> [i]n a neo-liberal discourse inequality is seen as a factor that promotes entrepreneurship and initiative. In a learning economy discourse it might be seen as something

*that makes it more difficult to build social capital and trust that is the basis for inter-active learning. . . . One mechanism through which equality promotes innovation is through its positive impact upon the active participation in organisational learning in working life.*

*(p. 35)*

Therefore, even in this strand of literature we find arguments to affirm that societies with an appropriate degree of equality and social cohesion promote equitable distribution of learning capabilities and economic and social change. Institutions and policies promoting greater inclusion can facilitate the broadening of the base on which the stock of knowledge and learning by interaction rest and, in this way, promote innovation and economic growth (Freeman, 2011; Arocena and Sutz, 2012).

The link between increased knowledge and the reduction of inequality, however, is only partly a natural and spontaneous factor, governed by market forces: it depends largely on public policies for training, education, high level education and research (Lundvall, 1992; Lundvall and Lorenz, 2010; Stiglitz and Greenwald, 2014). Moreover, the expansion of the stock of knowledge does not lead, *in itself*, to greater equality, as it emerges from Piketty's contribution. At the same time, more knowledge does not lead, *in itself*, to greater human development (see previous section). This will be further discussed in the chapters devoted to policies.

### b. 'Necessary' inequality

Since early contributions by Schumpeter, the innovation process is seen as intrinsically linked to the propagation of inequalities;[15] the continuous creative destruction that characterises the evolution of capitalism, the alternation of business cycles and resulting structural adjustments, new innovators replace the old, creating unemployment and imbalances between companies, sectors and territories (Schumpeter, 1939; Freeman, 2011).

*The opening up of new markets, foreign or domestic, and the organizational develop-ment from the craft shop and factory to such concerns as U.S. Steel illustrate the same process of industrial mutation – if I may use that biological term- that incessantly revolutionizes the economic structure from within, incessantly destroying the old one, incessantly creating a new one. It is what the capitalism consists in and what every capitalist concern has got to live in.*

*(Schumpeter, 2010, p. 73)*

According to Schumpeter, unemployment and business bankruptcy are temporary consequences of recessions. They are a recurring phenomenon in the capitalist system and play an important role in the reconstruction of a more efficient economy (Schumpeter, 1939). In the Schumpeterian model, the economy is re-built on a sounder basis after a crisis, it can grow unimpeded by exploiting the fruits of innovations, offering new opportunities to firms and workers adversely affected by a recession. (Schumpeter, 1936). In this way, the resulting temporary inequality between winners and losers is reabsorbed in the ascending phase of the cycle.

This idea of the crises' cleansing role and the related concept of "natural selection" which follows, however, clashes with the empirical evidence of some negative impacts that tend to persist after recessions (Stiglitz and Greewald, 2014). Productivity losses that occur during crises are seldom recovered in subsequent periods of expansion; failed companies hardly ever become operational when the crisis ends; these failures carry with them the loss of a lot of tacit knowledge that may not be recoverable. In addition, many workers are unable to adapt their skills to the emerging industries following the processes of structural economic change, and remain unemployed for long periods of time; the businesses that fail during crises are not always the least productive, but more often than not, simply the most indebted ones. Moreover, during crises businesses reduce those costs that have long-term impacts, such as investments in R&D and personnel training, which in turn reduces the growth potential of the economy.

Therefore, the idea that recessions have a Darwinian effect of eliminating the least-adapted businesses from the competitive arena and enabling the more able ones to contribute to the well-being of all clashes with the tendency of companies to become short-sighted and cut back crucial resources needed for growth and innovation in the areas of R&D, knowledge and learning. This in turn generates losses that are only partly compensated by the growth process of the innovative segment of the economic system.[16] 'While there may be some virtues in the process of 'creative destruction' that is associated with innovation, the destruction that occurs in the process of cyclical fluctuations is not offset by any creation, and the anticipation of future volatility dampens investment in learning and R & D . . . In short, volatility is bad for long-term growth of the economy' (Stiglitz and Greenwald, 2014, p. 98).

Even some important and influential studies on growth state that some degree of inequality is 'necessary'. Both the discussions by Kuznets (1955) on the initial increase and subsequent reduction of inequality in the various stages of growth, and Kaldor (1956) on the need to finance growth by focusing on the resource-rich, have, however, been refuted by recent studies that have put to use a better quality of statistical data (Piketty, 2014). Contrary to what was claimed by traditional analysis, and as it has been shown by a ponderous quantity of studies (World Bank, 2006),[17] greater equity has a significant influence on the processes of growth and development.[18]

### c. Equality and efficiency

The final issue to be examined here is the relationship between equality and efficiency. As we have seen (in Section 2.2.e), the arguments that consider inequality useful for the purpose of increasing efficiency are based mainly on two mechanisms: the first sees inequality as having an 'incentive' role that encourages a greater commitment to work (there are those who earn more, so I engage more to gain more income); the second considers inequality as 'just' because it is functional to the 'asymmetries' of skills and abilities that exist between people (I'm better, therefore it's right that I am paid more since the resources that I will use will then have a greater value). Both mechanisms contribute to an efficient use of resources.

Following this hypothesis, the increase in inequality experienced in recent decades in major developed countries should have stimulated the efficiency of the system and encouraged a higher rate of growth. This phenomenon, however, has not occurred. In contrast, long-term analysis (OECD, 2012) indicates, at least from the beginning of the new millennium, a progressive decrease in growth rates in industrialised countries. This slowdown has also been confirmed by the reaction of the global economy to the last Great Recession that began in 2008 (Ollivaud and Turner, 2015).

Looking at it through the Capabilities Approach lens, this contradiction could have a possible explanation. Let us assume that the repercussions of incentives and operational asymmetries on efficiency depend both on *static* and *dynamic* mechanisms. Static mechanisms work for a *given* number of parties involved in the economic system and assume that the only form of inequality occurring is income inequality. Dynamic mechanisms depend on the number of *new* players entering the market value and on the existing differences in terms of capabilities.

As highlighted above, CA's criticism of stimulus mechanisms generated by inequality is essentially based on the fact that these mechanisms do not consider the multiple causes of exclusion: gender, age, ethnicity, unemployment, religion, social context, land, etc. These causes can marginalise considerable segments of the population and lead to long-lasting exclusion from the development processes. Therefore, those who face these forms of inequality cannot 'be stimulated' by incentives such as the possibility of earning a higher income or the possibility of having an improved skill or job qualifications recognised, simply because these individuals are not part of the valorisation processes. Those individuals who instead are within the valorisation processes, in the absence of a significant number of newcomers, after having fully used the hypothesised stimuli generated by inequality, will run out of possibilities for efficient growth. A society with persistent and growing inequalities in capabilities will expand the number of excluded individuals, i.e., those who are not motivated to give their best and be rewarded for a better knowledge/competence. In turn, lack of new inputs and improvements leads to the stagnation of economies.

Policies targeting gender equality, improving access to health and learning of the most disadvantaged, facilitating the entry of young people into the labour market, and territorial balance, broaden the platform for those who can enter the valorisation process by setting in motion a *dynamic* process of economic and social change that creates new energy and new players contributing to efficient growth. Efficiency is greatly impacted by these dynamic processes, and it is a mistake to believe that it depends only on individual behaviour in a *static* context and a person's ability to add value to the material resources, as result of stimuli such as professional incentives and awards.

Over the past four decades, however, policies aiming at reducing inequality have not been at the centre of governments' concerns (Stiglitz, 2012; Atkinson, 2015). The stimuli resulting from the incentives and operational asymmetries have worked for an increasingly smaller number of persons (Stiglitz, 2012), limiting the dynamic processes of change and contributing to a decrease in efficiency of the system over the long run.

In his pioneering work on the relationship between efficiency and equality, Meade (1964) emphasised

> *In the highly developed industrialized countries a substantial proportion of the real product does accrue to the owners of property and the property is very unequally owned. There is already, therefore, a problem. The pattern of real wage rates which is required on efficiency ground may lead to a very high level of income per head for the small concentrated number of rich property owners. And it is possible, though not certain, that this problem will become more acute as a result of automation.*
>
> *(p. 25)*

The trend of wealth concentration in the hands of a few is in fact aggravated by the prevalence of labour-saving technologies. These would increase the average productivity and simultaneously reduce the amount of work required for a given amount of capital cost and therefore its total demand. This may also occur in the presence of a net accumulation of capital if the new labour demand for additional facilities is less than the sum of new workers coming onto the labour market and workers who have lost their jobs following the suppression of the activities they were engaged in. In such a case, jobs in the less-efficient industries and services will become available for workers engaged in low-productive activities. According to the forward-looking interpretation of Meade, this results in a reduction in the wage rate and a gap between the average output per worker and marginal productivity of labour. This implies a shift in income towards owners of capital and further inequality. Meade suggests that rather than worrying about what to do with the freed-up time resulting from technological progress,[19] it is appropriate to question as follows 'What shall we all do when output per man-hour of work is extremely high but practically the whole of the output goes to a few property owners, while the mass of the workers are relatively (or even absolutely) worse off than before?' (p. 26). In the event such a situation were to prevail without any government restrictions and interventions, it would lead to a strong concentration of ownership in the hands of a few and a progressive reduction of the impact of labour earnings on total output.

> *There would be a limited number of exceedingly wealthy property owners; the proportion of the working population required to manage the extremely profitable automated industries would be small; wage rates would thus be depressed; there would have to be a large expansion of the production of the labour-intensive goods and services which were in the high demand by the few multi-multi-multi-millionaires; we would be back in a super-world of an immiserized proletariat and of butlers,*

*footmen, kitchen maids, and others hangers-on. Let us call this the Brave New Capitalist's Paradise.*

Though extreme and colourful in his language, Meade described half a century ago a situation that is very similar to the one prevailing today in many industrialised countries where the state has failed to take action to limit inequality. It is characterised, as confirmed by the studies undertaken by Piketty and Atkinson, by an extreme concentration of ownership and a strong divergence of incomes, and as noted by Stiglitz, by an increase in the number of people engaged in precarious work yielding low productivity.

To prevent the emergence of a 'Brave New Capitalist's Paradise', Meade proposed interventions for a greater distribution and socialisation of properties that complement the policies of a Welfare State, already existing at the time in Great Britain. He called for raising property taxes, inheritance and gift taxes; public investments, policies favouring small holders, policies on basic education and interventions for population control. One of his students, Atkinson (2015), has recently developed this line of reasoning updating it to current conditions and proposing 15 measures to reduce inequalities, some of which will be discussed below (see Chapter 9).

The above analysis of Meade can help us interpret one of the most important institutional changes that contributed to the increase in inequality in recent decades, i.e., the weakening of trade unions. In almost all advanced countries, the presence of the unions is reduced, causing a major economic power imbalance and a political vacuum in employee representation. In many countries, employees face the difficulties of productive changes due to their weaker position and substantial individualisation of work conditions (Franzini-Pianta, 2016). Faced with labour-saving innovations and transfers of manufacturing abroad, workers with less bargaining power accept sharply deteriorated wage conditions and employment protection: a poorly paid job with little social security is preferred to unemployment. This weakened bargaining power of workers and the progressive reduction in average wages is consistent with the materialisation of the "Brave New Capitalist's Paradise" which, as we have seen earlier, leads to a strong polarisation of incomes and to the progressive rise in underpaid jobs requiring little qualification. This is the cause of major inefficiencies both of a micro and macro nature that will be discussed further in Chapter 9.

## 3.4 Innovation, public institutions and democracy

### Key ideas

The innovation process generates costs and benefits that tend to be distributed unevenly between individuals, businesses and territories. To ensure a more balanced distribution of these impacts, state intervention and an active presence of non-market institutions are required (section a.). The quality of institutions is closely linked to political freedoms. These have a direct role, as individual capabilities that allow people to learn from one another are at the core. They have an instrumental role, since they allow the control of political decision-making; and a constructive role, since they enable the identification of objectives and priorities for collective action. These functions of political freedoms are also important in the innovation processes and for the choices that institutions make to facilitate the learning process (section b.). Excessive inequality affects institutional effectiveness, which can be 'captured' by interest groups with greater economic power. These may in turn influence the use of public resources for research and innovation. This can lead to a vicious circle fuelled by the flow of public resources towards the strongest groups at the expense of the weak, and a gap between large (and few) public and private science, technology and innovation (STI) structures, on the one hand, and a growing number of excluded groups from the learning by doing, using and interacting processes (DUI), on the other (section c.). Citizens' effective participation, their motivation, the proper functioning of the institutional mechanisms and the extent of inequality influence the practice of democracy. The active presence of citizens gives them the opportunity to voice their opinion and steer the choices towards objectives of common interest (section d.).

### a. The costs and benefits of innovation

As we have seen, innovation feeds growth and generates extensive productive and social changes, resulting in benefits and costs. In terms of benefits, innovation meets (creates) new needs, increases productivity and generates new and greater profits and new job opportunities. In terms of costs, on the other hand, innovation destroys traditional practices and knowledge and creates instability in the financial markets, volatility in economic cycles, recurring crises and unemployment; the introduction of new activities, if not regulated, may cause problems in the market structures and the environment.

The impacts of change can be mitigated and better distributed by the intervention of the state and a wide network of non-market institutions. Over the past three decades, the idea that the state should play a neutral role, that of non-interference in market mechanisms, has become entrenched. State non-interference has widened inequalities and, as we shall see, impacted the very mechanisms of innovation and economic growth.

My working hypothesis is that innovation processes, if left to themselves without the presence of a stabilising role of the state and other non-market institutions, can lead to an extreme concentration of resources and power in the hands of a few and to an under-utilisation of the most valuable asset of the economy, i.e. the people (a condition described by Maede in "Brave New Capitalist's Paradise", discussed above). Over time, this condition can hinder the very processes of learning and innovation. On the contrary, a greater commitment of governments in the fields of education, health, social security and work organisation can generate innovation systems capable of increasing growth and dynamic effects of inclusion. The assumption of this increased commitment, however, is the establishment of an appropriate and participatory democratic system.

This subject is too vast and challenging to be treated exhaustively in this work. Thus, I will briefly address three questions which, although themselves broad and challenging, will help me to delimit the scope of the enquiry:

- Is democracy important for innovation?
- What are the consequences of inequality on the proper functioning of democracy?
- Could a better practice of democracy foster innovation?

### b. Democracy and innovation

Over the past two centuries, many parts of the world have witnessed the establishment of democratic institutions based on constitutional rights, overall independent judicial systems, functioning electoral systems, parliaments and national and regional elected assemblies and pluralist information systems (Acemoglu and Robinson, 2012). This has allowed some countries to attain a more general progress both on the economic and social front, through the respect of property rights, the encouragement of investment in new technologies and skills and access to well-being for a growing number of citizens, as well as inclusion of new strata of the population, and access to fundamental rights by historically marginalised classes and groups of people.

Historical factors and diverse interests within every community, however, led individual countries to follow paths of different institutional change that may not have always combined growth with full democracy (Acemoglu and Robinson, 2012; Reinert, 2007).

In this regard, it is not uncommon to encounter views on development issues that consider democracy as a luxury for poor countries. In some countries (e.g., China, Singapore) economic growth took off, with some success, in conditions of substantial political unfreedom. This experience strengthened the argument of those who advocate that economic growth has priority over political freedoms. This reasoning considers democracy an exclusive luxury of countries that have already addressed the major problem of subsistence and do not face the burden of material need. Questions such as: 'What would the poor do with political freedoms when they have nothing to live on? What comes first, the material need to survive or the freedom to choose political representatives?' are not uncommon and require a reasoned response.

According to Sen (1999b these arguments are not sound. He argues that the intensity of economic needs makes the expansion of political freedoms more urgent rather than less. This is the case because democracy fulfils the following the three functions: direct (or constitutive), instrumental and constructive (see above par. 2.i). Let me further elaborate on these three functions to highlight their importance in the process of innovation and growth.

The *direct or constitutive function* of democracy and the opportunities it offers people to learn from one another is definitely an essential starting point for the construction of dynamic systems of innovation. A context in which ideas do not circulate freely will hardly be conducive to the dynamic processes of full, critical and creative learning. There could certainly be contexts in which 'what' to learn and 'how' to learn are predetermined and imposed by a central entity. Over time, however, these contexts will sustain objective limitations in the ability to ensure the necessary diversity and complexity in the process of learning and innovation.

Stiglitz and Greenwald (2014) observe that there are considerable differences in the level of welfare between various national economies, which go beyond the differences in the availability of factors of production. This can be observed, for example, when a comparison is made between countries that until the beginning of the 1990s had a centralised economy with similar countries with a non-centralised economy. Immediately after the war, most of the former countries experienced a period of rapid economic development as compared to the 'democratic' countries. Finland was less developed than the Baltic countries of the former USSR, a large agricultural country like Spain was less rich than Poland, Taiwan was a relatively backward part of China, Vietnam and Cambodia were in better conditions than Thailand, and North Korea was more industrialised than South Korea. For the following forty years, however, countries with non-centralised economies extensively invested in capital and education at all levels, especially in technical disciplines, with high performance in the area of technological innovation (as in the space sector). This led to a substantial shift: the gap in terms of well-being between countries with centralised and non-centralised economies widened in favour of countries with non-centralised economy, and the latter achieved average per capita income three times higher and a life expectancy of 8 to 10 years longer than the former. The authors explain these differences in terms of the inability of the centralised economies 'to learn from the innovations and best practices that were going on the other parts of the world' (Stiglitz and Greenwald, 2014, p. 32).

In my view, the slow pace of these economies may also be explained by the role played by the unfreedoms. The relatively poor performance recorded by these countries was certainly caused by the fundamental characteristic of being *centralised, closed economies*. In other words, within these systems players, for the most part, had to follow directions about price, quantity, quality and distribution of resources and partly refrained from exchanging with the outside world beyond the Soviet system. An equally important role however, was played by *the political situation*, characterised by the enduring presence of authoritarian regimes during which there were serious limitations to fundamental freedoms of expression and political association. These limitations played a central role in terms of knowledge circulation, the ability 'to learn from one another' and, more generally, an affirmation of new economic and social paradigms that feed over time the process of change. In the long term, political limits to freedom and to the ability 'to learn from one another' that derive from these limitations, together with the inability 'to learn from best practices', were a serious setback in these countries.

The *instrumental function* of democracy also plays a crucial role in the processes of change. Innovation generates risks and uncertainties, as well as costs and benefits that tend to be unequally distributed. A better distribution of negative and positive impacts of change requires state intervention. However, both the intensity and the essence of state intervention result from political choices, the effectiveness of which depends on the democratic control and effective citizen participation (STEPS, 2010; Leach and Scoones, 2006; Arocena and Sutz, 2000, 2012) that limit the impact of bad decisions or decisions contrary to the collective well-being.[20]

Finally, *the constructive role* of democracy reminds us of the importance to focus on objectives that promote the well-being of the people. Many choices on the use of public funds for research and technological innovation are undertaken without deeply analysing the objectives to be achieved and without identifying clear priorities. This is typically the case of funding of programmes in the areas of defence, energy and biotechnology, for which it is rare that goals to be pursued are systematically debated in democratic fora[21] (Ely et al., 2011; UNDP, 2010).

A crucial starting point to trigger new processes of growth and development is that there is no innovation without full democracy. The idea that democracy will follow suit once growth and adequate material resources are ensured is inadequate. It is thus worth to experiment with paths of change in which democracy becomes a prerequisite rather than an outcome of growth.

For these reasons, 'a country does not have to be deemed fit for democracy; rather, it has to become fit through democracy. This is indeed a momentous change, extending the potential reach of democracy to cover billions of people, with their varying histories and cultures and disparate levels of affluence' (Sen, 1999b, p. 4).

### c. Institutions and economic power

The issue of democracy and its impact on innovation generally involves the nature of institutions and the practice of democracy. Recent studies have shown how political institutions play an essential role in determining the differences in a country's prosperity level (Acemoglu and Robinson, 2010, 2012; Cimoli et al., 2009; North, 1990, 2005; Knack, 2003; Reinert, 2007). They, in turn, depend on the de facto and de jure distribution of power between different social groups, which are in conflict over the distribution of resources. One of the reasons for the poor functioning of democratic practice outlined by Dreze and Sen (see Section 2.i) is the excessive inequality that restricts the proper functioning of institutions, even when the latter are formed based on free and fair elections with constitutionally guaranteed mandates.

In particular, Acemoglu and Robinson (2010) believe that there are two mechanisms of *persistence* and self-reproduction in the distribution of political power and economic resources. The first ensures that:

> *Political institutions allocate de jure political power, and those who hold political power influence the evolution of political institutions, and they will generally opt to maintain the political institutions that give them political power. A second mechanism of persistence comes from the distribution of resources: when a particular group*

*is rich relative to others, this will increase its de facto political power and enable it to push for economic and political institutions favourable to its interests, reproducing the initial disparity.*

*(Acemoglu and Robinson, 2010, p. 8)*

Therefore, the considerations laid out in Section 3.3 with reference to equality are closely linked to the functioning of political institutions. An unequal society is not simply deplorable *per se* but also because the high level of economic and political inequality leads to *institutions controlled ('captured')* by a minority with greater influence. This minority group tends to support policies which further consolidate the position of the privileged groups to which they belong. In such a way, public resources are channelled towards particular interest groups, with the middle and lower classes gradually being excluded from the distribution of the economic resources.

The processes of consumption, investment and innovation also weaken and the long-term opportunities for growth decrease. Most unequal societies tend to exclude certain groups of people from accessing opportunities that others with greater *de facto* power may instead have (better education, low-interest loans, risk insurance, etc.). This exclusion prevents those belonging to the discriminated groups from developing their full potential as economic actors (as workers, consumers, investors, etc.). 'Both theory and empirical evidence suggest that these incomplete realisations of economic potential are of concern not only to those who care about equity per se. They also affect aggregate economic potential, and therefore aggregate output and its rate of growth' (Ferreira, 1999, p. 13).

Along the same lines, Stiglitz (2012) argues that societies characterised by widespread inequality are inefficient and their economies suffer from stability and sustainability issues in the long-run. 'When one interest group holds too much power, it succeeds in getting policies that benefits itself, rather than policies that would benefit society as a whole' (p. 83).

On this point Piketty (2014) is even more forthright in stating that the excess of inequality undermines the very foundations of the rules of coexistence of modern democracies that developed in Western societies from the Declaration of 1789, which states in Article. 1: 'Social distinctions may be based only on common utility.' The recent huge concentration of economic and political power in the hands of a few is instead pushing modern democracies towards the protection of particular, rather than collective, interests.

One of the most important ways of 'institutional capture' by interest groups depends on the extent to which large corporations and financial centres can influence the functioning of political parties, and the decisions of national governments and international agencies. These big global powers influence the political decision-making process by not only providing financial resources to political parties, and directly participating in them, but also by owning and using the media and directly engaging in corruption. This is evident in every area of public decision-making, including research and innovation. The growing presence of these pressures distorts the process of decision-making and requires a democratic response. It is necessary to evaluate the consequences of these constraints on the capabilities of individuals and communities and to rethink the political interventions not only in national and regional but also global terms (Stewart and Deneulin, 2002).

Based on what has been discussed so far, we can identify a twofold effect that institutional capture by organised interest groups has on innovation processes. On one hand, the public resources devoted to R&D and technological innovation are directed to topics of interest promoted by dominant groups, as a result of their power to influence the political system and the decision-making process. Applied research topics are rarely driven by clear objectives and explicit priorities and are seldom deliberated in public discussion. Typically, they are defined through decision-making processes that involve political and administrative levels (such as ministries, big agencies, public research centres, large universities), influenced in particular by interest groups. In other words, this first effect promotes a RTI-based (Research, Technology and Innovation) innovation model, whose main, but not exclusive, actors are large companies, public and private laboratories, as well as universities, pushing for issues that rarely reflect collective interests.[22]

The second effect arises from the process of gradual exclusion of large sections of the population that, as we have seen, results from the concentration of resources. The underutilisation of people and the increase in excluded groups from the valorisation process reduce the potential for innovation based on interaction and learning (DUI). The growing exclusion leads to inadequate levels of complexity, diversity, creativity and unpredictability, all necessary agents for change, which can only be ensured by an inclusive and open system.

Therefore, in contexts where institutional capture is a prevailing phenomenon, innovation is based on the use of large amounts of public (and private) funds directed towards research areas supported by interests of large industrial groups. This model needs a few large centres of excellence (i.e., a few universities; a few, but top-ranking scholars in the world attracted by high remuneration, and a few large industrial groups). Against this model, we can outline an alternative approach based primarily on the interaction and involvement of a large number of public and private entities, which include and oversee the former group, directing it towards collective goals. In the case of institutional capture, this second approach will not be pursued, and the number of people who can participate in the process of change will reduce even further.

Furthermore, an unequal distribution of a country's resources reinforces the balances of power which determine the quality of the institutions and their ability to pursue policies that affect the quality of innovation and growth. The tendency for these balances to self-perpetuate can create a vicious circle which, by inhibiting society's new forces, adversely affects the processes of innovation and social and institutional changes.

As a result, only with a dramatic break from the unequal balances created within the institutions, and the assertion of 'democracy as a universal value', does it becomes possible to feed virtuous processes of growth and innovation. The extreme inequality would need government intervention, but this fails to materialise because the institutions are weak or 'captured'. In these situations, when a vicious cycle blocks a country, 'radical social innovations brought about by social movements might be necessary to overcome the stalemate' (Lundvall, 2007a, p. 117).

### d. The practice of democracy

Political freedoms and democratic institutions are not all: democracy should be seen as a system that creates a set of opportunities (Ocampo et al., 2007), whose concrete application depends also on *the practice of democracy*. Inequality makes the democratic practice less effective. Drèze and Sen (2002) identify two additional important elements: the lack of effective participation of citizens and the negative impacts of corruption, poor management of services, waste, etc. I will focus on the first cause, on which some general remarks can be made; I will not address, however, the second cause, as it is highly dependent on the historic and cultural context of each country as well as the forms of participation and control exercised by the citizens.

Today, the functioning of many democratic systems, even the most established ones as in North America and Europe, does not always guarantee choices that expand citizens' opportunities and improve their quality of life. In most cases, it is even difficult to clearly identify the priorities guiding governments' economic policy choices and among these, those for research and innovation (Mazzucato, 2013).

Even the current innovation policies for the benefit of developing countries are rarely subject to a democratic audit of the pursued objectives. They are mainly based on the transfer of technologies and innovation systems designed and tested in the context of more-developed nations (Lundvall et al., 2009; Arocena and Sutz, 2000), but have hardly allowed local economies to adopt, over time, an independent innovation system able to accelerate growth and induce development (STEPS 2010, UNDP, 2001). This occurred mainly because of the extreme weaknesses of political institutions in developing countries, which in actual practice tend to accommodate the needs of particular industrial and financial interests rather than those of their citizens.

This flags a problem with democratic practice, in particular with respect to lack of 'depth' and 'ability to control' (Crocker, 2008). In 'shallow' democracies citizens' concrete participation in public life is only through voting. The 'democratic decision-making' (see Section 2.i) is a form of indirect democracy, which merely entrusts the representatives elected to legislative bodies to protect common interests. 'Deeper' democracies include methods of participation that go beyond casting an election vote and identifying a majority and a minority in the representative bodies. This is a form of 'participatory decision making' in which citizens are directly involved in collective decisions. In such cases, democracy includes free discussions that assess different points of view: citizens' assemblies that examine and express opinions on the formulation of public budgets, on the opening of urban development projects, the organisation of public services, etc.

In the cases presented above, the extent of participation must be considered together with the size of *control (or influence)* that citizens exercise over public decisions. The deeper and more widespread the control, the greater the chance to operate in a full democracy (Crocker, 2008).

There is no doubt that the political choices concerning research and innovation have a particular importance to society as they affect its future and its possibilities for growth. However, in this type of decision-making, the participation of and control by citizens is indeed limited. The decision-making process includes a small circle of public and private decision-makers, mostly not subjected to public scrutiny and transparency. This phenomenon is observed both in the developed and less developed parts of the planet.

The capability approach provides some suggestions to overcome this problem. Its idea that the expansion of individual and social skills should be pursued through a process of empowerment (see Section 2.2) supports an idea of development that combines efficiency and the expansion of freedoms. As discussed in Section 3.1 focusing on technologies and inclusive innovation projects, the CA allows us to evaluate government choices and to establish different goals and priorities. According to Sen's approach, choices and priorities must stem from an 'evaluative exercise' to be performed by individuals and society in order to form judgments which embody a system of weighting. In Sen's view, 'for a particular person, who is making his or her own judgements, the selection of weights will require reflection, rather than any interpersonal agreement . . . in arriving at an 'agreed' range for *social evaluation* . . . there has to be some kind of reasoned 'consensus' on weights, or at least on a range of weights. This is a 'social choice' exercise, and it requires public discussion and a democratic understanding and acceptance' (Sen, 1999, p. 78). The starting point for reviewing of interventions will then have the widening citizens' freedoms of at its core and will certainly be different from the approach mentioned above, in which political and administrative entities seek to increase in profits, open new markets and maximise competitiveness.

The link between the changes introduced by innovation, the distribution of its costs and benefits, the regulatory intervention of the state, and the quality of institutions and democratic practices can trigger both virtuous and vicious circles. This depends on the mix of historical, social, political and cultural factors of each country. In some countries and for some periods of time, innovation, economic and social policies and democratic control have interlaced in favour of virtuous circles, which have been self-perpetuating and have produced decades of well-being fairly distributed among the citizens. This is the case of the Scandinavian countries (Lundvall, 2002; Castell and Himanen, 2002; Veggeland, 2007; Miettinen, 2013) that have, in past decades, been a top of world rankings in innovation (EC, 2016) and at the same time, virtuously combined equity and efficiency (Sapir, 2006) with good systems of distribution of economic and social risks (Andersen et al., 2007). Even during the most recent wave of crisis and despite the changes in the political balance of power, these countries remained a good example of how high competitiveness, social equity, institutional trust, high-quality education and proper democratic control can co-exist and reciprocally reinforce one other.

## 3.5  Innovation, social networks and social security

*Key ideas*

Innovation and capabilities are influenced by the social context in which individuals and communities coexist. Within the CA, the importance of the social context is captured by the reference to 'structures of living together'. For the CA, these can have a positive but also a negative impact on the freedom of individuals. In innovation studies, however, the context is analysed in terms of social capital, which is a more limited concept. Social capital refers to social relations relevant to economic activities (section a.). One factor that could undermine trust between people and weaken democratic participation is the risk of marginalisation and social exclusion. A sense of insecurity can be generated by many factors, both exogenous and endogenous factors to contemporary societies, and is amplified by the increased interdependence of economies and cultures. Social protection systems can improve the sense of individual and collective security. In addition, the proper operationalisation of these systems is a prerequisite for creating a more dynamic economy in which people are more likely to take risks and introduce innovations (section b.).

### a.  Structures of living together and social capital

Innovation and growth strongly benefit from contexts in which the relationships between individuals are based on networks of trust. (Soete et al., 2010; Akçomak and ter Weel, 2012; Neira et al., 2009, see Section 2.1). As previously discussed (Section 2.2), capabilities are determined by social context and structures of living together, as well as by the trust and transparency governing relations among individuals.

> *In social interactions, individuals deal with one another on the basis of same presumption of what they are being offered and what they can expect to get. In this sense, the society operates on some basic presumption of trust . . . . When that trust is seriously violated, lives of many people – both direct parties and third parties- may be adversely affected by the lack of openness. Transparency guarantees (including the right to disclosure) can thus be an important category of instrumental freedom. These guarantees have a clear instrumental role in preventing corruption, financial irresponsibility and under-hand dealings.*
>
> *(Sen, 1999a, p. 40)*

According to Deneulin and Stewart (2002), in order to promote citizens' capabilities, we cannot focus exclusively on individual interactions. Rather, it is also necessary to improve the structures of living together. Positive structures of living together improve individual well-being, enable individuals to be free agents, and encourage them to set valuable goals. 'In other words, flourishing individuals generally need and depend on functional families, cooperative and high-trust societies, and social contexts which contribute to the development of individuals who choose 'valuable' capabilities' (p. 68). An important objective of development policies is thus to identify interventions that lead to major changes in these structures of living together and limit the emergence of negative (dysfunctional) structures.

As I discussed in Section 2.1, the concept of social capital, in both its interpretations (civic-ness and networks), primarily focuses on the benefits that social cohesion and trust trigger within the economy in terms of information flow, transfer of tacit knowledge and reduction of transaction costs.

There are undoubtedly some similarities between the structures of living together and social capital, as they both pertain to the social dimension of collective activities. However, the two approaches diverge significantly because of the differences between the points of view they reflect. Interest in the structures of living together is linked to the role they can play in influencing and shaping the capabilities of individuals. The interest in social capital is triggered by the contribution it can make towards the good or bad functioning of economic relations between agents. In the first case the focus is on the growth of community and individuals, a factor that has value *per se*, while in the second case the focus is on a factor that has an *instrumental* value to the proper functioning of economic relations. In this sense, social capital is another important factor for growth, together with physical, financial and human capital.

### b. Innovation and social security

One factor that can undermine trust between people is the risk of marginalisation and social exclusion (Edwards and Glover, 2001; Taylor-Gooby and Zinn, 2006). In recent years, despite some undeniable improvements in terms of human and technological progress, a strong sense of insecurity has spread worldwide, both with respect to disposable resources of individuals and families, and with respect to personal and environmental safety (UNDP, 2014). Local political tensions, migration pressures, wars, corruption, economic and financial crises, policies that reduce public services, ecological and health disasters and much more have contributed to the spreading of a sense of vulnerability both individual and collective, in particular among the weakest groups (UNDP, 2014). A greater interconnection between states, favoured by the advancement in ICT, reduction in transport costs, increased market liberalisation and greater political integration among countries, as compared to the divisions during the Cold War, contributed to the 'shrinking space, shrinking time and disappearing borders' (Giddens, 1990) and to the rapid spread of these threats from one country to another (Fukuda-Parr, 2003).

The rapid spread of insecurity and of individual and collective vulnerability have called into question the preconditions for 'human security' (UNDP, 1994).

> *The concept of human security stresses that people should be able to take care of themselves: all people should have the opportunity to meet their most essential needs and to earn their own living. This will set them free and help ensure that they can make a full contribution to development – their own development and that of their*

*communities, their countries and the world. Human security is a critical ingredient of participatory development.*

*(UNDP, 1994, p. 24)*

As we have seen, innovation processes set in motion mechanisms that feed forms of insecurity while, at the same time, being influenced and limited by excessive and widespread insecurity of individuals and communities (UNDP, 2001, Chapter 3).

Indeed, structural change favours the emergence of new activities and, at the same time, condemns the existing ones to a slow decline. The increase in the resulting structural unemployment can lead to a more rigorous process of selection in the work force and to the exclusion of less-qualified workers, who find it increasingly difficult to find work in the new sectors of expansion or who see their salaries reduced to a level close to or below subsistence levels. The absence of interventions by the government – through income support, active work policy interventions or professional retraining courses – can cause progressive forms of social marginalisation and disintegration of the social fabric (Fukuda-Parr, 2003), with negative impacts on the structures of living together (and social capital), individuals' capabilities (and human capital), equality (and social mobility) and citizens' participation of in public affairs (and the functioning of democracy).

The sense of insecurity induced by change and the financial crisis connected to it can, if not regulated, seriously limit the very process of innovation. In fact, if those involved know they can count on a system that guarantees a social safety net, they will be more inclined to participate in the change – investing savings, changing work qualifications, changing work sites – taking individual risks with less apprehension. In contrast, the lack of risk protection can limit the processes of change, as it threatens not only the crucial factors of growth but also the individual and collective willingness to change.

> *Risk markets – giving individuals the ability to buy insurance in the private market against the important risks that individuals face, like unemployment- are imperfect and absent; that imposes a huge burden on those with limited resources. Because risk markets are imperfect, in the absence of social protection, individual welfare is lower – and the willingness to undertake high return and high-risk ventures is lower. Providing better social protection can help create a more dynamic economy.*
>
> *(Stiglitz, 2012, p. 175)*

As a result, a solid social protection system provides a powerful incentive to the widening of the innovators' base and of new capacities for change. More generally, 'a common commitment – national and global – towards universal provision of social services, strengthening social protection and assuring full employment would constitute a profound societal and political decision that would lay the foundation for building long-term resilience, for countries and for their citizens as individuals' (UNDP, 2014, p. 5).

### 3.6 Innovation, growth and freedom: the virtuous circles

The above survey points to an interesting, even if partial, series of interactions between CA and IS. This supports the idea that there are many common areas of interest for innovation process (as interpreted by the IS theory) and human development, and that combining these two literatures can trigger virtuous circles of mutual interaction.

One of the first economists who tried to interpret development in terms of virtuous and vicious circles of cumulative causation was Myrdal (1957). His contributions were complemented by the work of economists of the post-Keynesian tradition, who built on Kaldor's (1957, 1970) work. These authors focused on the spatial polarisation processes of development and the consequent link between leading areas where the cumulative impact of development is positive (the core) and the dependent areas where, at least initially, the impact is negative (the periphery). In the former, institutional conditions and the growing accumulation of knowledge set in motion self-sustaining mechanisms of growth; in the latter, institutional weaknesses and the impact of the low demand for goods and services generate a progressive impoverishment and distancing from the more dynamic areas (regions, nations, business systems).

Within the literature on human development, some studies (UNDP, 1996; Ranis et al., 2000; Ranis and Stewart, 2006; Suri et al., 2011) focus on the connection between human development (HD) and economic growth (EG), separately considering two relations: one moving from economic growth to human development (Chain A); the other (Chain B) going in the opposite direction (Suri et al., 2011). Putting together the two relations results in a circular diagram demonstrating how important HD is for EG and how relevant economic growth is for human development.

The basic idea of these contributions[23] is that a dual relationship exists. In the first, growth secures, for state and families, resources to invest in the overall improvement of people's conditions (health, education, housing, social security, poverty reduction), therefore increasing human development; in the second, human development contributes to the advancement of the quality of workers (human capital), thus leading to a higher degree of productivity and economic growth.

Only one study, within the literature on the capability approach, focused on the relationship between HD and technologies describing it in terms of virtuous circle (UNDP, 2001). In this case, not only does technological change (see UNDP, 2001, diagram 2.1) contribute indirectly to human development through economic growth and increased resources for social policies, but it also directly contributes to increasing the set of capabilities that individuals consider as valuable. This is experienced in all areas, particularly in the healthcare sector (vaccines and medicines), communications (reducing isolation and facilitating better information and participation), agriculture (with increased production and decreased prices), energy (alternative and cheaper sources) and manufacturing (providing new and more solid opportunities for growth and employment). The relationship between human development and technology also runs in the opposite direction, with the former fostering the growth in human capital in terms of knowledge, creativity and participation. Better education significantly contributes to the creation and diffusion of technology; a greater number of scientists engaged in R&D and more educated workers can use technologies more effectively; greater participation and social and political freedoms create the conditions for more vibrant creativity. This model describes and interprets in a more complete way the relationship between human development and technological change, giving the latter a central role, rather than considering it merely ancillary to economic growth.

To conclude my analysis on the interconnections between HD and IS, a diagram was developed to illustrate the relationship between these two lines of research (see Figure 3.1). Figure 3.1 differs in the following two ways from the contributions considered above:

1   The presence of the *public decision-makers and policy choices* that affect and are affected by human development, innovation systems and growth. As discussed at length in this chapter, 'policy matters', and the explicit presence of public institutions in our diagram helps us to focus on some important interrelationships.
2   The presence of *innovation systems* clarifies that technology does not flow from a black box, but is always generated by a process of interaction between individuals, public and private organisations.

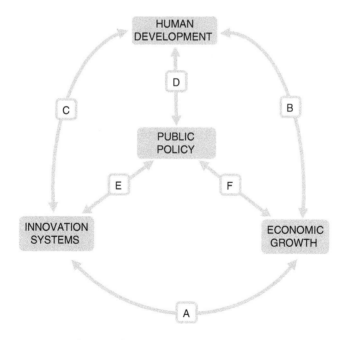

*Figure 3.1* Connections between human development, economic growth, innovation systems and public policy

Figure 3.1 illustrates six interactions, denominated by letters A to F that will help us summarise the connections highlighted in our review.[24]

A    IS→EG – virtuous *innovation systems* respond to the transformative pressures induced by the rapid change in science and technology, changes in markets and public choices. Good interaction between individuals, companies and institutions is a precondition for increased resilience of innovation systems and their *capability to innovate*. It translates into *innovation and technological change* that allows economic systems to meet needs and generate new resources. This feeds the process of *economic growth.*

EG→IS – Economic growth creates an environment conducive to economic and social change: new markets, economies of scale, new learning processes, new jobs and new skills. A stagnant economy can never stimulate innovation and social dynamism.

B    EG→HD – The process of *economic growth*, as mentioned several times in the sections above, is not an end but a mere means of development. The greater the income and the quantity of private goods and services, the more and better technologies extend the possibilities of individuals to live a life that they value. As it was emphasised above, however, the availability of these resources is not sufficient to ensure high levels of human development.

HD→EG – Human development is an end in itself. This does not entail that it has no direct and indirect effects on economic growth. An educated and healthy population has a direct effect on learning processes and economy's productivity; similarly, greater social cohesion and more trust between people foster the reduction of transaction costs, as well as improve the organisation and efficiency of enterprises and public administrations.

C    HD→IS – Human development has a direct effect on innovation systems, by improving individual, collective and institutional learning abilities. *Learning capabilities* benefit from the improvement of all individual capabilities: not just the capabilities that directly affect individual productivity (education, health), but also those that result from participation and social relations, from culture and greater awareness and ownership of community goals. The interactions between individuals in different positions, such as producers, users, workers, researchers, etc., benefit from a context in which inequalities (both income and non-income) are not exacerbated, where there are high levels of interpersonal trust and solid conditions for the rapid circulation of information and where common values and customs are shared. In addition, a cohesive and well-informed community exercises greater democratic control and contributes to a greater transparency in public decisions on investments which affect research and innovation, and, more generally, in political decisions that affect innovation systems. A society with solid social safety nets stimulates enterprise and risk taking.

IS➔HD – Innovation systems help increase learning capabilities as well as technologies available to individuals and in this way, expand their *capability set*. The actual impact on human development, however, will depend on *factors of individual conversions and the social context*.

D  PP➔HD – All *public policies* have an impact on the distribution of costs and benefits of economic and social change. For instance, choices about taxation (regressive or progressive, more or less heavy on wealth, more or less lenient on financial and real income, etc.), choices about expenditure (more or less directed to social sectors, more or less public presence in the healthcare, social, education and training, energy, industrial sectors, etc.), regulatory interventions (in the areas of health, environment and markets), institutional and administrative choices (more or less centred on transparency and participation); these and other areas of government intervention have fundamental redistributive impacts. The choices made by public institutions have an important, though not exclusive, impact on *instrumental freedoms*, namely the fields that promote social opportunities, political freedoms, economic infrastructures, transparency and security, contributing directly or indirectly to an individual's freedom to live as he or she wishes, and thus to the *human development* of a community.

HD➔PP – *Human development* affects the work of public institutions in two important ways: the first concerns the growth of the *structures of living together*. Individuals are placed in a context that influences *their agency* and their opportunities to live a life that they deem valuable; this context in turn affects both formal and informal institutions. The second, deriving from the first, is *democratic control*. A greater participation, less inequality, more transparency and public information promote more equitable public choices and a greater attention to goals of collective interest.

E  PP➔IS – Public choices affect both 'non-core' components (particularly those relating to education, labour market, financial market, intellectual property, market regulation, and welfare policies) as well as 'core' components (particularly through industrial policies, and policies pertaining research and innovation). Public policies can encourage high-tech activities and STI-led (science, technology and innovation) modes of innovation, as well as stimulate experience-based innovation strategies, focusing more on the interactions between individuals, businesses and institutions (DUI); they can be directed towards the strengthening of high-tech activities and/ or the background conditions. They can also strengthen of a few large centres of excellence or support a more widespread and diverse system of skills and innovation.

IS➔PP – Part of the public system (universities, public research laboratories, education) is a direct and important actor in innovation systems. The IS thus has a direct impact on these public institutions. Also, the IS indirectly impacts the entire public administration through "efficiency transfers" occurring through the adoption of new technologies and the introduction of new forms of work organisation.

F PP→EG – This is a typical context of macroeconomic policies. According to the Keynesian approach, public policies have a direct impact on aggregate demand and thus on employment and overall growth rates of national income. In addition, economic policies have an impact on the supply structure, as well as on the static and dynamic efficiency of the production system.

EG→PP – *Economic growth* plays an important role in providing, through taxation, resources to finance public projects.

The first three relations (A, B and C) in Figure 3.1 are the basis for the empirical analysis of the next three chapters; the following three (D, E and F) lay the foundation for Chapters 7, 8 and 9, which focus on public policies.

## Notes

1 In fact, in his doctoral thesis (1960) and in the text entitled 'Employment, Technology and Development' (1975), Sen addressed the issue of technology but outside of the capabilities approach, with a particular focus on capital accumulation and employment.
2 We will explore this topic further in this section, when discussing inclusive innovation.
3 We will resume discussing issues on innovation policies in Chapter 8.
4 We will discuss these issues in more detail in Chapters 7 and 8 dedicated to innovation policies.
5 We will further discuss and deepen the issue of democracy. See section 5 and Chapter 8.
6 See Chapter 8.
7 The major contribution within this strand is the meritorious work done by the Globelics association (www.globelics.org) and its journal "Innovation and Development".
8 See Chapter 2
9 We will resume this approach when discussing innovation policies in Chapter 8
10 On the theme of education and capabilities, see the special issue of the Journal of Human Development and Capability Approach, 13 (3), 2012.
11 It is good to recall that the stock of knowledge is influenced by two streams, the first is the learning, which increases it and the second is the forgetting, which reduces it. There is then a maintenance of what has been learned, the remembering, which helps to avoid damaging the knowledge already acquired. Learning and forgetting have a relationship similar to that between innovative activities that are established and obsolete activities that decline and disappear (Johonson and Lundvall, 1994). In what follows we focus only on the process of growth of the stock of knowledge, and on the learning.
12 We will discuss this in more depth in par. 3.3.
13 Chapters 7, 8 and 9 are dedicated to these topics.
14 Policies to curb inequality will be discussed in Chapter 9.
15 See Chapter 2.
16 We will resume the theme of economic fluctuations and cyclical policies in Chapter 9.
17 Refer to the bibliography.
18 We will resume these themes in the chapters devoted to policies.
19 Subject treated by Keynes in his 'Economic Possibilities for our grandchildren' (1930).
20 We will discuss this issue in greater depth in Chapter 7.
21 The topic will be discussed in detail in Chapter 8 dedicated to innovation policies.
22 We will resume this theme with reference to the large Mission-oriented programmes in Chapter 8.

23 It will be further discussed in Chapter 4.
24 The diagram merely summarises some of the connections that emerged from the review and therefore cannot be either exhaustive or analytically comprehensive. Every relationship is a two-way relation, thus the type of relationship that is being discussed is distinguished by a directional arrow and the initials PP (Public Policy), IS (Innovation Systems), EG (Economic Growth) and HD (Human Development).

## References

Acemoglu, A. and Robinson, J. 2010. The Role of Institution in Growth and Development, *Review of Economics and Institutions*, 1(2), 1–33.

Acemoglu, A. and Robinson, J. 2012. *Why Nations Fail: The Origins of Power, Prosperity, and Poverty*, New York, Crown Publishers.

Akçomak, İ.S. and ter Weel, B. 2012. The Impact of Social Capital on Crime: Evidence From the Netherlands, *Regional Science and Urban Economics*, Elsevier, 42(1–2), 323–340.

Altenburg, T. 2009. Building Inclusive Innovation Systems in Developing Countries: Challenges for IS Research. In: Lundvall et al. 2009, 33–57.

Andersen, T., Holmström, B., Honkapohja, S., Korkman, S., Söderström, H.T., and J.Vartiainen (2007), *The Nordic Model: Embracing globalization and sharing risks*, Helsinki, Taloustieto.

Arocena, R. and Sutz, J. 2000. Looking at National Systems of Innovation From the South, *Industry and Innovation*, 7(1), 55–75.

Arocena, R. and Sutz, J. 2012. Research and Innovation Policies for Social Inclusion: An Opportunity for Developing Countries, *Innovation and Development*, 2(1), 147–158.

Atkinson, A.B. 2015. *Inequality: What Can Be Done?* Cambridge, MA, London, UK, Harvard University Press.

Biggeri, M. and Ferrannini, A. 2014. Opportunity Gap Analysis: Procedures and Methods for Applying the Capability Approach in Development Initiatives, *Journal of Human Development and Capabilities*, 15(1), 60–78.

Bowles, S. 2012. *The New Economics of Inequality and Redistribution*, Cambridge, Cambridge University Press.

Burton-Jones, A. and Spender, J.C. (eds.) 2011. *The Oxford Handbook of Human Capital*, Oxford, Oxford University Press.

Capriati, M. 2013. Capabilities, freedom and innovation: exploring connections, *Innovation and Development*, n. 1, 1–17.

Castells, M. and Himanen, P. 2002. *The Information Society and the Welfare State: The Finnish Model*, Oxford, Oxford University Press.

Chataway, J., Hanlin, R. and Kaplinsky, R. 2014. Inclusive Innovation: An Architecture for Policy Development, *Innovation and Development*, 4(2), 33–54.

Chiappero-Martinetti, E. and Sabadash, A., 2014. Integrating Human Capital and Human Capabilities in understanding the value of Education, in Tiwari, M. and Ibrahim, S. (eds.) 2014 *The Capability Approach: From Theory to Practice* Palgrave MacMillan pp. 206–230.

Cimoli, M., Dosi G. and Stiglitz J.E. (eds.) 2009. *Industrial Policy and Development: The Political Economy of Capabilities Accumulation*, Oxford, Oxford University Press.

Coeckelbergh, M. 2011. Human Development or Human Enhancement? A Methodological Reflection on Capabilities and the Evaluation of Information Technologies, *Ethics and Information Technology*, 13, 81–92.

Cozzens, S. and Sutz, J. 2014. Innovation in Informal Settings: Reflections and Proposals for a Research Agenda. *Innovation and Development*, 4(1), 5–31.

Crocker, David A. 2008. *Ethics of Global Development: Agency, Capabilities and Deliberative Democracy*, New York, Cambridge, Cambridge University Press.

Deaton, A. 2013. *The Great Escape: Health, Wealth and the Origins of Inequality*, Princeton, NJ, Princeton University Press.

Deneulin, S. 2006. *The Capability Approach and the Praxis of Development*, Basingstoke, UK, New York, Palgrave Macmillan.

Deneulin, S. and Stewart, F., 2002. Amartya Sen's Contribution to Development Thinking, *Studies in Comparative International Development*, 37 (2), 61–70.

Drèze, J. and Sen, A. 2002. *India: Development and Participation*, Oxford, Oxford University Press.

EC (European Commission) 2016. European Innovation Scoreboard, Bruxelles.

Edwards, R. and Glover, J. (eds.) 2001. *Risk and Citizenship: Key Issues in Welfare*. London, Routledge.

Ely A., Van Zwanenberg P. and Stirling A. 2011. *New Models of Technology Assessment for Development STEPS*, Working Paper 45, Brighton, STEPS Centre.

Fagerberg, J. and Srholec, M. 2009. Innovation System, Technology and Development: Unpacking the Relationship. In: Lundall et al. 2009, 83–118.

Fagerberg, J., Mowery, D.C. and Nelson, R.R. (eds.) 2005. *The Oxford Handbook of Innovation*, Oxford, Oxford University Press.

Fagerberg, J., Srholec, M. and Verspagen, B. 2010. Innovation and Economic Development. In: Hall, B. and Rosenberg, N. (eds.), *Handbook of Economics of Innovation*, Amsterdam, Elsevier, 833–872.

Ferreira, F.H.G. 1999. Inequality and Economic Performance: A Brief Overview to Theories of Growth and Distribution, Text for World Bank's Web Site on Inequality, Poverty, and Socio-economic Performance.

Franzini, M. and Pianta, M. 2016. *Explaining Inequality*, London and New York, Routledge.

Freeman, C. 2011. Technology, Inequality and Economic Growth. *Innovation and Development*, 1(1), 11–24.

Fukuda-Parr, S. 2003. New Threats to Human Security in the Era of Globalization, *Journal of Human Development*, 4(2), 167–179.

Giddens, A. 1990. *The Consequences of Modernity*. Stanford, CT, Stanford University Press.

Heeks, R. 2010. Information and Communication Technologies (ICTs) Contribute to Development? *Journal of International Development*, 22, 625–40.

Heeks, R., Foster, C. and Nugroho, Y. 2014. New Models of Inclusive Innovation for Development, *Innovation and Development*, 4(2), 175–185.

Hellsten, S.K. 2007. From Information Society to Global Village of Wisdom? The Role of ICT in Realizing Social Justice in the Developing World. In: Rooksby, E. and Weckert, J. (eds.), *Information Technology and Social Justice*, Hershey, Information Science Publishing, 1–28.

Hirschman, A.O. 1958. *The Strategy of Economic Development*. New Haven, CT, Yale University Press.

Hirschmann, A.O. 1967. *Development Projects Observed*, Washington, DC, The Brooking Institute.

Johnstone, J. 2007. Technology as Empowerment: A Capability Approach to Computer Ethics, *Ethics and Information Technology*, 9(1), 73–87.

Joseph, K.J. 2014. Exploring Exclusion in Innovation Systems: Case of Plantation Agriculture in India, *Innovation and Development*, 4(1), 73–90.

Kaldor, 1970. The Case for Regional Policies, *Scottish Journal of Political Economy*, 67, 591–624.

Kaldor, N. 1956. Alternative Theories of Distribution, *Review of Economic Studies*, 23(2), 83–100.

Kaldor, N. 1957. A Model of Economic Growth, *The Economic Journal*, 67(268), 591–624.

Keynes, J.M. 1930. Economic Possibilities for Grandchildren, *The Nation and Athenaeum*, 11 and 18 October.

Kleine, D. 2011. The Capability Approach and the 'Medium of Choice': Steps Towards Conceptualising Information and Communication Technologies for Development, *Ethics and Information Technology*, 13(2), 119–30.

Kleine, D. 2013. *Technologies of Choice? ICTs, Development, and the Capabilities Approach*, Cambridge, MA, MIT Press.

Knack, S. (ed.) 2003. *Democracy, Governance, and Growth*, Lanham, MD, The University of Michigan Press.

Kuznets, S. 1955. Economic Growth and Income Inequality, *American Economic Review*, 45(1), 1–28.

Leach, M. and Scoones, I. 2006. *The Slow Race: Making Technology Work for the Poor*, London, Demos.

Liu, X. 2009. National Innovation Systems in Developing Countries: Chinese National Innovation System Intransition. In: Lundvall et al. 2009, 119–139.

Lundvall, B.A. 2002. *Innovation, Growth and Social Cohesion: The Danish Model*, Cheltenham, UK, Northampton, MA, Edward Elgar.

Lundvall, B.A. 2007a. National Innovation Systems: Analytical Concept and Development Tool, *Industry and Innovation*, 14(1), 95–119.

Lundvall, B.A. 2007b. *Innovation System Research: Where It Came From and Where It Might Go*, Globelics Working Paper, No. 2007–01.

Lundvall, B.A. 2011. Notes on Innovation Systems and Economic Development, *Innovation and Development*, 1(1), 25–38.

Lundvall, B.A. (ed.) 1992. *National System of Innovation: Towards a Theory of Innovation and Interactive Learning*, London, Pinter Publishers.

Lundvall, B.A. and Johnson, B. 1994. The Learning Economy, *Journal of Industry Studies*, 1, 23–42.

Lundvall, B.A., Joseph, K.J., Chaminade, C. and Vang, J. 2009. *Handbook of Innovation System and Developing Countries: Building Domestic Capabilities in a Global Setting*, Cheltenham, UK; Northampton, Edward Elgar Publishing Ltd.

Lundvall, B.Å. and Lorenz, E. 2010. Accounting for Creativity in the European Union: A Multi-Level Analysis of Individual Competence, Labour Market Structure, and Systems of Education and Training, *Cambridge Journal of Economics*, 35(2), 269–294.

Mazzucato, M. 2013. *The Entrepreneurial State: Debunking the Public vs. Private Myth in Risk and Innovation*, London, Anthem.

Meade, J.E. 1964. *Efficiency, Equality and the Ownership of Property*, London, George Allen & Unwin.

Miettinen, R. 2013. *Innovation, Human Capabilities, and Democracy: Towards an Enabling Welfare State*, Oxford, Oxford University Press.

Myrdal, G. 1957. *The Economic Theory and Underdeveloped Regions*, London, Duckworth.

Myrdal, G. 1973. *Against the Stream: Critical Essays on Economics*, London, Palgrave Macmillan.

Neira, I., Vászquez, E. and Portela, M. 2009. An Empirical Analysis of Social Capital and Economic Growth in Europe (1980–2000), *Social Indicators Research*, 92(1), 111–129.

North, D.C. 1990. *Institutions, Institutional Change, and Economic Performance*, Cambridge, Cambridge University Press.

North, D.C. 2005. *Understanding the Process of Economic Change*, Princeton, NJ, Princeton University Press.

Ocampo, J.A., Jomo, K.S. and Khan, S. (eds.) 2007. *Policy Matters. Economic and Social Policies to Sustain Equitable Development*, London, ZED.

OECD (Organisation for Economic and Co-operation and Development) 2012. Looking to 2060: Long-Term Global Growth Prospects, *Economic Policy Paper*, n. 3.

OECD (Organisation for Economic and Co-operation and Development) 2013. Innovation and Inclusive Development, Conference discussion report.

Ollivaud, P. and Turner, D. 2015. The Effect of the Global Financial Crisis on OECD Potential Output, *OECD Journal: Economic Studies*, 2014, 7 (1), 41–60.

Oosterlaken, I. 2011. Inserting Technology in the Relational Ontology of Sen's Capability Approach. *Journal of Human Development and Capabilities*, 12(3), 425–432.

Oosterlaken, I. 2015. *Technology and Human Development*, London and New York, Routledge.

Oosterlaken, I. and van den Hoven, J. 2012. *The Capability Approach, Technology and Design*, Berlin, Springer.

Papaioannou, T. 2014. How Inclusive Can Innovation and Development Be in the Twenty-First Century? *Innovation and Development*, 4(2), 187–202.

Piketty, T. 2014. *Capital in the Twenty-First Century*, Cambridge, MA; London, UK, Harvard University Press.

Ranis, G. and Stewart, S. 2006. *Successful Transition Towards a Virtuous Cycle of Human Development and Economic Growth: Country Studies*, Yale University, Center Discussion Paper No. 943.

Ranis, G., Stewart, F. and Ramirez, A. 2000. Economic Growth and Human Development, *World Development*, 28(2), 197–219.

Reinert, E.S. 2007. *How Rich Countries Got Rich . . . and Why Poor Countries Stay Poor*, London, Constable.

Sapir, A. 2006. Globalization and the Reform of European Social Models, *Journal of Common Market Studies*, 44(2), 369–390.

Schumpeter, J.A. 1936. *The Theory of Economic Development: An Inquiry Into Profits, Capital, Credit, Interest, and the Business Cycle*, Cambridge, MA, Harvard University Press.

Schumpeter, J.A. 1939. *Business Cycles: A Theoretical, Historical and Statistical Analysis of the Capitalism Process*, New York, McGraw-Hill.

Schumpeter, J.A. 2010. *Capitalism, Socialism and Democracy*, London and New York, Routledge.

Sen, A. 1960. *Choice of Techniques*, Oxford, Blackwell.

Sen, A. 1975. *Employment, Technology and Development*, Oxford, Oxford University Press.

Sen, A. 1997. Human Capital and Human Capabilities, *World Development*, 25(12), 1959–61.

Sen, A. 1999a. *Development as Freedom*, Oxford, Oxford University Press.

Sen, A. 1999b. Democracy as Universal Value, *Journal of Democracy*, 10(3), 3–17.

Sen, A. 2000. Social Exclusion: Concept, Application and Scrutiny. *Social Development Papers* No. 1, Asian Development Bank, Manila.

Sen, A. 2010. The Mobile and the World. *Information Technologies & International Development*, 6(SE), 1–3.

Soete, L., Verspagen, B. and Ter Weel, B. 2010. System of Innovation. In: Hall, H. and Rosenberg, N. (eds.), *Economics of Innovation*, 2, 1159–1180.

STEPS Centre. 2010. *Innovation, Sustainability, Development: A New Manifesto*, Brighton, University of Sussex.

Stewart, F. 1977. *Technology and Underdevelopment*, London, Palgrave Macmillan.

Stiglitz, J.E. 2012. *The Price of Inequality*, New York, London, W.W. Norton and Company.

Stiglitz, J.E. 2015. *The Great Divide: Unequal Societies and What We Can Do About Them*, London, New York, W.W. Norton & Company.

Stiglitz, J.E. and Greenwald, B.C. 2014. *Creating a Learning Society*, New York, Columbia University Press.

Suri, T., Boozer, M.A., Ranis, G. and Stewart, F. 2011. Paths to Success: The Relationship Between Human Development and Economic Growth, *World Development*, 39(4), 506–522.

Taylor-Gooby, P. and Zinn, J.O. 2006. *Risk in Social Science*, Oxford, Oxford University Press.

Toboso, M. 2011. Rethinking Disability in Amartya Sen's Approach: ICT and Equality of Opportunity, *Ethics and Information Technology*, 13(2), 107–118.

UNDP (United Nations Development Programme) 1994. *Human Development Report 1994*, Oxford, Oxford University Press.

UNDP (United Nations Development Programme) 1996. *Human Development Report 1996*, Oxford, Oxford University Press.

UNDP (United Nations Development Programme) 2001. *Human Development Report 2001, Making New Technologies Work for Human Development*, Oxford, Oxford University Press.

UNDP (United Nations Development Programme) 2010. *Human Development Report 2010: The Real Wealth of Nations: Pathways to Human Development*, New York, UNDP.

UNDP (United Nations Development Programme) 2014. *Human Development Report 2014, Sustaining Human Progress: Reducing Vulnerabilities and Building Resilience*, New York, UNDP.

Veggeland, N. 2007. *Paths of Public Innovation in the Global Age: Lessons From Scandinavia*, Cheltenham, UK, Edward Elgar.

Verspagen, B. 2005. Innovation and Economic Growth. In: Fagerberg et al. 2005, 487–513.

Voeten, J.J. and Naudè, W.A. 2014. Regulating the Negative Externalities of Enterprise Cluster Innovations: Lesson From Vietnam, *Innovation and Development*, 4(2), 203–222.

WB (World Bank) 2006. *World Development Report 2006*. Equity and Development, Washington, DC.

WB (World Bank) 2013. *China: Inclusive Innovation for Sustainable Inclusive Growth*, Washington, DC: World Bank Group.

Zheng, Y. 2009. Different Spaces for e-Development: What Can We Learn From the Capabillity Approach? *Information Technology for Development*, 15(2), 66–82.

Zheng, Y. and Stahl, B.C. 2011. Technology, Capabilities and Critical Perspective: What Can Critical Theory Contribute to Sen's Capability Approach? *Ethics and Information Technology*, 13(29), 69–80.

Zheng, Y. and Stahl, B.C. 2012. Evaluating Emerging ICTs: A Critical Capability Approach of Technology. In: Oosterlaken-Van den Hoven 2012, 57–76.

# Part II

# Empirics

# 4 Innovation, human development and economic growth

Interpretations and empirical analysis

What transpired from the analysis elaborated in the previous chapter are three main interrelationships[1] between:

1 Innovation systems and economic growth;
2 Economic growth and human development; and
3 Human development and innovation systems.

There is an extensive body of empirical literature focusing on the first inter-relationship, identifying different ways in which processes of innovation and technological change can increase per capita GDP (Verspagen, 2005; Fagerberg et al., 2010; Andersson et al., 2012; OECD, 2009). On the other hand, the literature on the other two interrelationships is rather limited.

The interface between human development and growth has been investigated by a group of authors linked to UNDP and, in particular, by development economists Ranis and Stewart. The empirical literature on the interrelationship between human development and innovation systems, as we shall see, is indeed minimal and relatively recent.

Accordingly, the contributions from the innovation-growth nexus will be considered briefly, with rather more attention given to the two other interrelations.

## 4.1 Innovation and growth

*Key ideas*

With the exception of Smith and Marx, the classical and later the neoclassical economists tended to either neglect innovation or to regard it as an essentially exogenous factor (section a.). With 'growth accounting' emerged the existence of a 'residual' which could not be explained by production factors, but could be attributed to the technological change. At the time, technological change was considered exogenous and freely available. According to this approach, in the long run the free movement of technology fosters the convergence of income levels amongst countries (section b.). The Neo-Keynesian school of thought does not regard knowledge, except in a very limited way, as a public good; the appropriation and the growth of knowledge depends on the initial conditions of national economies. Empirical and historical analyses suggest that there is a gap between countries with an ability to learn and those without (section c.). A crucial role in the relationship between innovation and growth is played by the absorptive capacities each system can acquire. Developing countries can, through appropriate policies, build the innovation capacity needed to catch up. Models analysing the convergence and divergence processes of a country's growth pattern consider the diverging forces creating a gap (innovation) and the stabilising forces allowing the recovery of lost ground (imitation/adaptation). One of these two tendencies can prevail and either instigate or discourage the catch-up process (section d.).

### a. Early interpretations

The relationship between technological change and economic growth has been the object of intermittent interest through the evolution of economic thought. Classical scholars such as Smith and Marx certainly did not fail to analyse innovation's contribution to the increased productivity and living standards of countries. Smith implicitly looked at it in his analysis of the division of labour, while Marx explicitly argued that technological progress was the driving factor of capitalist development, as well as the cause of productivity gaps and industrial concentration. Despite these important inputs from the classical school of thought, technological change remained for a long time in the shadows of other economic theories, advanced both by the other 'classics' such as Malthus, Ricardo, Mill and the neoclassics that emerged starting from the second half of the nineteenth century. The latter remained anchored to a static view of the combination of factors of production processes, in which the 'technology is given', and have never conceived technological progress in dynamic terms. Consequently, they could not grasp the importance of innovation in long-term growth processes (Nelson and Winter, 1974). For this school of thought, technological progress remained an 'awkward' factor, difficult to consistently include in analytical models. The basic assumptions of the latter proponents, in fact, were such that it became difficult to explain both the origins and the dynamic impacts of technological progress.

Chapter 2 looked already at the contributions made by Schumpeter and how this author considered innovation a fundamental factor for the structural change and the long-term growth of economies. Despite Schumpeter's (2010) harsh criticism of Marxism, he claimed that there were some points of agreement between his line of thought and that of the German economist and philosopher. He referred, in particular, to his idea of change being driven by the emergence of dominant positions and the arising of cyclical crises (Schumpeter, 1936, preface Japanese edition).

### b. Growth accounting

The weakness of the neoclassical tradition was further underscored when sixty years ago, with the introduction of economic growth models (Solow,

1956) – that viewed technological change as an exogenous factor – and the subsequent empirical application of the 'growth accounting' (Abramovitz, 1956; Solow, 1957), it became clear that this approach was unable to consider innovation a key factor of growth.

The Solow model relied on the standard options of the neoclassical theory, such as perfect competition, free flow of information, diminishing returns of factors, no externalities, etc. In this context, an increase in productivity is generated by an increase in capital per worker. Following the law of diminishing returns, at a certain amount of capital stock, this growth eventually slows down and then halts completely. In the long run, the economy grows at a steady and exogenous rate influenced by the population growth and technological progress. Based on this interpretation, technological progress is not only considered exogenous, but is also seen as a 'public good', i.e., more companies can simultaneously use knowledge without it being exhausted (non-rivalry) and at the same time, once this knowledge is acquired by others, its use cannot be prevented (non-excludability). These assumptions have two important consequences. First, since technological knowledge is freely available, no company would engage in generating it internally (Arrow, 1962). Second, since it can be enjoyed by all even at the international level, it implies that there will be a convergence of the growth capacity of the countries with different levels of development. In particular, developing countries with a low level of capital, following the law of diminishing returns, will enjoy a higher return on capital. If we assume that both capital and knowledge circulate freely, such countries will experience an inflow of these resources and will have the opportunity to grow at a faster rate than the developed countries. In the long run, this mechanism will ensure a convergence, i.e., the coming closer of the levels of income between the countries.

The empirical research that analysed the extent to which this model fits the data immediately pointed out some inconsistencies. First, the breakdown of the GDP growth rates into the contributions of different factors (the so-called 'growth accounting') proved that only a part of the growth could be attributed to the growth of capital and labour, and that a significant proportion (the so-called 'residual') remained unexplained. This residual which does not result from the increase of factors was referred to by Abramovitz (1956), as a 'measure of our ignorance about the causes of economic growth' (p. 11). Second, empirical research that analysed long-term growth trends indicate that, far from converging, the levels of countries' wealth showed a tendency to diverge (Landes, 1998; Islam, 2003).

'Growth accounting' helped to stimulate an empirical approach based on a 'knowledge production function', namely on the econometric estimation of the relationship between investment in R&D and GDP. In these empirical models, the *stock of knowledge* is considered an additional factor, besides the traditional ones, i.e., capital and labour. The stock of knowledge is estimated from investment in R&D, accumulated and amortised over the years (Griliches, 1979, 1984, 1986). These analyses highlight the positive and significant impacts that investments in R&D have on the productivity growth of firms, sectors and countries.

From the 1980s, the focus on the role of knowledge in growth and development processes gained prominence even within the tradition of neoclassical thought. Proponents of the 'new growth theory' hold that economic growth is influenced by the investment in both R&D and human capital (Romer, 1990; Lucas, 1988; Barro, 1991; Aghion and Howitt, 1992, 1998). They hold that this accumulation does not depend on external factors, but is rather the result of an intentional internal process, which is a fundamental part of an economic system. An important role in these processes is played by legal restrictions to the dissemination of knowledge, such as Intellectual Property Right (IPR), that ensure the innovator most benefits from investing in the new knowledge. Advocates of endogenous growth reject the assumption that knowledge is a pure public good, and thus freely available. They therefore also reject the claim that countries converge towards the same steady state. They argue that different steady states can be achieved from a given resource endowment. Policies supporting the growth of the knowledge stock are able to foster growth, and thus bring about a better equilibrium. However, in so doing, proponents of endogenous growth take the relation between knowledge and growth to be linear and deterministic, neglecting those mechanisms (be it social, institutional or entrepreneurial) that can in reality affect the path of an economy. And those paths, as we have seen, play a crucial role in the Schumpeterian approach.

### c. Neo-Keynesian interpretations

In the '50s and '60s, an alternative approach explicitly considered the *demand*, and it did not consider knowledge a public good. Unlike the neoclassical school of thought, the neo-Keynesian models interpreted the tendency of economies to diverge as a result of the principle of 'cumulative causation'. Knowledge is linked to the agents and to the countries that generate it and so is diffused with difficulty; this is due to the interplay of learning by doing and learning by using processes that enable one to acquire knowledge directly from the production processes and products. The larger the market that is being supplied, the more intense is the learning process, and the greater is the ability to sell new products and attract new processes, and to further expand the market. This interpretation of the cumulative process between knowledge and the market size goes back to Smith's analysis (1776) reiterated by Young (1928) and Verdoorn (1949) and used by Myrdal (1957) and Kaldor (1970) in their territorial development models. The basic idea of these models is that, far from being available to and easily acquired by all, technological knowledge benefits those who are already at a certain level of well-being and creates a gap between those who are able to follow this process of accumulation and those who are not.

### d. Absorptive capacities and catching-up strategies

This gap, however, is not unbridgeable. Historical studies (Gerschenkron, 1962; Reinert, 2007) have shown that appropriate policies and the implementation of appropriate institutional tools (such as the establishment of investment banks as seen in the German experience) can trigger ways of catching up. This was the case of the United States and Germany as compared to the United Kingdom in the nineteenth century and more recently the experience of Asian countries against the US leader in the '60s till the '80s.

A strategic role in the catching-up process is played by a set of conditions that Abramovitz (1986) calls the 'social capabilities'. These include technical qualifications and a general level of education; experience in the organisation and management of large companies; a capital market able to mobilise resources necessary for innovation; stability of government and its ability to define and guarantee the respect of rules which will enable growth; as well as honesty and trust.

A concept similar to the one outlined by Abramovitz is the one of 'absorptive capacity', or the ability to absorb knowledge and technology. According to Cohen and Levinthal (1990), this can be defined as 'the ability of a firm to recognise the value of new, external information, assimilate it and apply it to commercial ends' (p. 128). Although it originally refers to single companies, this concept has also been used at a larger scale, for regions and countries.

The Schumpeterian approach takes growth to be a process of disequilibrium created by the interaction of two forces: that of innovation, which tends to increase technological differences among countries, and that of imitation/diffusion which tends to decrease them (Fagerberg, 1988; Verspagen, 1991). This can result in either divergent or convergent paths. In order to benefit from innovation, countries/territories need a wide range of absorptive capacities (Abramovitz, 1986): in terms of adequate institutional and social conditions, human capital, R&D, and so on. The literature on the technological gap (Fagerberg, 1987, 1988; Verspagen, 1991), and in particular the one focusing on the regional scale (Rodiguez and Pose, 2001; Crescenzi, 2005; Sterlacchini, 2008), has shown that there is a minimum threshold of absorptive capacities, below which it is difficult to move from knowledge (both internal and external) to innovation and growth.

Achieving a threshold level of these capacities is a precondition to start an innovation-fuelled process of growth. But much depends on political choices, on the initial conditions of the country, and its institutional framework. 'Technological catch-up is not a question of replacing an outdated technological set up with a more modern one, but to continually transform technological, economic and institutional structures' (Fagerberg and Verspagen, 2002, p. 1292).

## 4.2 Growth and human development

### Key ideas

The first studies undertaken by the UNDP indicated that there is no close correlation between per capita income and human development. Some countries showed that they could improve the well-being of their citizens regardless of the available material resources (section a.). Other studies highlighted that it was possible, *in the short run*, to record progress in human development despite limited or no economic growth, but *in the long run* human development must go hand in hand with a significant rate of growth. There seems to be no 'trickle down' effect from the economic growth to human development, but rather a process of reverse causality comes into play, especially in countries that over time have reached sustainable growth (section b.). The latest work in the area has focused on the two-way relationship between economic growth and human development. When analysing the impact of economic growth on human development, an important role is played by governments, mostly through expenditure on education and health, and by women. On the other hand, the impact of human development on income appears to be positive even in association with a greater investment in physical capital and lower inequality (section c.). The studies on long-term impacts revealed a variety of strategies: there are countries that permanently benefit from virtuous circles between HD and EG, others that are trapped in the vicious circles and others still that prefer to focus more on EG or on HD. No country has been able to achieve high levels of growth without first improving its HD (section d.). The countries with high human development are those which have retained a high share of social expenditure and women's participation in training activities, as well as an equitable distribution of income. The paths, however, are far from being similar and differ greatly depending on the country's history, political choices and point of departure (section e.).

### a. Preliminary evidence

Since the first Human Development Report (HDR) in 1990, the UNDP has focused particularly on the relationship between human development and economic growth. For the first time, a report developed an index aiming to replace the GNP in evaluating the well-being of nations. With the introduction of the Human Development Index (HDI), it became possible to compare the levels of well-being as measured traditionally by the GNP, with that measured in a broader manner, by the HDI. The latter is focused on the three essential elements of human life: life expectancy, education and a decent standard of living. An indicator is attributed to each of these elements. Longevity is measured in terms of life expectancy at birth; education is measured by adult literacy rates (then supplemented with enrolment rates at secondary level and more recently, average number of years of schooling); while the standard of living is measured by the logarithm of GNP per capita. To build the HDI, these three indicators are standardised and added together with an equal weight.[2]

The two rankings, i.e., the one classifying countries based on GNP per capita and the other based on the HDI, lead to very different results: many countries scoring high in their GNP per capita (such as Switzerland, Luxembourg and Hong Kong) underperformed in the ranking which took into account elements that measure longevity and health (life expectancy) and education (literacy). On the other hand, low-income countries such as Costa Rica, Cuba, and Sri Lanka scored better when assessed in terms of the HDI.

'Life does not begin at $11,000, the average per capita income in the industrial world. Sri Lanka managed a life expectancy of 71 years and an adult literacy rate of 87% with a per capita income of $400. By contrast, Brazil has a life expectancy of only 65 years, and its adult literacy rate is 78% at a per capita income of $2,020. In Saudi Arabia, where the per capita income is $6,200, life expectancy is only 64 years and the adult literacy rate is an estimated 55%' (UNDP 1990, p. 2).

It was evident from the beginning that there is no strong correlation between income and human development. The two rankings based on the two indicators did not agree, and this demonstrated that it was possible to think of development in a different way and to employ a new indicator (that can still be improved) to define an alternative set of priorities to assess human well-being. As mentioned earlier, income is included in the human development index, hence a positive relationship, although not exclusive, between the standard of living and human development is implicit. As we have also seen, the initial UNDP reports tried to explore the potential and the limits of this relationship. However, because the CA sees human development as an end in itself and not as a means, the inverse relationship going from the latter to the income had not been adequately explored. This opened a wide gap for interesting analysis defined by the relationships that could empirically be identified between the two variables. As already mentioned in Chapter 3, extensive empirical work was undertaken in the second phase of UNDP's Human Development Reports by a group of researchers who have worked with this organisation, led by two important economists in the field of development: Gustav Ranis and Frances Stewart. These authors have made an important contribution to the analysis of the links between Human Development and Economic Growth, in at least four aspects: the short and long-term relationships between growth and human development; the identification of factors that influence the relationship between the two; the long-term strategies; and success stories in human development processes.

### *b. Relationships between growth and human development*

The first empirical analyses confirmed that *short-term* improvements in human development are possible even in the absence of sustained economic growth. In fact, the UNDP studies (1990, 1996) highlighted that with a well-aimed public expenditure policy and a sufficiently equitable income distribution, major development achievements were possible even in the absence of satisfactory income levels, as in the cases mentioned earlier – Costa Rica, Cuba and Sri Lanka. However, it emerged that a good redistributive policy is important only in the short to medium term; in *the long run* the redistribution policy must be accompanied by a significant increase in income, in order to sustain further human development progress (UNDP 1996, Ranis et al., 2000). The fact that there is no close link between growth and human development, in the sense that an increase in material well-being does not automatically translate into human progress, does not imply that growth is not necessary. It is necessary because it provides the community a greater amount of resources, which in turn can increase the opportunities of individuals to live a decent life. It is equally necessary to pay attention to the *quality* and *distribution* of growth in order to ensure that it is directed to supporting human development (UNDP, 1996). In fact, another finding from the studies that compared growth and human development was that growth benefits are not automatically accessible to people, and that, in other words, do not spontaneously "trickle down" (UNDP, 1996). As it has been indicated, a good distribution of the benefits of growth can only happen when driven by policies aimed at achieving a better distribution of resources and opportunities (such as education and health programmes, progressive taxation, land reform and social security). In countries where distribution and social expenditure proved to be more balanced (such as in South Korea, Taiwan and Sri Lanka), growth has been accompanied by an improved well-being in terms of increased life expectancy and school enrolment rates. On the other hand, in countries where income distribution has been uneven and social expenditures have been low and/or poorly distributed (such as in Pakistan, Nigeria and Brazil), human development has not expanded significantly despite the rapid growth of GNP (UNDP, 1996).

### c. Factors influencing the relation between economic growth and human development

The first studies analysing the relationship between Human Development (HD) and Economic Growth (EG) focused on the influences of growth on human development. Is it possible to identify a reverse relationship? Also, is there any reason to believe that these relationships influence each other, resulting in circular causal chains? The answers to these questions have emerged from studies that have assumed the existence of a dual relationship outlined in Chain A (EG → HD) and Chain B (HD → EG).[3] The empirical work on these two interrelations was undertaken mainly in a sample of developing countries (about 70–80) over a long period of time (on average 40 years) using life expectancy at birth and infant mortality rates as indicators of human development.

As we have seen, *the growth of income can promote HD* in several ways, mainly through the behaviour of households and governments. In the first case, the spending choices can be more or less directed towards elements affecting human development: good nutrition, health, education. In the second case, governments may or may not prioritise expenditures linked to the capacity building of individuals and poverty reduction. At the household level the empirical studies have highlighted that women's empowerment (which is typically measured by school attendance rate) plays a key role in HD. Numerous studies (Suri et al., 2011; Gray Molina and Purser, 2010; Ranis and Stewart, 2006; Boozer et al., 2003; Ranis et al., 2000) have shown that the higher the education of women, the greater their economic autonomy, which in turn channels the family spending towards the most important elements of human development: healthy nutrition and education. In the case of governments, a key role is played by the choices of tax and expenditure policies made at the national level. Studies show that these policies impact human development when they focus on sectors such as social security, health and education, rather than on sectors that are unlikely to improve human development, such as spending on the military, unnecessary infrastructure, privileges for top bureaucrats, etc. The impact of public policies is usually assessed by calculating the percentage of public spending employed for social purposes (health and education) over GDP. According to the various estimates, this value is significant for obtaining a greater HD (Suri et al., 2011; Ranis and Stewart, 2006; Boozer et al., 2003). It should be noted that directing public expenditure towards social purposes is not a goal in itself, and by itself does not guarantee the achievement of a greater capacity of individuals. The amount of expenditure is certainly important, but its effectiveness in facilitating the various dimensions of human well-being (Ranis and Stewart, 2000) is equally critical. The empirical analysis carried out in these studies highlighted that several factors have a positive impact on HD (measured by life expectancy): in addition to the expenditure on social sectors (health and education), these included the growth rate of the GDP per capita, adult literacy and girls' school attendance rate (Ranis et al., 2000; Boozer et al., 2003).

*Human development* is the ultimate end. However, *it can also be considered an important means* if we take into account the way it can improve an economic system's capacity to progress. Growth is certainly stimulated by a healthy and well-educated population. The main purpose of well-organised social policies is not to support only of the active segment of the population, but also those who, because of their age, health and social status, are unable to enter the labour market; nonetheless, the presence of a higher number of fully productive and creative people favours the ability to innovate and grow. This increased availability can help attract and adapt new technologies from the outside, and (if the level of development is high enough) improve autonomous production. From an empirical point of view, studies point out the high impact that the HDI, investment rates and their variation over time have on economic growth. The underlying assumption is that the growth of the human factor has a higher impact on the overall growth if accompanied by a greater quantity and better quality of both domestic and foreign investments. Policies that are designed to improve HD, but which neglect to also stimulate investments, are likely to generate an excess of a well-trained work force (educated unemployed). Therefore, it is important to give due attention not only to the supply of high-quality human capital, but also to the demand side, which is influenced by saving and investment choices (Amsden, 2010; Hartmann, 2014). For the HD→EG nexus a significant (but less stable) effect of the income distribution indices (mainly the Gini and poverty headcount) has been detected. The idea in this case is that a more equitable distribution of income could encourage a more widespread use of favourable reforms of capabilities and thus increase the productivity of the economic system. These studies also highlight how the HD-EG connection is positively influenced by the levels of adult literacy (Ranis et al., 2000; Boozer et al., 2003; Ranis and Stewart, 2006) and good governance (Gray Molina and Purser, 2010).

### d. Long-term strategies

The analysis of the possible combinations of growth and human development and the long-term changes between the two helps to classify countries into four groups (Ranis et al., 2000, Ranis and Stewart, 2000, Boozer et al., 2003).

1   Countries that see positive changes in both HD and EG, which are in turn reinforced by positive feedbacks. These countries are within *a virtuous*

*circle* where a well-directed economic growth leads to an improved HD, which, in turn, further strengthens the EG. Typically, once a high level of human development is reached, there is a tendency to maintain it, both because a better-educated population can influence more consciously the political choices that are being made, and because once good levels of education and health are reached, fewer resources are needed to maintain them.

2    Countries that are locked in the trap of *vicious circles* created by low EG and low HD. In these cases, a low availability of resources makes the investment in education and health more difficult. At the same time, a poorly educated population that is in poor health has a lower chance of contributing to the economic growth. In the absence of a radical reform, countries that find themselves in a vicious circle are likely to remain in this condition.

3    Countries that have decided to focus more on economic growth, while experiencing a low level of HD (EG-loopsided).

4    Countries that have invested more in the human development of its citizens and less in economic growth (HD-lopsided).

The analysis of the growth paths recorded between 1960 and 2001 indicates that no country has been able to achieve high levels of growth without first improving its human development (Ranis and Stewart, 2005).

In fact, the empirical evidence highlights that: 1) in the long run, the improvements in HD and EG tend to move synchronously, thus highlighting an intense interaction; 2) a country's EG can only be sustained if, at first, the HD level is improved. This implies that it is only through a strong investment in HD that a virtuous circle can be set in motion. Attempts to strengthen EG without first improving HD can, at best, lead to a temporary increase in EG, to then lead back into a vicious circle (Boozer et al., 2003).

Largely, a situation of perpetual imbalance (either in favour of the HD or EG) has not been experienced. Empirical evidence indicates that countries are able to shift from a situation of high HD and low EG (known as lop-sided HD) to a situation of high HD and high EG resulting in a virtuous circle; on the other hand, no country has been able to move from a situation of lopsided EG to a situation resulting in a virtuous circle. This evidence supports the idea that economic growth alone does not guarantee the attainment of wider outcomes in terms of human progress and well-being. It may be a necessary but not a standalone tool. At the same time, almost no country remains in the situation of disequilibrium in favour of HD, indicating what has been referred to earlier: in order to sustain a high level of HD in the long run, a country needs to expand its economic resources, which can be generated only by an adequate economic growth.

> *Economic and social policy have tended to focus priority on getting the economic fundamentals 'right' as a necessary precondition for economic growth, arguing that HD*

*improvement must await such economic growth – for example, in the classic 'Washington Consensus'. In sharp contrast, our findings contradict the view that HD improvement may be postponed until economic resource expansion makes it affordable. If HD improvement is postponed in this way, EG itself, will not be sustained.*

(Ranis-Stewart, 2005, p. 13)

### e. Success cases

As we have seen, the most relevant factors to attain high levels of HD, as analysed by the various scholars within the existing literature, are: the rate of participation of women in training activities; the percentage of GDP allocated to social spending; the growth rate of the GDP; and income distribution (Ranis and Stewart, 2000). These elements, however, interact in different ways based on the specific history of each country. There is, in fact, no single path towards attaining a high level of HD (Ranis and Stewart, 2012). From the analysis undertaken so far, three relevant approaches can be identified: the first consists of a high level of growth accompanied by a reasonable income distribution and by a sustainable social public expenditure (as in the case of Korea and Taiwan over the past 40 years); the second is based on moderate growth linked to good wealth redistribution and the presence of a strong public sector (as experienced in Mauritius and Sri Lanka); the third consists in directing public spending towards priority sectors such as health and education for the most excluded segments of the population and in achieving good income distribution even if accompanied by unsatisfactory growth (Cuba, Costa Rica) (Ranis and Stewart, 2000).

On the other hand, a common element in all the cases with weak HD is very low or moderate growth. According to this school of thought, human development is not easily replaceable by other inputs to generate economic growth. An improvement in human development must either precede or accompany the increase of a country's EG to achieve sustainable growth. In terms of sequence in policies, without improvements in HD, policies that attempt to improve EG are highly unlikely to lead to sustainable growth.

In principle, every country has a specific ability to translate growth into human development and human development into growth, with relationships of varying intensity, depending on the initial conditions of the country, changes in the environment and policy choices. In the next chapters, we will introduce innovation, within this general framework, as a connecting element between human development and growth, and examine how these interactions can have positive or negative outcomes for countries.

## 4.3 Innovation and human development

### Key ideas

The preliminary analyses of the relationship between innovation and human development have shown a significant correlation between a composite index of technological level (the Technological Achievement Index) and HDI (section a.). More recent analyses have used as a proxy for innovation the TFP (Total Factor Productivity) along with various indices of product diversification. In the first case, the joint positive effect of innovation and human development on growth is highlighted (section b.); while the second case (section c.) illustrates the emerging correlation between human development and diversification.

### a. Technological achievement index

As we have seen, it is only recently that scholars have become interested in the relationship between technological innovation and human development. For the first time, the 2001 HDR placed 'the use of new technologies' firmly at the core of human development mechanisms with the intention of creating 'a new *partnership* between technology and development' (UNDP 2001, p. 1). It can thus be understood from these quotes that the report focused on the relationship between technology as an 'artefact' and the various dimensions of human development. Technology is still seen as a given, a tool that can be used either positively, benefiting humans, or negatively, generating risks.

Based exclusively on the empirical data, the UNDP report (2001) introduced a new Technological Achievement Index (TAI), taking into consideration the following four dimensions:

- Technological creations, measured by the number of patents and income generated from royalties and licenses;
- Diffusion of new technologies, such as the use of Internet and export of products with high technological content;
- Dissemination of existing technologies, such as telephones and electricity; and
- Human capital, in terms of years of schooling and attendance of scientific, math and engineering degree programmes.

The index helps to classify countries into four groups: the leaders (such as Finland, USA, Sweden and Japan), potential leaders (including Italy, Spain and Hungary), dynamic adopters (e.g., Uruguay, South Africa and Thailand) and the marginalised (Tunisia, Paraguay and Ecuador). In the report, the index is not used for an in-depth comparison with human development; there is only a brief reference to the empirical link that is of interest to us in that 'the TAI shows a high correlation with the human development index (HDI), and it correlates better with the HDI than with income' (UNDP, 2001, p. 47). The strong relationship between human development and technological innovation has been the focus of other contributions that have not used the TAI, and have chosen other specifications of technological progress.

### b. TFP and human development

The contribution made by Ranis and Zhao (2013) is, to my knowledge, the first to empirically analyse the relationship between technological advancement, human development and growth. It shows the importance of combining human development with technology to generate growth as an instrument to further improve human development. Their empirical analyses focus on 22 developing countries in Latin America and Asia during the period 1960–2010. The regression technique is a Pooled OLS analysis. In the first relationship assessed, the researchers show how technology (measured by the Total Factor Productivity) associated with human development (measured by non-income components of the HDI) affects growth. The results indicate that both components have a positive effect on growth. Among the regressors, Ranis and Zaho inserted an interactive variable between TFP and HDI,⋆ which is significant and has a high but negative coefficient. This implies that with greater technology there are actually decreasing returns to human development. In other words, human development and technology may in fact be substitutes for each other in their effects on growth. This is in line with other results showing that the contribution of human development to economic growth gradually decreases and that it becomes relatively less important than technological progress. In the long run, when high levels of human development are attained, innovation becomes the main engine for growth.

From the second relationship analysing the factors influencing TFP it emerged that open markets (measured either by the share of exports of GDP or through the average tariff rate) and FDI (Foreign Direct Investment) have positive effects. This is consistent with the idea that external flows of technology and knowledge can contribute to local innovation capacity. In addition, another interesting outcome of this analysis indicates that national patents are more important than foreign ones. The former are the manifestation of the efforts made by local manufacturers to adapt the technologies that come from abroad and generate new knowledge, while the latter mainly aim at achieving strategic goals and preventing competing patents.

### c. Diversification and human development

Hartmann (2014) adopted an important perspective in the empirical examination of the relationship between innovation and human development. In his work, he analyses the relationship between diversification 'defined as the change in the degree, type, composition and quality of the economic sectors in an economy' (p. 63), and human development. Diversification can be seen as an aspect of the broadest process of institutional and technological change, resulting in an expansion of job opportunities and of quality and quantity of goods. This expansion of opportunities, brought about by diversification, has a profound influence on people's capabilities. Greater diversification determines wider opportunities of agency and well-being. According to the author, a person living in a context where fewer goods are produced has fewer employment opportunities than a person living in a context where there are many companies engaged in various activities requiring a high degree of specialised knowledge.

In the empirical analysis of the relationship between diversification, human development and per capita income, Hartmann measures diversification through various indices[4] that capture the variety of a country's exports, and uses the HDI for human development. The analysis is performed for the year 2000 for 121 countries at different stages of development; it shows a strong and important relationship between diversification and human development and a weaker one between diversification and income per capita.

Hartmann concludes stressing that 'qualitative economic diversification is not only crucial for sustained economic growth, but appears to be even more important for human development' (p. 85) because it demands human capabilities and tends to distribute economic and political power.

## Notes

1 As shown in Figure 3.1, each of these relationships influences and is influenced by the public decision-maker. The last part of the book will discuss the role of policy makers in innovation, growth and human development.
2 See Chapter 5 for an empirical application and for more details on index construction
3 See paragraph 3.6
4 Entropy Index, Hirschman-Herfindal Index, the number of revealed comparative advantages and product ubiquity.

## References

Abramovitz, M.A. 1956. Resources an Output Trends in the United States since 1870, *America Economic Review*, 46, 5–23.

Abramovitz, M. 1986. Catching Up, Forging Ahead, and Falling Behind, *The Journal of Economic History*, 46(2), 385–406.

Aghion, P. and Howitt, P. 1992. A Model of Growth Through Creative Destruction, *Econometrica*, 60, 323–51.

Aghion, P. and Howitt, P. 1998. *Endogenous Growth Theory*, Cambridge, MA, MIT Press.

Amsden, A. 2010. Say's Law, Poverty Persistence, and Employment Neglect, *Journal of Human Development and Capabilities*, 11(1), 57–66.

Andersson, M., Johansson, B., Karlsson, C. and Lööf, H. (eds) 2012. *Innovation and Growth: From R&D Strategies of Innovating Firms to Economy-Wide Technological Change*, Oxford, Oxford University Press.

Arrow, K. 1962. Economic Welfare and the Allocation of Resources for Invention. In: Universities-National Bureau (ed.), *The Rate and Direction of Inventive Activity: Economic and Social Factors*, Princeton University Press, 609–626.

Barro, R.J. 1991. Economic Growth in a Cross-Section of Countries, *Quarterly Journal of Economics*, 106, 407–43.

Boozer, M., Ranis, G., Stewart, F. and Suri, T. 2003. *Paths to Success: The Relationship Between Human Development and Economic Growth*, Yale University, Center Discussion Paper No. 874.

Cohen, W.M. and Levinthal, D.A. 1990. Absorptive Capacity: A New Perspective on Learning and Innovation, *Administrative Science Quarterly*, 35(1), 128–152.

Crescenzi, R. 2005. Innovation and Regional Growth in the Enlarged Europe: The Role of Local Innovative Capabilities, Peripherality, and Education. *Growth and Change*, 36, 471–507.

Fagerberg, J. 1987. A Technology Gap Approach to Why Growth Rates Differ. *Research Policy*, 16, 87–99.

Fagerberg, J., 1988. Why Growth Rates Differ. In: Dosi, G., Freeman, C., Nelson, R., Silverberg, G. and Soete, L. (eds.), *Technical Change and Economic Theory*, London, Pinter Publishers, 432–457.

Fagerberg, J., Srholec, M. and Verspagen, B. 2010. Innovation and Economic Development. In: Hall, B. and Rosenberg, N. (eds.), *Handbook of Economics of Innovation*, Amsterdam, Elsevier, 833–872.

Fagerberg, J. and Verspagen, B. 2002. Technology-Gaps, Innovation – Diffusion and Transformation: An Evolutionary Interpretation. *Research Policy*, 31, 1291–1304.

Gerschenkron, A. 1962. *Economic Backwardness in Historical Perspective*, Cambridge, MA, Harvard University Press.

Gray Molina, G. and Purser, M. 2010. *Human Development Trends Since 1970: A Social Convergence Story*. *Human Development Research Paper* n. 2.

Griliches, Z. 1979. Issues in Assessing the Contribution of Research and Development to Productivity Growth, *The Bell Journal of Economics*, 10, 92–116.

Griliches, Z. 1984. *R&D, Patents and Productivity*, Chicago, Chicago University Press.

Griliches, Z. 1986. Productivity, R&D and Basic Research at the Firm Level in the 1970s, *American Economic Review*, 76, 141–54.

Hartmann, D. 2014. *Economic Complexity and Human Development: How Economic Diversification and Social Networks Affect Human Agency and Welfare*. London, New York, Routledge.

Islam, N. 2003. What Have We Learnt From the Convergence Debate? *Journal of Economic Surveys*, 17, 309–362.

Kaldor, N. 1970. The Case for Regional Policies, *Scottish Journal of Political Economy*, 67, 591–624.

Landes, D. 1998. *The Wealth and Poverty of Nation*, London, Abacus.

Lucas, R.E.B. 1988. On the Mechanics of Economic Development, *Journal of Monetary Economics*, 22, 3–42.

Myrdal, G. 1957. *The Economic Theory and Underdeveloped Regions*, London, Duckworth.

Nelson, N.N. and Winter, S.G. 1974. Neoclassical vs Evolutionary Theories of Economic Growth: Critique and Prospectus, *The Economic Journal*, 84(336), 886–905.

OECD (Organisation for Economic and Co-operation and Development) and WB (World Bank) 2009. *Innovation and Growth: Chasing a Moving Frontier*, Paris, OECD.

Ranis, G. and Stewart, F. 2000. Strategies for Success in Human Development, *Journal of Human Development*, 1(1), 49–69.

Ranis, G. and Stewart, F. 2005. *Dynamic Links Between the Economy and Human Development*. DESA Working Paper No. 8.

Ranis, G. and Stewart, F. 2006. *Successful Transition Towards a Virtuous Cycle of Human Development and Economic Growth: Country Studies*, Yale University, Center Discussion Paper No. 943.

Ranis, G. and Stewart, F. 2012. Success and Failure in Human Development, 1970–2007, *Journal of Human Development and Capabilities*, 13(2), 167–195.

Ranis, G., Stewart, F. and Ramirez, A. 2000. Economic Growth and Human Development, *World Development*, 28(2), 197–219.

Ranis, G. and Zhao, X. 2013. Technology and Human Development, *Journal of Human Development and Capabilities*, 14(4), 467–482.

Reinert, E.S. 2007. *How Rich Countries Got Rich . . . and Why Poor Countries Stay Poor*, London, Constable.

Rodriguez and Pose, A. 2001. Is R&D Investment in Lagging Areas of Europe Worthwhile? Theory and Empirical Evidence. *Papers in Regional Science*, 80, 275–295.

Romer, P. 1990. Endogenous Technological Change. *Journal of Political Economy*, 98, S71–S102.

Schumpeter, J.A. 1936. *The Theory of Economic Development: An Inquiry Into Profits, Capital, Credit, Interest, and the Business Cycle*, Cambridge, MA, Harvard University Press.

Schumpeter, J.A. 2010. *Capitalism, Socialism and Democracy*, London and New York, Routledge.

Solow, R.M. 1956. A Contribution to the Theory of Economic Growth, *Quarterly Journal of Economics*, 70, 65–94.

Solow, R.M. 1957. Technical Change and the Aggregate Production Function, *Review of Economics and Statistics*, 39(3), 312–320.

Sterlacchini, A. 2008. R&D, Higher Education and Regional Growth: Uneven Linkages Among European Regions, *Research Policy*, 37, 1096–1107.

Suri, T., Boozer, M.A., Ranis, G. and Stewart, F. 2011. Paths to Success: The Relationship Between Human Development and Economic Growth, *World Development*, 39(4), 506–522.

UNDP (United Nations Development Programme) 1990. *Human Development Report 1990*, Oxford University Press, Oxford.

UNDP (United Nations Development Programme) 1996. *Human Development Report 1996*, Oxford University Press, Oxford.

UNDP (United Nations Development Programme) 2001. *Human Development Report 2001, Making New Technologies Work for Human Development*, Oxford, Oxford University Press.

Verdoorn, P.J. 1949. Fattori che Regolano lo Sviluppo della Produttivitá del Lavoro, *L'Industria*, 1, 45–53.

Verspagen, B. 2005. Innovation and Economic Growth: In: Fagerberg, J., Mowery, D.C. and Nelson, R.R. (eds.), *The Oxford Handbook of Innovation*, Oxford University Press, Oxford, 487–513.

Verspagen, B. 1991. A New Empirical Approach to Catching Up and Falling Behind. *Structural Change and Economic Dynamics*, 12, 374–397.

Young, A. 1928. Increasing Returns and Economic Progress, *Economic Journal*, 38, 527–42.

# 5 Innovation, human development and economic growth in national and regional innovation systems

## A descriptive analysis

### 5.1 Introduction

In this and the next chapter, the empirical relationship between innovation, human development and growth will be discussed in-depth by comparing national and regional economic systems. Subsequently, two main questions will be addressed: how do countries and regions rank with respect to these three dimensions? Is it possible to identify groups of countries and regions at similar stages in terms of innovation, growth and human development? To respond to these questions, two sets of data will be used: one focusing on 40 middle- and high-income countries covering the period 1995–2012 (Panel 1) and the other on 266 European regions covering the period 2000–2012 (Panel 2).[1]

As we shall see, the analysis undertaken at the national level took advantage of the available data that proved to be sufficient for this purpose. However, one of its limitations is that it considers the processes that are being analysed as uniformly distributed within the national territories. This greatly reduces the significance of the analysis, especially for large countries. Innovation processes, human development and growth of large countries like the US, China, India and Russia, but also of medium-size countries such as Italy, France and Germany, are not evenly distributed geographically. To analyse hierarchies, interdependent relationships and dissemination processes at the territorial level of the analysed dimensions, it is necessary to adopt a sub-national scope. This, however, implies an availability of data which, although much improved in recent years, is still very limited. For several years, Eurostat has been building a regional database large enough to allow us to explore data in line with our interest, but only within regions of member countries of the European Union.

The analysis included in this chapter will begin with a comparison between countries based on the relative levels and changes over time, of innovation indices and human development as well as of per capita income (Section 5.2). The same type of analysis will be extended to European regions (Section 5.3).

### 5.2 National systems

#### a. Levels of income, innovation and human development

The results from the calculation of the indices for the 40 countries under consideration[2] are shown in Tables 5.1 and 5.2. In the first table, the states are

*Table 5.1* Per capita income, ICI and HDI in 40 countries, year 2012

| COUNTRY RANKING | | | COUNTRY RANKING | | | COUNTRY RANKING | | |
|---|---|---|---|---|---|---|---|---|
| | GNI | | | ICI | | | HDI* | |
| 1 | NO | 64,163 | 1 | KR | 0.81 | 1 | AU | 0.97 |
| 2 | LU | 58,695 | 2 | AU | 0.70 | 2 | NZ | 0.95 |
| 3 | CH | 53,043 | 3 | US | 0.70 | 3 | NO | 0.93 |
| 4 | US | 51,707 | 4 | FI | 0.69 | 4 | IE | 0.92 |
| 5 | DE | 42,965 | 5 | DK | 0.69 | 5 | NL | 0.92 |
| 6 | SE | 42,902 | 6 | CH | 0.69 | 6 | IS | 0.91 |
| 7 | AT | 42,874 | 7 | IS | 0.68 | 7 | DE | 0.91 |
| 8 | NL | 42,849 | 8 | SE | 0.68 | 8 | KR | 0.90 |
| 9 | DK | 42,780 | 9 | NO | 0.66 | 9 | CH | 0.90 |
| 10 | CA | 41,539 | 10 | JP | 0.66 | 10 | IL | 0.90 |
| 11 | AU | 41,045 | 11 | IL | 0.66 | 11 | US | 0.90 |
| 12 | BE | 39,610 | 12 | NZ | 0.66 | 12 | CA | 0.90 |
| 13 | FI | 38,062 | 13 | NL | 0.65 | 13 | UK | 0.89 |
| 14 | FR | 36,692 | 14 | CA | 0.64 | 14 | DK | 0.89 |
| 15 | JP | 36,113 | 15 | DE | 0.63 | 15 | SI | 0.89 |
| 16 | IE | 34,922 | 16 | SI | 0.59 | 16 | JP | 0.89 |
| 17 | UK | 34,604 | 17 | AT | 0.58 | 17 | SE | 0.89 |
| 18 | IS | 34,382 | 18 | UK | 0.58 | 18 | FR | 0.88 |
| 19 | IT | 33,449 | 19 | BE | 0.57 | 19 | CZ | 0.88 |
| 20 | NZ | 32,102 | 20 | IE | 0.56 | 20 | ES | 0.87 |
| 21 | ES | 30,835 | 21 | FR | 0.55 | 21 | FI | 0.87 |
| 22 | KR | 29,654 | 22 | EE | 0.53 | 22 | IT | 0.87 |
| 23 | IL | 29,638 | 23 | CZ | 0.50 | 23 | BE | 0.87 |
| 24 | SI | 27,152 | 24 | ES | 0.48 | 24 | AT | 0.86 |
| 25 | EL | 25,507 | 25 | LU | 0.45 | 25 | EL | 0.86 |
| 26 | SK | 25,130 | 26 | IT | 0.45 | 26 | EE | 0.85 |
| 27 | CZ | 24,776 | 27 | PT | 0.44 | 27 | PL | 0.85 |
| 28 | PT | 24,484 | 28 | EL | 0.44 | 28 | LU | 0.84 |
| 29 | EE | 23,051 | 29 | HU | 0.41 | 29 | CL | 0.83 |
| 30 | RU | 22,319 | 30 | RU | 0.38 | 30 | SK | 0.83 |
| 31 | PL | 21,156 | 31 | PL | 0.38 | 31 | HU | 0.82 |
| 32 | HU | 20,893 | 32 | SK | 0.36 | 32 | PT | 0.82 |
| 33 | CL | 20,137 | 33 | CN | 0.33 | 33 | RU | 0.76 |
| 34 | TR | 18,011 | 34 | TR | 0.29 | 34 | MX | 0.75 |
| 35 | MX | 15,867 | 35 | CL | 0.29 | 35 | TR | 0.74 |
| 36 | BR | 14,081 | 36 | BR | 0.28 | 36 | BR | 0.74 |
| 37 | ZA | 11,726 | 37 | ZA | 0.25 | 37 | CN | 0.72 |
| 38 | CN | 10,712 | 38 | MX | 0.20 | 38 | ID | 0.69 |
| 39 | ID | 8,601 | 39 | IN | 0.14 | 39 | ZA | 0.62 |
| 40 | IN | 5,000 | 40 | ID | 0.08 | 40 | IN | 0.58 |

sorted in descending order by gross national income per capita (GNI), then by the innovation capacity index (ICI) and finally by the human development index, net of income component (HDI*), all referred to the latest year available, i.e., 2012.[3] Table 5.2 shows the ranking positions of countries and

Table 5.2 Country ranking by indices and differences in their relative positions, year 2012

| | RANKING | | | DIFFERENCE IN RANKING | | |
|---|---|---|---|---|---|---|
| | *GNI* | *ICI* | *HDI★* | *GNI-ICI* | *GNI-HDI★* | *HDI★-ICI* |
| AU | 11 | 2 | 1 | 9 | 10 | −1 |
| AT | 7 | 17 | 24 | −10 | −17 | 7 |
| BE | 12 | 19 | 23 | −7 | −11 | 4 |
| BR | 36 | 36 | 36 | 0 | 0 | 0 |
| CA | 10 | 14 | 12 | −4 | −2 | −2 |
| CL | 33 | 35 | 29 | −2 | 4 | −6 |
| CN | 38 | 33 | 37 | 5 | 1 | 4 |
| CZ | 27 | 23 | 19 | 4 | 8 | −4 |
| DK | 9 | 5 | 14 | 4 | −5 | 9 |
| EE | 29 | 22 | 26 | 7 | 3 | 4 |
| FI | 13 | 4 | 21 | 9 | −8 | 17 |
| FR | 14 | 21 | 18 | −7 | −4 | −3 |
| DE | 5 | 15 | 7 | −10 | −2 | −8 |
| EL | 25 | 28 | 25 | −3 | 0 | −3 |
| HU | 32 | 29 | 31 | 3 | 1 | 2 |
| IS | 18 | 7 | 6 | 11 | 12 | −1 |
| IN | 40 | 39 | 40 | 1 | 0 | 1 |
| ID | 39 | 40 | 38 | −1 | 1 | −2 |
| IE | 16 | 20 | 4 | −4 | 12 | −16 |
| IL | 23 | 11 | 10 | 12 | 13 | −1 |
| IT | 19 | 26 | 22 | −7 | −3 | −4 |
| JP | 15 | 10 | 16 | 5 | −1 | 6 |
| KR | 22 | 1 | 8 | 21 | 14 | 7 |
| LU | 2 | 25 | 28 | −23 | −26 | 3 |
| MX | 35 | 38 | 34 | −3 | 1 | −4 |
| NL | 8 | 13 | 5 | −5 | 3 | −8 |
| NZ | 20 | 12 | 2 | 8 | 18 | −10 |
| NO | 1 | 9 | 3 | −8 | −2 | −6 |
| PL | 31 | 31 | 27 | 0 | 4 | −4 |
| PT | 28 | 27 | 32 | 1 | −4 | 5 |
| RU | 30 | 30 | 33 | 0 | −3 | 3 |
| SK | 26 | 32 | 30 | −6 | −4 | −2 |
| SI | 24 | 16 | 15 | 8 | 9 | −1 |
| ZA | 37 | 37 | 39 | 0 | −2 | 2 |
| ES | 21 | 24 | 20 | −3 | 1 | −4 |
| SE | 6 | 8 | 17 | −2 | −11 | 9 |
| CH | 3 | 6 | 9 | −3 | −6 | 3 |
| TR | 34 | 34 | 35 | 0 | −1 | 1 |
| UK | 17 | 18 | 13 | −1 | 4 | −5 |
| US | 4 | 3 | 11 | 1 | −7 | 8 |

the differences between the positions in each indicator with respect to the other two.

The comparison between the rankings highlights some common aspects and some interesting peculiarities. Let's first tackle the aspects in common. Ten countries – Australia, Canada, Denmark, Germany, Japan, Netherlands, Norway, Sweden,[4] Switzerland and the United States – have the three indices simultaneously in the first 16 positions (the first two quintiles, see Table 5.1). The same countries were at the same level 18 years ago (see Annex Table A.3). It therefore *appears*[5] that these countries are in a virtuous circle where high levels of innovation and human development go hand in hand with high levels of income. The three dimensions of our focus then appear to have reached a good degree of harmony and persistence in this group of leading states. This group will be referred to as the 'Club of 10'.

At the other extreme are the countries with the lowest ranking of the indices (i.e., the last 8 positions), which comprise of the middle-income countries included in the sample: China, India, Indonesia, South Africa, Chile, Mexico, Turkey and Brazil.[6] Another pattern is observed in the prevailing ranking of medium-low indices in the three dimensions of a group of countries from the Eastern bloc (Czech Republic, Estonia, Hungary, Poland, Russia and Slovakia) as well as from the Southern part of the European continent (Italy, Spain, Portugal and Greece).

Let us now consider some peculiarities. Norway has an interesting ranking, in that it ranks first in terms of GNI per capita and third for human development, but 'only' ninth in the innovation index. Following our model discussed in Chapter 3, we could say that the resources generated in this country (mainly from the export of raw materials) appear to have been directed by public policies primarily to the education and health sectors, at the expense of investment in innovation. Luxembourg's ranking is also noteworthy, with its high level of income (ranks second), which is not linked to an expansion in the innovation capacity (ranks 25th, see Table 5.2) or human development (ranks 28th). In this case, the characteristics of this country (in terms of size, specialisation in financial services and taxation system) probably led to the lack of interest amongst policy makers to promote efficiency (measured by innovation) and/or equity (measured by HDI★). Among the top rankings, also Australia presents distinctive features, as it ranks second in innovation and first in HDI, but 11th in income – a ranking that indicates a high interest in innovation and human development. It could be said that it adopts the opposite strategy to Luxembourg.

The rankings for the innovation capacity index is led by Korea; the high index for innovation is accompanied by a high level of HD (ranking 8th) and an average level of income, slightly lower than that of Spain. The comparison between the Asian country and the two European countries of more ancient industrialisation, Italy and Spain, is very interesting. With an income slightly lower than those in Spain and Italy, Korea, as we have seen, ranks 8th in HDI★ and 1st in ICI, while the two Southern European countries rank 22nd and 20th respectively in HDI★ and 26th and 24th in ICI (Table 2). As we will see later in this chapter when discussing the analysis of long-term changes, the performance of this Asian country is the result of intense efforts undertaken over the past decades. Korea's ranking is similar to that of Iceland; the income of both countries is slightly higher than that of Italy, but the human development and innovation indices ranked the country 6th and 7th respectively.

Two more countries deserve to be highlighted here, namely Finland and New Zealand. The first country ranks 4th for the innovation index, but 21st for HDI and 13th for income. In this case the high level of investments in innovation (especially those undertaken by some large national firms) has generated a medium-high level of income, which, however, has not yet been followed by adequate levels of health and knowledge.

New Zealand's development profile is similar to that of Korea and Iceland: with an income level close to that of Italy and Spain (ranked 20th), this country retains a high HDI (ranked 2nd) and a medium-high index for innovation (ranked 12th).

### a. Variations during the period 1995–2012

In the previous section, we have compared the levels of innovation, income and human development of countries in the year 2012. These are a result of different pathways pursued by countries in previous years. Thus, in order to get a complete picture with the aim to make comparisons based on the level of indices, it is relevant to also include the analysis of variations over the period 1995–2012.

A variety of measurement methodologies are available to assess variation over the period, this study adopted the divergence from expected performance (deviation from fit). This measurement, as discussed in Appendix A.2, appears to be more suitable for the purpose of comparison between countries at different levels of development, as it is able to avoid the shortcomings of measurements that assume a hypothesis of linear evolution of phenomena. Table 5.3[7] reports for each indicator and country the deviation from the fit values.

Korea is the only country that simultaneously appears in the first quintile across the three rankings. When comparing these data with the previous set reporting the levels, the distinctiveness of the Korean catching-up strategy proves to be effective: despite starting initially with medium-low income levels (relative to the analysed sample, see Appendix Table A.5), this country has engaged in a major innovation effort (with regards to research and technological infrastructures), consolidated with a significant investment in the health and education of its people. With reference to our rankings, the country advanced by 17 positions in the index of innovation, 12 positions for human development and 'only' 5 for income per capita (see Appendix Table A.6). Six other countries – Ireland, Australia, Estonia, China, Germany and Slovenia – are in the first sixteen positions (first two quintiles) of the three rankings. This group of seven countries has therefore made important progress simultaneously in the three dimensions – economic growth, human development and innovation. Within this group, Germany and Australia are the only countries belonging to the 'Club of 10', i.e., countries with simultaneously high levels of income, innovation capacity and human development (see above). In the case of the remaining countries within the group, we note that Ireland is an upper-middle income country, Korea a medium- income country, Slovenia and Estonia are countries in transition and China is a developing country.

*Table 5.3* Selected countries: progress in GNI, HDI★ and ICI measured by deviation from fit

| RANK | country | devfit-GNI | country | devfit-ICI | country | devfit-HDI★ |
|------|---------|-----------|---------|-----------|---------|------------|
| 1 | CN | 2.17 | KR | 1.86 | TR | 1.48 |
| 2 | SE | 1.70 | CN | 1.77 | KR | 1.42 |
| 3 | EE | 1.64 | EE | 1.76 | IE | 1.40 |
| 4 | KR | 1.56 | TR | 1.35 | AU | 1.34 |
| 5 | FI | 1.52 | PT | 1.30 | DE | 1.30 |
| 6 | IE | 1.46 | IS | 1.27 | NZ | 1.26 |
| 7 | SK | 1.45 | SI | 1.26 | IS | 1.24 |
| 8 | AU | 1.42 | DK | 1.23 | SI | 1.23 |
| 9 | CA | 1.36 | IN | 1.20 | NO | 1.23 |
| 10 | US | 1.31 | AU | 1.15 | EL | 1.19 |
| 11 | PL | 1.30 | CH | 1.13 | EE | 1.19 |
| 12 | AT | 1.27 | EL | 1.12 | IT | 1.19 |
| 13 | RU | 1.26 | IE | 1.07 | CZ | 1.17 |
| 14 | SI | 1.24 | DE | 1.05 | CN | 1.17 |
| 15 | DE | 1.21 | CZ | 1.04 | ID | 1.17 |
| 16 | IL | 1.11 | AT | 1.04 | CH | 1.13 |
| 17 | NL | 1.06 | FI | 1.03 | DK | 1.11 |
| 18 | NO | 1.06 | NL | 1.03 | CL | 1.08 |
| 19 | NZ | 1.04 | US | 1.02 | BR | 1.05 |
| 20 | UK | 1.00 | IL | 0.99 | IL | 1.03 |
| 21 | CL | 0.94 | ES | 0.98 | MX | 0.99 |
| 22 | IN | 0.89 | NZ | 0.98 | LU | 0.97 |
| 23 | CZ | 0.85 | JP | 0.94 | NL | 0.96 |
| 24 | IS | 0.85 | SE | 0.91 | FR | 0.96 |
| 25 | TR | 0.82 | NO | 0.89 | AT | 0.95 |
| 26 | BE | 0.79 | BR | 0.83 | ES | 0.94 |
| 27 | DK | 0.79 | BE | 0.83 | HU | 0.93 |
| 28 | CH | 0.77 | LU | 0.82 | PL | 0.92 |
| 29 | FR | 0.74 | CL | 0.82 | PT | 0.90 |
| 30 | HU | 0.71 | HU | 0.82 | UK | 0.86 |
| 31 | ES | 0.70 | PL | 0.81 | IN | 0.84 |
| 32 | JP | 0.54 | IT | 0.77 | SK | 0.80 |
| 33 | MX | 0.48 | CA | 0.73 | JP | 0.79 |
| 34 | EL | 0.48 | FR | 0.72 | FI | 0.74 |
| 35 | ID | 0.47 | UK | 0.71 | RU | 0.73 |
| 36 | BR | 0.43 | RU | 0.70 | SE | 0.58 |
| 37 | PT | 0.43 | MX | 0.67 | US | 0.57 |
| 38 | ZA | 0.33 | ID | 0.65 | CA | 0.56 |
| 39 | IT | 0.28 | SK | 0.47 | BE | 0.41 |
| 40 | LU | | ZA | 0.37 | ZA | −0.12 |

With regards to *growth* (see Figure 5.1 and Table 5.3), in the top rankings, in addition to those already mentioned, are both high-income countries such as Sweden, Finland, Austria, Canada and the United States, and countries in transition like Slovakia, Poland and Russia. In the lowest rankings are some

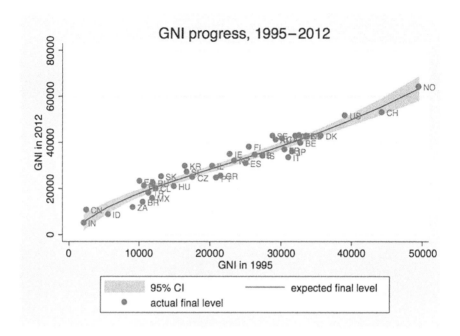

*Figure 5.1* GNI progress relative to expectations

countries considered in the current literature as rapidly growing, which how-ever, according to the methodology followed, are not confirmed as such: South Africa, Brazil, Indonesia and Mexico. This group of countries is placed along-side Greece, Portugal and Italy, the latter being the last in the rankings with the worst performance in terms of economic growth among the 39 countries under consideration.

The performance according to *the innovation index* is much more varied. In the top three ranks are the three most dynamic countries of the period: Korea, China and Estonia, followed (see Figure 5.2 and Table 5.3) by high-income countries such as Iceland, Denmark, Australia, Switzerland, Ireland, Germany and Austria; countries in transition such as Slovenia and the Czech Republic; Southern European countries (Portugal and Greece) and low-income coun-tries (Turkey and India). Similarly, at the bottom of the ranking appear devel-oped countries (UK, Canada, France, Italy, Norway, Belgium and Luxembourg), countries in transition (Russia, Slovakia, Poland and Hungary) and low-income countries (South Africa, Indonesia, Mexico, Chile and Brazil). The decision to invest in innovation does not seem to depend on the development level of countries. Leading countries which have slowed down over the two decades under consideration (the case of the United States and Sweden) are placed together with leading countries which continue to invest (as in the case of Denmark and Switzerland); developing countries or countries in transition

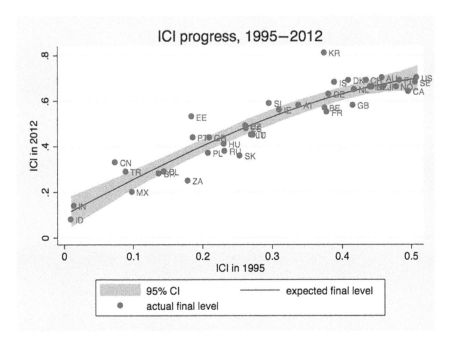

*Figure 5.2* ICI progress relative to expectations

that are advancing innovation (China, Turkey, Slovenia, Estonia and India), are placed side by side with countries which instead have done little or nothing in this direction (all others). Curious, for example, is the path followed by Canada which in 1995 ranked third in the innovation index, after the USA and Sweden, and which in 2012 slipped down to 14th rating, losing 11 positions due to a period of modest performance, amongst the worst of the countries analysed (see Appendix Tables A.5 and A.6).

Finally, Turkey ranks at the top when considering the progress achieved in *human development* (see Figure 5.3 and Table 5.3). During the period under consideration, this country demonstrated a certain level of vitality, as we have seen, also in terms of innovation (ranking 4th), although not backed by economic growth (ranking 25th). Turkey, along with China, is a low-income country in our sample which, taking into account its starting point, invested largely in human development and innovation, but unlike China, achieved lower-than-expected levels of growth.

The other top positions (with significant advances in the human development, i.e., of at least 20% above the expected figure) are occupied by four European countries (Ireland, Germany, Iceland and Slovenia) and two from the Pacific region (Australia and New Zealand). On the other side of the ranking (the bottom quintile) emerged some of the developed countries such as Japan, Sweden, USA, Canada, Belgium and Finland, who underinvested in human

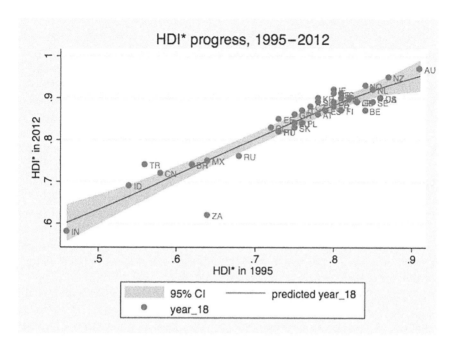

*Figure 5.3* HDI★ progress relative to expectations

development. The first four are members of the 'Club of 10' (see above), a club formed by countries with high levels in all three indices. In these cases, the low progress in human development, at least in two of the dimensions considered by the model, could be interpreted as caused by the already high levels of education and life expectancy attained by these countries which make it difficult to record further significant progress. This interpretation however, contradicts the performance of other countries such as Australia and Germany. In 1995 Australia had the highest human development index, and despite this, it ranked fourth among countries that in subsequent years invested more in education and health.

Finally, let's bring our attention to some low-income countries, which despite the limited material resources at their disposal, have intensively directed their efforts towards health and education. These are Brazil, Chile, Indonesia and China, whose performance index values are all greater than one. The performance index values of other low-income countries are below one, with an advancement that is lower than expected.

### b. Correlation between variations

With the aim of establishing whether there are common trends and regularities among countries, let's proceed to analyse the changes in each pair of indicators:

at first the changes in GNI and HDI; then those in ICI and GNI and finally the variations in HDI and ICI.[8]

Let's start with comparison of variations in *human development*[9] *and economic growth* (Figure 5.4). The chart's distribution does not show any pattern of regularity and countries are distributed almost evenly across the four quadrants.[10] Within the timeframe analysed, ten countries have simultaneously achieved a significant improvement in HDI★ and an economic performance above average. Three of these are in Central and Northern Europe (Germany, Norway and Ireland), two are countries in transition (Estonia and Slovenia), two are Asian (China and Korea), in addition to New Zealand, Australia and Israel. These countries seem to foster conditions in which growth and human development improve hand in hand.

On the opposite side (SW quadrant), nine countries have variations lower than expected for both human development index and economic growth and seem to have fallen into a vicious circle. Six of these countries are either an EU Member State (France, Spain, Portugal, Hungary and Belgium) or a high-income country (Japan), while three (South Africa, India and Mexico) belong to the low-income group of countries.

Ten more countries belong to the group of EG-lopsided countries (SE quadrant), with an economic performance above average and an HDI★ improvement below average. Seven are from the group of the most developed countries (UK, the Netherlands, Austria, Finland, USA, Canada and Sweden) and three

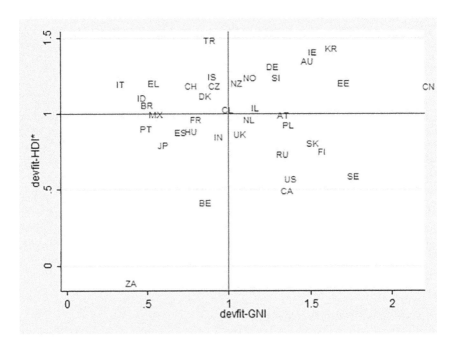

*Figure 5.4* Correlation between HDI★ and GNI progress, 1995–2012

are countries in transition (Russia, Poland and Slovakia). For these countries, therefore, resources generated by the rapid growth have not been sufficiently directed to expand health and education of the population.

Ten other countries have invested more intensely in human development than in growth performance (NW quadrant). This group is dominated by six European countries along with Chile, Brazil, Indonesia and Turkey.

The exercise of linking income growth and human development index builds on related work, mentioned earlier (Ranis et al., 2000; Ranis and Stewart, 2000; Boozer et al., 2003), which explored the relationship between growth and human development, focusing in particular on developing countries. In the following sections, this approach will be extended to the two other relationships, i.e., between growth and innovation and between innovation and human development.

Let us see then if there are any regularities when comparing variations of the *innovation capacity index and economic growth* (see Figure 5.5). In this case too, there appears to be no regularity in the country distribution on the chart. Among those which have simultaneously made significant advances in the innovation capacity and GNI (NE quadrant) is a small group of countries, which positively stands out. This consists of Korea, Estonia and China. Also in this quadrant but with lower indices are Slovenia, Ireland, Austria, Germany, Finland, Holland, USA and Australia. Equally numerous, however, are countries that have a low growth performance alongside a low increase in innovation capacity (SW

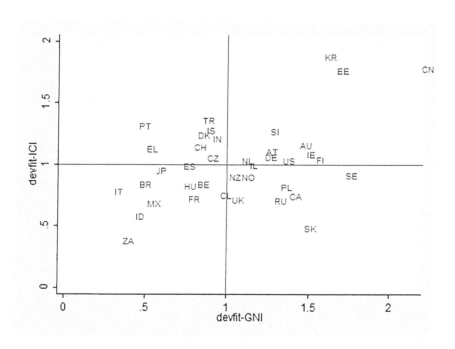

*Figure 5.5* Correlation between ICI and GNI progress, 1995–2012

quadrant). Eleven countries are part of this group: five European (Belgium, Spain, Hungary, France and Italy), Japan and five low-income countries (South Africa, Brazil, Indonesia, Mexico and Chile)

There are also a number of countries (Norway, Sweden, Slovakia, Russia, Canada, Great Britain, Poland, New Zealand and Israel) that, during the period 1995 to 2012, have experienced high economic growth unaccompanied by a low growth of innovation capacity. An even more diverse group is found in the NW quadrant, in which low growth is combined with high investment in innovation. Here we find countries like Greece, Portugal, Iceland, Czech Republic, Switzerland and Denmark along with Turkey and India.

Finally, let us compare the changes in the *innovation capacity index (ICI★)*[11] *and human development* in terms of the deviation from the expected value in the same timeframe (see Figure 5.6). The countries are arranged along an ideal rising curve,[12] suggesting the existence of a correlation between innovation and human development. In this figure, unlike the previous two, the majority of countries (25 out of 40) are found in the SW and NE quadrants. This arrangement leads us to presume that the processes of both innovation and human development have a similar trend in the long run and as we shall see, are mutually reinforcing. This does not happen in the case of economic growth. As we have seen, even very significant increases in per capita income can go hand in hand with modest changes in human development and/or innovation; or vice versa, a low rate of growth can co-exist with high advances in innovation and/ or human development.

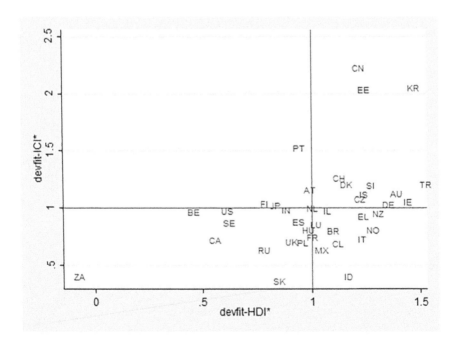

*Figure 5.6* Correlation between HDI★ and ICI★ progress, 1995–2012

There are 12 countries in the quadrant representing the virtuous circle between innovation and human development (NE), and 13 in the opposite quadrant (SW) which includes countries with low performance both in innovation and in human development. Only four countries are in the quadrant characterised by low innovation capacity and high human development (NW); and ten are found in the quadrant with low growth in innovation and high human development (SE). In the first group of virtuous countries, two sub-groups stand out: the first consists of Korea, China and Estonia, with very high values for both indices, and the other 9 countries, for the most part European, with more moderate values. In the SW quadrant there are, as we have seen, 13 countries mostly from Europe, but also the two North American nations (US and Canada), India and South Africa. These countries seem to have some difficulty in pursuing virtuous paths leading to a simultaneous improvement in human and innovation capacity. For the more developed countries, probably this is caused by the high levels in innovation and human development already attained. In the case of the least-developed countries this could signal a difficulty in undertaking paths of change that can promote sustainable development over time. In the NW quadrant, there are countries where the process of enhancing innovation capacity is intense, but it is accompanied by low efforts in terms of improving human development. In this quadrant, only Portugal records high levels of innovation performance, while the other three (Austria, the Netherlands and Finland) are very close to the average value of advancement in terms of innovation. In the SE quadrant, we find European countries (Italy, Norway, Greece and Luxembourg), some developing countries (Brazil, Indonesia, Chile and Mexico) as well as Israel and New Zealand.

### c. A general picture

The analysis conducted so far on the levels and variations of the indices provides us with an array of innovation-growth-human development combinations. Let's try to re-classify them. To do this, we will refer to four groups of countries, showing a certain degree of similarity in aspects related to the levels of the three indices: the 'Club of 10' (Australia, Canada, Denmark, Germany, Japan, Netherlands, Norway, Sweden, Switzerland and the United States), 'other developed countries' (Austria, Belgium, South Korea, Finland, France, Greece, Iceland, Israel, Ireland, Italy, Luxembourg, New Zealand, Portugal, Spain and UK), 'countries in transition' (Estonia, Hungary, Russia, Slovenia, Slovakia, the Czech Republic and Poland), and 'developing countries' (India, Indonesia, China, South Africa, Chile, Brazil, Mexico and Turkey). For each of these groups, I will try to identify similar variations and trends. In order to do this, I will use Figure 5.7.[13]

Let us start with the group of leading countries, the *'Club of 10'*. Despite the fairly homogeneous level of development of the 10 countries that are part of this group, the group is characterised by a difference in paths pursued by the countries. The first path is that of countries which have continued to invest in innovation and human development even though the levels of these

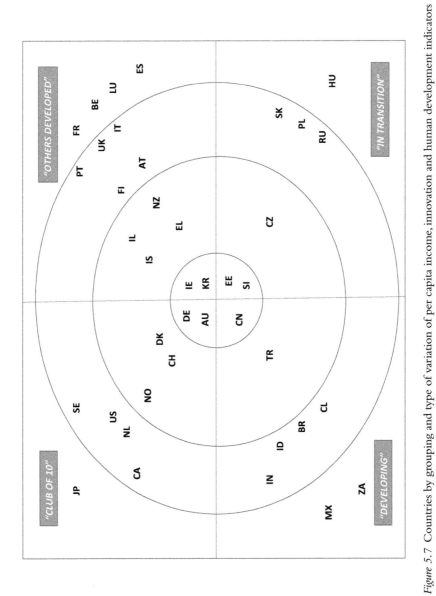

*Figure 5.7* Countries by grouping and type of variation of per capita income, innovation and human development indicators

two dimensions were high. Some recorded good results in terms of economic growth (Australia and Germany), and others grew less than expected (Denmark and Switzerland). As we have seen, Norway can be added to this sub-group, as it has focused its resources on health and education at the expense of innovation. These are countries with an already high level of wealth that have laid the foundations for further future development. The second sub-group is characterised by countries which failed to adequately invest in human development still obtaining high economic growth levels, in some cases accompanied by good performance in innovation (The Netherlands and USA), in other cases without positive results in this area (Sweden and Canada). One way to interpret these results, as we have already pointed out, is the high level of human development already achieved by these countries. This interpretation, however, does not seem to hold when the opposite results are observed (as we have just seen) in countries belonging to the same group. Japan is a particular case, as in the 18 years under study, while still maintaining high rankings in the three dimensions, its performance was below expectations in all three indices.

Let us look now at the largest group of countries (15) consisting of other developed nations that have not always held top positions in terms of growth, innovation and human development. Again we recognise a sub-group of countries that have heavily invested in innovation and human development, formed by Korea and Ireland (which have also achieved high levels of growth) and Israel and Greece (recording low levels of economic growth). It is surprising to note the ranking of Greece if we take into account the difficulties that the country manifested especially after 2011 and the economic policies set by the EEC organisations (OECD, 2011, 2013). Before the surge of these difficulties therefore, the country implemented policies aimed at strengthening its innovation capacity along with education and health sectors. This, in my opinion, is a virtuous path that could have paid off over time had it not been interrupted by the financial crisis and the austerity policies imposed by European partners. This sub-group includes two other countries (Israel and New Zealand). Like Norway, these two countries have high economic growth rates and high investments in human development, but have limited capacity for innovation.

The second sub-group consists of two countries, Austria and Finland, which have channelled the resources generated by their high growth towards strengthening their innovation capacity. The third sub-group consists of four countries (France, Belgium, Luxembourg and Spain), to which we can add yet another three European nations: Italy (which records a positive value only in the variation of human development), the United Kingdom (with a level of growth slightly higher than expected) and Portugal (with a positive variation only in innovation capacity). This sub-group, which we could provocatively call 'Old Europe', has apart from the exceptions mentioned above, lower than expected levels of growth across all three indices, and overall difficulties rooted in the European stagnation and uncertainties in the EU project.

Let us now consider *the countries in transition*. Within this group too, there is a cluster that directed its efforts into innovation and human development, comprising Estonia, Slovenia (which also had good growth performance) and the

Czech Republic (which did not have good growth outcomes). On the opposite side is a cluster of countries which have not invested in either innovation or human development. This sub-group consists of three countries that have had good performance in terms of growth (Slovakia, Russia and Poland) and Hungary, which had disappointing results in all three indices.

Last, let us examine the group of *developing countries*. In this cluster, we can distinguish countries that have simultaneously focused on the improvements of innovation and human development: China, which also recorded high performance in economic growth, and Turkey. The second cluster consists of countries that have had a positive performance in at least one indicator. This is the case of Indonesia, Brazil and Chile (HDI★), and India (ICI). These countries are viewed as having high growth rates, but this is not observed in our analysis. Efforts directed towards human development, if supported by policy choices favouring innovation, will lay the foundations for more sustainable future growth.[14]

### d. Convergence and divergence processes

Finally, let us compare the dynamics of convergence. According to the traditional approach (see Appendix A.2e), if the relationship between the levels of ICI, HDI and EG in 1995 and their respective variations is inverse, we observe a recovery of developing states over developed nations, i.e., a catching-up phenomena. Conversely, if the relationship between initial levels and variations during the timeframe is positive, diverging processes come into play.

Convergence is observed in all three indicators, as clearly revealed in Table 5.4: the negative coefficient, highly significant in all regressions,[15] indicates in fact, a negative relationship between income growth, improvements in terms of human development and innovation capacity, and the different levels of departure of each country. On average thus, those who started from lower levels have actually advanced more quickly.

This approach, which I consider statistically obvious for reasons discussed in Appendix A.2e, seems insufficient to analyse the convergence processes. It is therefore appropriate to complement these results with those obtained from the analysis of the sigma convergence. Figure 5.8 in fact illustrates a decreasing trend over time of the variation coefficients[16] of the three indices under consideration, more prominent in GNI and ICI than in HDI. The differences in the

*Table 5.4* Countries. Beta convergence test: impact of initial values on performance, 1995–2012

|  | GNI | ICI | HDI★ |
| --- | --- | --- | --- |
| coefficient | −1.7000★★★ | −2.7867★★★ | −0.2930★★★ |
|  | (0.3676) | (0.2539) | (0.0547) |
| constant | 18.9580★★★ | −0.1399 | 0.0308★★ |
|  | (3.7275) | (0.3090) | (0.0122) |
| n. of obs. | 40 | 40 | 40 |
| R-squared | 0.6258 | 0.8589 | 0.5282 |

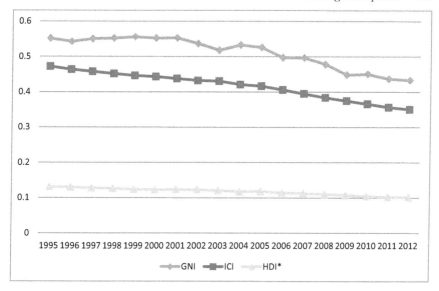

*Figure 5.8* Countries. Sigma convergence test: coefficient of variation over time, 1995–2012

first two cases are much more distinct than in human development. In the latter case, the differences between countries are restrained and decrease over time in a less-prominent way. This implies that the levels of human development in the countries under consideration have become with time more and more similar and that this similarity increases very slowly.

## 5.2 Regional systems

Our focus on the European regions will follow a three-stage descriptive analysis: an analysis of the indices (in 2012) for each region and their ranking, performance analysis over the time period, and finally a verification of the convergence/divergence processes. It will be done, however, in a slightly different way, mainly based on maps and rankings that will be limited to the regions with the highest position.

### a. Income, innovation and human development levels

It would be particularly difficult to interpret a ranking for 266 European regions. In Table 5.5 we have limited ourselves to indicating, with reference to the year 2012, the top 53 regions (first quintile of regions arranged by descending values of indices) for per capita income, innovation and human development. Maps will be used to provide an overall picture of the three indices and to highlight regional differences.

The top three regional[17] rankings in terms of *GDP per capita* are held by London, Brussels and Luxembourg. The German regions are widely present, even though, as we shall see, to a lesser extent compared to the other two rankings,

*Table 5.5* European regions by per capita income, innovation and human development indices, first 53 rankings, 2012

| | *REGIONS* | *GDPpc* | *REGIONS* | *ICI* | *REGIONS* | *HDI★* |
|---|---|---|---|---|---|---|
| | | | *Regional Indices, 2012* | | | |
| 1 | UKI1 | 82,528 | BE31 | 0.61 | DED2 | 0.89 |
| 2 | LU00 | 69,400 | DE11 | 0.59 | DE21 | 0.88 |
| 3 | BE10 | 57,021 | DE21 | 0.55 | DED4 | 0.87 |
| 4 | DE60 | 51,942 | DE14 | 0.53 | DE13 | 0.87 |
| 5 | SK01 | 48,005 | DE12 | 0.51 | SE11 | 0.87 |
| 6 | FR10 | 46,505 | DE25 | 0.51 | DE11 | 0.87 |
| 7 | NL11 | 45,972 | FI1B | 0.51 | DE14 | 0.87 |
| 8 | SE11 | 44,774 | DE91 | 0.50 | AT32 | 0.87 |
| 9 | CZ01 | 43,716 | SE11 | 0.48 | DED5 | 0.86 |
| 10 | DE21 | 43,233 | DK01 | 0.48 | UKJ2 | 0.86 |
| 11 | AT13 | 42,609 | SE22 | 0.46 | DE71 | 0.86 |
| 12 | DE71 | 41,492 | UKD6 | 0.44 | SI02 | 0.86 |
| 13 | UKM5 | 40,956 | DE13 | 0.44 | UKJ1 | 0.85 |
| 14 | DE50 | 40,672 | DE71 | 0.44 | DEG0 | 0.85 |
| 15 | DK01 | 39,312 | DEB3 | 0.44 | DE12 | 0.85 |
| 16 | FI1B | 39,023 | AT34 | 0.43 | DE26 | 0.85 |
| 17 | DE11 | 38,931 | DED2 | 0.42 | AT21 | 0.85 |
| 18 | AT32 | 38,689 | BE24 | 0.42 | UKK2 | 0.85 |
| 19 | NL31 | 38,511 | SE12 | 0.42 | DE27 | 0.85 |
| 20 | ITH1 | 37,318 | FR62 | 0.42 | FR62 | 0.85 |
| 21 | IE02 | 37,132 | NL41 | 0.42 | DE40 | 0.85 |
| 22 | NL32 | 36,898 | SE23 | 0.41 | DEB2 | 0.85 |
| 23 | UKJ1 | 36,850 | DE30 | 0.41 | UKI1 | 0.85 |
| 24 | BE21 | 35,690 | DE26 | 0.41 | UKJ3 | 0.84 |
| 25 | AT34 | 35,490 | AT22 | 0.41 | UKI2 | 0.84 |
| 26 | FI20 | 35,253 | UKJ1 | 0.40 | AT22 | 0.84 |
| 27 | DEA1 | 35,242 | UKH1 | 0.40 | SE23 | 0.84 |
| 28 | DE12 | 34,833 | DEA2 | 0.40 | FR10 | 0.84 |
| 29 | AT33 | 34,459 | DE23 | 0.40 | DEE0 | 0.84 |
| 30 | DE14 | 34,116 | FI19 | 0.39 | UKK1 | 0.84 |
| 31 | DE25 | 34,116 | FR10 | 0.39 | AT33 | 0.84 |
| 32 | RO32 | 33,600 | FR71 | 0.38 | FI1B | 0.84 |
| 33 | ITC4 | 33,576 | DK04 | 0.37 | CZ01 | 0.84 |
| 34 | AT31 | 33,530 | FI1D | 0.37 | SE33 | 0.83 |
| 35 | ITC2 | 33,373 | AT13 | 0.37 | UKE2 | 0.83 |
| 36 | DE23 | 33,296 | DEA4 | 0.36 | DE25 | 0.83 |
| 37 | DEA2 | 33,193 | DE27 | 0.36 | DE73 | 0.83 |
| 38 | NL41 | 33,168 | UKM5 | 0.35 | DE60 | 0.83 |
| 39 | ES21 | 32,934 | AT31 | 0.35 | AT34 | 0.83 |
| 40 | BE24 | 32,613 | DE60 | 0.35 | FR71 | 0.83 |
| 41 | SE33 | 32,572 | DE72 | 0.35 | DE22 | 0.83 |
| 42 | NL33 | 32,261 | DEA1 | 0.35 | DE80 | 0.83 |
| 43 | DE22 | 32,169 | DE92 | 0.35 | UKH1 | 0.83 |
| 44 | DE26 | 32,169 | UKK1 | 0.34 | UKH2 | 0.83 |

|  | REGIONS | GDPpc | REGIONS | ICI | REGIONS | HDI* |
|---|---------|-------|---------|-----|---------|------|
| 45 | DE27 | 32,067 | FI1C | 0.34 | DE72 | 0.83 |
| 46 | DE91 | 32,067 | DE24 | 0.34 | DEF0 | 0.83 |
| 47 | ES30 | 31,921 | AT33 | 0.34 | BE24 | 0.82 |
| 48 | ITH5 | 31,755 | BE21 | 0.34 | SE21 | 0.82 |
| 49 | ES22 | 31,516 | SI02 | 0.33 | DE30 | 0.82 |
| 50 | NL34 | 31,253 | UKJ3 | 0.33 | DE93 | 0.82 |
| 51 | DEA4 | 31,042 | AT21 | 0.33 | SE12 | 0.82 |
| 52 | DE13 | 30,940 | UKJ2 | 0.33 | DE92 | 0.82 |
| 53 | DEC0 | 30,940 | UKH2 | 0.32 | SE22 | 0.82 |

*Regional Indices, 2012*

with 18 out of a total of 38 regions in the country. The country that is relatively the most represented is Austria with 5 regions out of 9, followed by the
Netherlands (6 out of 12) and Finland (2 out of 5).[18] There are 11 countries,
whose regions have not ranked high in terms of per capita income. All of these
are either countries in transition or from southern Europe.

The map illustrating *the level of GDP per capita* (see Map 5.1) shows a concentration of high-income regions along an axis running from Austria to the
Netherlands, through the regions of Western Germany. This core extends to
a number of regions in Northern Italy, Catalonia and the Basque regions of
Spain, the south-eastern parts of Ireland and the Scandinavian countries. In
general, there is a greater concentration of income in the regions that are home
to the country capitals or large metropolitan centres.

The leading region in the rankings for the *innovation index* (see Table 5.5) is
the Belgian province of Brabant Walloon, home of the prestigious university of
Louvain, and of a major scientific and technological park with innovative companies in the field of life sciences, fine chemistry, information technologies and
engineering. In the top rankings of the innovation capacity index there are 21
German regions (out of a total of 38 regions in the country). Other countries
that are relatively well represented are Finland with 4 regions out of 5, followed
by Austria with 6 regions out of 9 and Sweden with 4 regions out of 8. Seven-
teen countries (out of 27) do not have any region ranking at the top; with the
exception of Luxembourg and Ireland, these regions are found in the southern
and central-eastern part of the Union.

The innovation excellence map (see Map 5.2) in Europe extends from Zahodna
in Slovenia to Austria, reaches the South of England through the regions in
west-central Germany, Belgium and the Netherlands. This central axis has an
important extension to the North-East, starting from Denmark and stretching
to Finland, reaching across the South of Sweden with an important offshoot in
France in the regions of Paris, Midi-Pyrenees and Rhone-Alpes. Around this
central axis and its branches, are situated regions with medium to high levels
of innovation capacity in Eastern Germany, North-Central Sweden, Estonia,

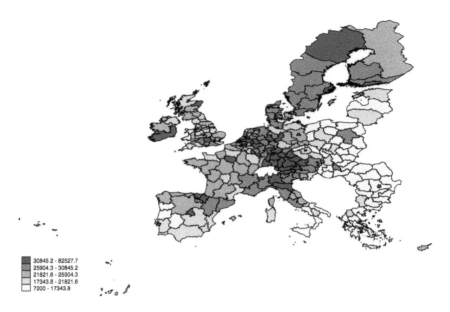

*Map 5.1* Gross domestic product (GDP) at current market prices by NUTS 2 EU regions. Purchasing power standard per inhabitant (2012)

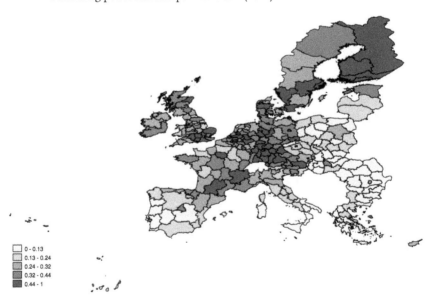

*Map 5.2* ICI by NUTS 2 EU regions (2012)

the Czech Republic and most of the other regions in France and Great Britain. The area comprising this group of European regions leading in innovation is delimited on the East by the Baltic countries, Poland, Slovakia, Hungary, Bulgaria and Romania, and on the South by Greece, Italy, Spain and Portugal.

The top seven rankings for the *human development index* are held by six regions in Germany and one in Sweden. More precisely, these are two regions in East Germany (Dresden and Chemnitz), three in South Germany (Oberbayern, Stuttgart and Tubingen) and the Stockholm region. This ranking has a large presence of German regions: 25 of 38, which makes the country more prominent than in the two previous indices. In addition, Sweden with 6 out of 8, and Austria with 5 out of 9 regions are also prominent. Two regions from Eastern Europe (one in Slovenia and one in the Czech Republic) can be flagged in this ranking. For this index, 18 countries have no regions ranking in the first 53 positions.

Unlike the two previous maps, the one based on the Human Development Index (Map 5.3) shows relatively lower indices for the Netherlands, Belgium and Luxembourg; the higher rates are concentrated in eastern and southern regions of Germany, Sweden and France. Beyond the differences in details, the overall trend is confirmed: in the case of the Human Development Index, the leading regions are the central and northern parts of the continent ranging from Slovenia to England and extending to the Scandinavian regions, while eastern and southern regions result marginal.

### b. Variations during the period 2000–2012

It is interesting to understand also in the case of European regions, whether there are differences in the investments made across the three dimensions – that of growth, human development and innovation. The top six rankings for performance in terms of economic growth (see Table 5.6) are achieved by regions hosting the six capitals of Eastern European countries: Slovakia, Romania,

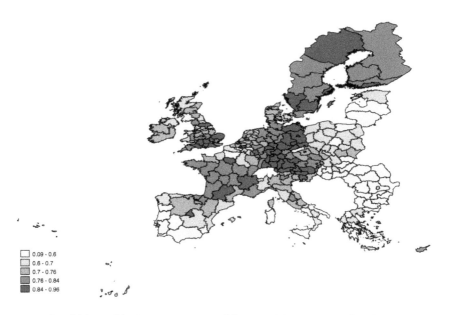

| | |
|---|---|
| 0.09 - 0.6 | |
| 0.6 - 0.7 | |
| 0.7 - 0.76 | |
| 0.76 - 0.84 | |
| 0.84 - 0.96 | |

*Map 5.3* HDI (net of the income component) by NUTS 2 EU regions (2012)

*Table 5.6* European Regions. Progress in GDP, HDI and ICI measured by deviation from fit

| RANK | GDP, ICI, HDI* VARIATIONS, 2000–2012 | | | | | |
|---|---|---|---|---|---|---|
| | Region | GDP pc | Region | ICI | Region | HDI* |
| 1 | SK01 | 4.62 | BE31 | 12.81 | EE00 | 15,761 |
| 2 | RO32 | 4.39 | DE11 | 9.92 | FR83 | 15,613 |
| 3 | PL12 | 2.77 | DE14 | 6.20 | IE01 | 14,461 |
| 4 | CZ01 | 2.33 | FR62 | 4.71 | UKI1 | 13,924 |
| 5 | HU10 | 2.32 | DE25 | 4.30 | ES30 | 13,649 |
| 6 | BG41 | 2.29 | UKD6 | 4.19 | DED2 | 13,630 |
| 7 | NL11 | 2.19 | BE24 | 4.08 | SI02 | 13,580 |
| 8 | DE22 | 2.01 | AT22 | 4.07 | DK05 | 13,356 |
| 9 | SE33 | 1.96 | DK04 | 4.07 | SI01 | 13,234 |
| 10 | LT00 | 1.93 | EE00 | 3.78 | IE02 | 13,165 |
| 11 | DE23 | 1.89 | SI02 | 3.62 | ES21 | 12,952 |
| 12 | PL51 | 1.86 | AT34 | 3.55 | DE21 | 12,797 |
| 13 | SK02 | 1.77 | UKM5 | 3.50 | LU00 | 12,721 |
| 14 | DE91 | 1.76 | DK03 | 3.47 | UKI2 | 12,704 |
| 15 | EE00 | 1.75 | DE12 | 3.41 | ES13 | 12,618 |
| 16 | DEC0 | 1.69 | UKJ2 | 3.22 | ES23 | 12,546 |
| 17 | DE24 | 1.69 | DED2 | 3.06 | LV00 | 12,487 |
| 18 | DE14 | 1.65 | AT31 | 3.02 | UKJ3 | 12,448 |
| 19 | DE27 | 1.65 | CZ06 | 2.98 | UKK2 | 12,420 |
| 20 | DE26 | 1.64 | DE73 | 2.97 | RO42 | 12,411 |
| 21 | DEA3 | 1.63 | AT33 | 2.96 | HU10 | 12,404 |
| 22 | PL22 | 1.63 | DEA4 | 2.87 | ES11 | 12,363 |
| 23 | ES21 | 1.63 | IE01 | 2.78 | DE13 | 12,238 |
| 24 | LV00 | 1.62 | ES22 | 2.78 | UKH1 | 12,197 |
| 25 | DED5 | 1.58 | UKJ4 | 2.66 | ES24 | 12,192 |
| 26 | DEA5 | 1.56 | AT21 | 2.60 | ES22 | 12,086 |
| 27 | DED4 | 1.55 | ES21 | 2.57 | ES12 | 12,080 |
| 28 | DEA1 | 1.54 | UKJ1 | 2.57 | RO11 | 12,071 |
| 29 | ES11 | 1.54 | UKN0 | 2.56 | AT32 | 12,053 |
| 30 | LU00 | 1.54 | NL21 | 2.53 | RO32 | 12,050 |
| 31 | DED2 | 1.54 | FR71 | 2.44 | RO12 | 12,026 |
| 32 | DE73 | 1.52 | BE23 | 2.42 | CY00 | 11,932 |
| 33 | NL34 | 1.51 | BE21 | 2.35 | PT17 | 11,832 |
| 34 | PL41 | 1.51 | UKG1 | 2.33 | RO41 | 11,796 |
| 35 | DEE0 | 1.51 | DE23 | 2.30 | UKK3 | 11,788 |
| 36 | DEG0 | 1.49 | DE13 | 2.28 | EL14 | 11,744 |
| 37 | ES12 | 1.49 | UKM3 | 2.24 | UKJ4 | 11,705 |
| 38 | DE25 | 1.48 | CZ03 | 2.23 | UKJ1 | 11,678 |
| 39 | CZ08 | 1.46 | FR43 | 2.22 | PT15 | 11,644 |
| 40 | DE40 | 1.46 | SI01 | 2.18 | DED4 | 11,631 |
| 41 | DEB1 | 1.45 | ES13 | 2.17 | UKJ2 | 11,593 |
| 42 | PT30 | 1.44 | UKM6 | 2.16 | ES42 | 11,557 |
| 43 | ES24 | 1.43 | IE02 | 2.15 | DE11 | 11,492 |
| 44 | DEB2 | 1.42 | DE80 | 2.09 | DK01 | 11,455 |

| RANK | GDP, ICI, HDI* VARIATIONS, 2000–2012 | | | | | |
|------|--------|--------|--------|------|--------|--------|
|      | Region | GDP pc | Region | ICI  | Region | HDI*   |
| 45 | DE72 | 1.42 | UKH1 | 2.05 | UKG2 | 11,451 |
| 46 | DEB3 | 1.42 | PT11 | 2.04 | DE14 | 11,449 |
| 47 | ES41 | 1.42 | BE32 | 2.04 | DE26 | 11,436 |
| 48 | EL30 | 1.42 | PT17 | 1.99 | FI1B | 11,430 |
| 49 | DE92 | 1.41 | UKF1 | 1.96 | ES52 | 11,413 |
| 50 | DE13 | 1.4  | FR52 | 1.93 | UKC2 | 11,394 |
| 51 | DE11 | 1.39 | CZ01 | 1.93 | UKH3 | 11,322 |
| 52 | DE94 | 1.38 | PL32 | 1.92 | AT22 | 11,301 |
| 53 | BE31 | 1.38 | AT12 | 1.92 | UKD6 | 11,292 |

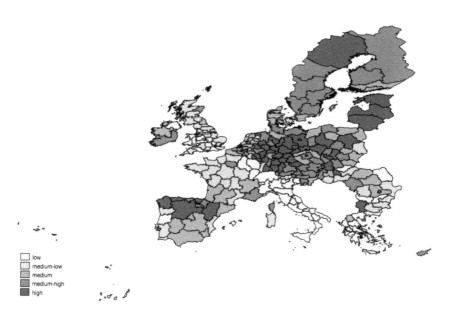

low
medium-low
medium
medium-high
high

*Map 5.4* Variations in GDP during the period 2000–2012 by NUTS 2 EU regions

Poland, Czech Republic, Hungary and Bulgaria. With the exception of Slovenia, all of the countries in transition (that are under consideration) have at least one region present in the first 53 positions. Germany, with 28 regions out of 38, is still the most represented European country. Some important European countries, such as France, UK, Italy, Austria, Denmark, Ireland and Finland, do not have any regions ranking in the top 53 positions.

The graphical representation of the *GDP growth* between 2000 and 2012 (Map 5.4) is very clear: the most dynamic area in this period extended from the regions in Germany to Scandinavia, covering all eastern regions, in particular

Poland, the Czech Republic, Hungary, Slovakia, the Baltic countries and to a lesser extent, Romania and Bulgaria. Economic growth is very low in almost all the Italian and Greek regions, medium-high in the north of Spain and medium-low to low in the regions of France and Britain. Map 5.4, therefore, confirms that economic growth concentrated around the central-eastern part of the continent during the period considered. This is due to the expansion of the European Union[19] that triggered an important trade flow. The benefits of trade have not been evenly distributed, but instead have focused substantially on the central and eastern regions of the Union.

A mirroring pattern can be observed across the 53 positions in the relative regional rankings when we consider the variation in *innovation capacity* (Table 5.6): the first nine positions are occupied by the regions of 'old' Europe, all present also in the ranking of regions with high levels of innovativeness. The most represented countries in this first part of the ranking are the UK (with 11 regions) and Germany (10), followed by Austria with 6 out of 9 regions.

The map illustrating variations in the index of innovation capacity (see Map 5.5) is characterised by a greater dispersion of results. Many German regions together with many regions of Eastern Europe, Spain and Portugal, Ireland, Finland, Denmark and Great Britain have high variation indices. On the other hand, countries such as Romania, Bulgaria, the southern regions of Italy and the regions of central and northern Sweden appear to be less dynamic.

The top rankings for variations in the *human development index* (Table 5.6) show a less distinct separation between regions of the old and new Europe, and

low
medium-low
medium
medium-high
high

*Map 5.5* Variations in ICI during the period 2000–2012 by NUTS 2 EU regions

*Map 5.6* Variations in HDI* during the period 2000–2012 by NUTS 2 EU regions (2012)

especially a lower concentration of virtuous regions in a few countries. The first in the rankings is Estonia, followed by Corsica and then the Northern region of Ireland. None of these regions appeared in the first quintile of regions ranked by level of HDI* (see Table 5.5). The country with the most regions that recorded variations appearing in the first 53 positions is Great Britain (13), followed by Spain (10) and Germany (7). Comparatively, Romania (5 out of 8), Ireland (2 out of 2) and Slovenia (2 out of 2) are also very present. Important progress in the *human development index* (Map 5.6) is thus concentrated in the area between Romania, the Austrian regions and the southern German Länder, reaching England and Ireland. Significant increases are also observed in the North-East of Spain, Denmark, Latvia, Estonia and Finland. The dynamism of some Greek regions which confirms the results at national level shown above (in Section 5.2) should be highlighted as well.

### c. Convergence and divergence processes

As in the case of the national data, the convergence processes for the period 2000–2012 were measured for the regional data, following the same measurement techniques applied in Section 5.2.b (see also Appendix A.2). The results are summarised in Table 5.7 for beta convergence and in Figure 5.9 for sigma convergence. In the first case, I was able to validate the previous results showing negative and significant regression coefficients, confirming, according to the

*Table 5.7* European regions. Beta convergence test: impact of initial values on performance, 2000–2012

|  | GDP | ICI | HDI* |
|---|---|---|---|
| coefficient | −0.2728*** | −0.5030*** | −0.9069*** |
|  | (0.0192) | (0.0225) | (0.0086) |
| constant | 2.9710*** | −0.6804*** | 2.9710*** |
|  | (0.18752) | (0.0471) | (0.0107) |
| n. of obs. | 266 | 266 | 266 |
| R-squared | 0.432 | 0.6542 | 0.9766 |

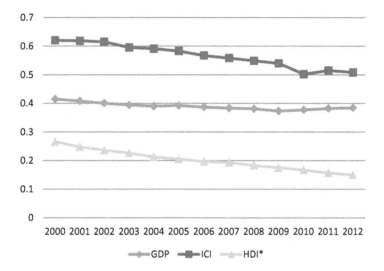

*Figure 5.9* European regions. Sigma convergence test: coefficient of variation over time

traditional approach, the hypothesis of convergence for GDP, ICI and HDI* of the European regions.

A few significant differences can be drawn from the trend of the variation coefficient. First, considering income: the index remains largely constant over the period, with a slight tendency to decrease until 2009, and an equally slight tendency to increase after that year. The highest variability is detected at the regional level in the index of innovation, contrary to the situation at the national level where the major differences between countries were in income. In the thirteen years under study, the variation of the innovation capacity index decreased from just over 0.6 to 0.5 in 2010 and remained at that level in the following years. The human development index, too, had a tendency to reduce during this period from 0.27 to 0.15 indicating, probably, the recovery of the most disadvantaged regions, particularly those in Eastern Europe, as discussed earlier.

### Summing up

The descriptive analysis in this chapter has explored the levels, variations and convergence of the three indicators that are at the core of my analysis. This study covered a sample of 40 countries as well as 266 European regions. It emerged that countries with different levels of development, such as Estonia, Korea, Ireland, Slovenia, Australia and Germany, have invested in innovation, economic growth and human development, implementing harmonic and sustainable strategies of change. On the other hand, developed countries such as Japan, France, Belgium, Luxembourg, Spain and Hungary and developing countries such as Mexico and South Africa appear to have fallen into a spiral of difficulties, with limited progress in all three aspects. Between these two extremes there are other strategies: countries that have focused more on growth rather than innovation or human development (such as in the case of Sweden, the USA, Russia and Poland); and countries that have invested more in human development and innovation, despite their low levels of growth (Turkey, Denmark, Iceland and the Czech Republic). The average differences between the countries in terms of income and innovation capacity are high but tend to rapidly reduce during the period that was studied. Conversely, the differences in terms of human development are much smaller and show a slight tendency to decline further.

Additional interesting findings are revealed from the descriptive analysis of data at the regional level. Differences in the per capita income are still high and within the timeframe of the study did not show any clear trend to decrease, on the contrary after 2009, they tend to increase. Regions with the highest income are concentrated in countries in Central Europe. The dynamics of the period highlighted processes of growth intensification along the Central-Eastern axis of the continent, with a lower dynamism in the western and southern regions. The innovation excellence regional map shows concentrations mainly in the central and northern regions of the continent, with southern and the majority of eastern regions lagging behind. The dynamism of recent years affected the majority of these same regions (with the exception of the Scandinavian regions) as well as regions mainly located in France, Great Britain, Ireland and Spain. These new dynamics allowed a sharp reduction in the innovation capacity gap, which in recent years seems to have been contained. The human development in European regions, as represented by HDI, appears to follow its own long-term trend irrespective of the trends in economic growth. The differences between regions are much smaller compared to the other two indices and decrease progressively, contrary to innovation and economic growth, which experienced a slowdown with the recent crisis. The regions that have experienced the most increase in levels of human development are predominantly in Eastern Europe, but also in Northern Spain, Greece, England and Ireland.

## Notes

1 See Appendix A.1 for further details on the compiled database.
2 See Appendix A.2 for details on the development of the indices.
3 For each index, the states are divided into five groups of eight countries: the first group comprises those with high indices, the second medium-high, the third medium, the fourth medium-low and the fifth low indices. For the purpose of this study, this classification of indices will be referred to. For example, according to our classification and based on the sample size, China would be defined as a low-income country, different from its ranking at the global level done by international organisations such as the World Bank, which classifies China as an upper-middle income country.
4 Although Sweden ranks 17 for HDI★ in our classification, I have included it in the top group because of the small difference separating its HDI★ from the country that precedes it.
5 We'll see how well the dynamics for this group are anything but homogeneous.
6 Roughly the same positions of 1995, except for the rearmost position of some countries in transition. Estonia, for example, in 1995 ranked 36th in terms of per capita income, preceding South Africa and after Brazil.
7 When calculating the deviation from fit for GNI, the data of outlier Luxembourg were omitted. This is because a major distortion in the calculation of the index resulted from the drastic fall in income experienced by the country mainly between 2008 and 2012.
8 For this analysis too, variations throughout the period are measured by deviation from the expected performance (deviation from fit).
9 For this comparison, too, I chose to use the human development index net of income component, denoted as HDI★. This is in line with the cited literature (see Chapter 4).
10 The chart is divided into four quadrants: the first (NW) with indices higher than the average index indicated only on the Y axis (Y loop-sided); the second (NE) with above-average growth of both indices (virtuous circle); the third (SE) with growth above the average index shown only on the X axis (X- loop-sided); and the fourth (SW) with both indices growing by less than average (vicious circle). See Chapter 4 for further details on the use of this approach in the literature.
11 Similar to what I have done for the HDI, in order to avoid improper correlations between the variations of the two indices, the innovation capacity index is considered here in its net value, that is, without adding the 'development of human skills' component (see Appendix A.2). This results in a slight change compared to the rankings in Table 5.3.
12 Unlike the previous two charts in which it was not possible to identify any trend line, in this case it is possible to draw a curve of polynomial interpolation with an $R^2$ of 0.25.
13 Figure 5.7 was developed for a purely descriptive purpose. The placement of each country in the plane is not based on a precise metric calculation, but takes into account the following graphical-descriptive elements: 1) in every quadrant the areas nearer to the intersection of $x$ and $y$ axes represent more positive values while those external represent more negative values; 2) variations within the studied timeframe that are always superior to 1 for the three indices represent the highest positivity, and variations that are always less than 1 for the three indices represent the highest negativity; in-between situations will be evaluated based on variations of indices in this order of importance: human development, innovation, economic growth. For example, New Zealand (with a high growth, low innovation and high human development) is placed nearer to the origin of axes than Canada (with a high growth only) but not as near as Denmark (with high innovation and human development and low growth). The inner circle of the figure represents countries with variations greater than 1 in all three indices; countries comprised between the inner circle and the next are those with variations in two indices – one of which is HDI★ – greater than 1. Among countries within the second and third circles are those that do not meet the previous condition, but for which at least one index

variation is greater than 1. Beyond the boundaries of the last circle are countries with variations lower than 1 in all three indices.

14 For India, the opposite is true.

15 All figures are obtained by a simple OLS regression of the growth rate on the initial levels of the single variable.

16 The variation coefficients have been used here rather than the standard deviation, to have a variability index independent from the measuring unit

17 The list of regions and their acronyms is in Appendix Table A.3.

18 When referring to the relative presence of countries in terms of regions, countries with less than 5 regions will not be considered

19 The timeframe under consideration includes the years preceding the EU expansion in 2004, when 10 new countries were admitted. Almost all of the new members (except Malta and Cyprus) are countries from Eastern Europe. During the second phase of enlargement (2007) that occurred during the time covered by the study, Bulgaria and Romania were included.

## References

Boozer, M., Ranis, G., Stewart, F. and Suri, T. 2003. *Paths to Success: The Relationship Between Human Development and Economic Growth*, Yale University, Center Discussion Paper No. 874.

OECD. 2011. *OECD Economic Surveys*, Greece, Paris.

OECD. 2013. *OECD Competition Assessment Reviews*, Greece, Paris.

Ranis, G. and Stewart, F. 2000. Strategies for Success in Human Development, *Journal of Human Development*, 1(1), 49–69.

Ranis, G., Stewart, F. and Ramirez, A. 2000. Economic Growth and Human Development, *World Development*, 28(2), 197–219.

# 6 Innovation, human development and economic growth

## An empirical analysis

### 6.1 Introduction

The descriptive analysis presented some general guidelines on the performance of income and indices for innovation capacity and human development at the international and regional levels. In this chapter, we will examine the cause-and-effect relations, setting aside the performance of individual regions and states, and focusing on the relationships between the variables. A first step in the analysis of the causal links between the three dimensions, i.e., innovation, human development and income, consists of performing a correlation analysis (Section 6.2). As in the previous chapter, the analysis will be supported by graphical representations. In Section 6.3 we will continue with the analysis of some simple econometric models that will help us explore, in more detail, the relationship between the three dimensions. This will allow us to examine the relationships in both directions, as highlighted in Figure 3.1.

### 6.2 Correlation analysis

Tables A.11 and A.12 present the coefficients of correlation for the variables used in the two data panels – at the international (Panel 1) and regional (Panel 2) levels. With respect to the indices measuring the levels of innovation, human development and income,[1] the tables indicate the existence of a high correlation (always greater than 0.5) for all combinations. The correlation between human development and innovation is particularly high for both samples, amounting to 0.81 for the national sample and 0.59 for the regional one, and confirming other analyses (UNDP, 2001; Ranis and Zhoa, 2013), which highlighted the same trend. The values for the correlation between innovation and average income are also positive and high (0.71 and 0.60), again supporting the extensive literature on these two dimensions (see overview in Chapter 4). Finally, the relationship between human development and income shows high and positive coefficients, higher at the national (0.70) than at the regional (0.57) level. Here again, this preliminary result confirms the empirical evidence on the relationship between growth and human development *in the long run*.

The figures below present the relationships between human development and innovation (INN★), between innovation and income and between human development (HDI*) and income.[2] A line delineating a trend and a functional expression of the relation are added in the chart to illustrate both the type of interaction and its intensity.[3]

Let's begin with the relationship between innovation and human development (Figures 6.1 and 6.2). Both at the international and regional levels, the two dimensions are linked in a positive relation that has been modelled, in both cases, by an exponential function. The two graphs depict a growing relationship between the two indices that after a certain level of HDI results in increasing increments in innovation. In particular, following the great number of observations, the graph generated by regional data allows us to better read the link between the two dimensions – up to a certain level of the human development index (approximately around 0.6), the contribution that HDI gives to innovation is limited; beyond this level the curve shoots up and small increments in HDI trigger high levels of innovation.

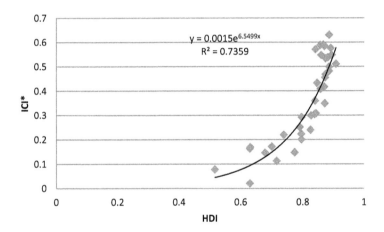

*Figure 6.1* Countries. Correlation between ICI* and HDI, annual averages 1995–2012

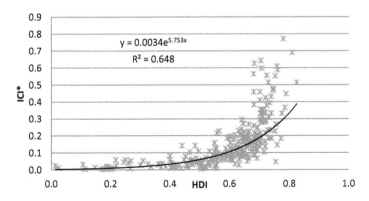

*Figure 6.2* European regions. Correlation between ICI and HDI, annual averages 2000–2012

The second pair of graphs (Figures 6.3 and 6.4) depicts the relationship between human development (HDI*) and the average level of per capita income. As in the previous case, the relationships that we interpolated with an exponential are more clearly positive in the case of national data ($R^2 = 0.82$) and less so for regional data ($R^2 = 0.49$). National data point to a level, similarly around an index level of 0.6, above which the contribution of human development to income is increasingly higher. The data from the regional sample is more dispersed than in previous cases, making the detection of minimum thresholds harder.

The last two graphs (Figures 6.5 and 6.6) illustrate the relationship between innovation and income. In this case the data is distributed along a straight line, i.e., unlike the other two relationships, there appears to be no threshold beyond which increases in an index trigger an increasing rise in the other. Also

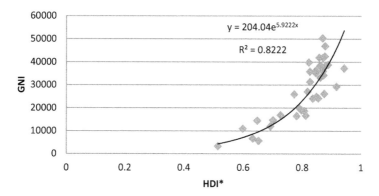

*Figure 6.3* Countries. Correlation between human development and per capita income, annual averages 1995–2012

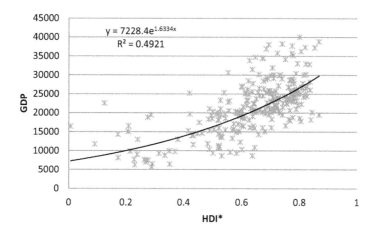

*Figure 6.4* European regions. Correlation between human development and per capita income, annual averages 2000–2012

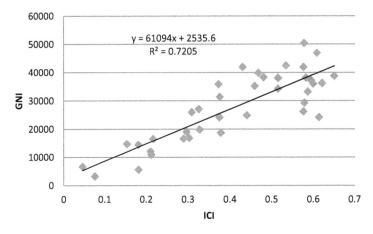

*Figure 6.5* Countries. Correlation between innovation and per capita income, annual averages 1995–2012

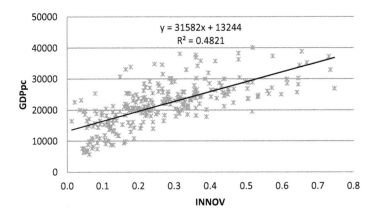

*Figure 6.6* European regions. Correlation between innovation and per capita income, annual averages for 2000–2012

in this case, the intensity of the relationship is greater in the national sample ($R^2 = 0.72$) than in the regional ($R^2 = 0.48$).

## 6.3 Empirical analysis: the model and econometric strategy

In this section, we will explore in depth the causal relationships between income, innovation and human development, using Figure 3.1 as a reference. We will focus on the 'external' relationships, i.e., relations involving only innovation, growth and human development – ignoring the *quantitative* impact of policies on each of these relationships.[4] Such analysis would require a more extensive and detailed set of data and analytical framework, which go beyond the scope and limits of this work. We will instead focus on the *qualitative* aspects of the policies in the following chapters. Here we will try to answer the questions: is there a circular relationship between innovation, human development and growth? What impact do democracy, transparency and equality, studied in Chapter 3, have on such a relationship? To what extent does geographical proximity influence the interaction between these three dimensions? This will be done through two approaches. The first is aimed at identifying the existence of a simultaneous and circular relationship between the three dimensions; to do that, we will use the national and regional data to test an econometric model that allows us to measure the intensity and significance of the relationships between these dimensions (Section a). The second aims at analysing the spatial dimension of the relationship between income, innovation and human development and will focus on regional data using spatial econometric methods (Section b).

### a. The virtuous circles

The model for investigating the 'virtuous circle' of income, innovation and human development is as follows:

$$
\begin{aligned}
{}^{1}Income_{it} &= \alpha_{0} + \alpha_{1} \ (Innovation_{it}) + \alpha_{2} \ (Human \ development_{it}) \\
&\quad + \alpha_{3} \ (Controls_{it}) + \varepsilon_{it} \\
{}^{2}Innovation_{it} &= \beta_{0} + \beta_{1} \ (Income_{it}) + \beta_{2} \ (Human \ development_{it}) \\
&\quad + \beta_{3}(Controls_{it}) + \varepsilon_{it} \\
{}^{3}Human \ Development_{it} &= \gamma_{0} + \gamma_{1} \ (Income_{it}) + \gamma_{2} \ (Innovation_{it}) \\
&\quad + \gamma_{3} \ (Controls_{it}) + \varepsilon_{it}
\end{aligned}
\tag{1}
$$

where $i$ and $t$ indicate, respectively, country and year. The error term $\varepsilon$ is in standard components form, i.e., including both time invariant and time variant part.

The main variables of interest – income, innovation and human development – are all in log scale. Note that, in order to reduce potential problems due to circular causality and high correlation between the variables, the human development index employed here is computed without the income dimension; likewise, innovation is calculated without education.

For Panel 1, additional regressors, included as controls, are: democracy, transparency, income inequality, gender equality, employment rate and social expenditure.[5] These control variables serve to model, to the extent possible, the instrumental freedoms discussed in Chapters 2 and 3. They have been included to test the impact they have on the processes of innovation, growth and human development. Democracy is measured by the Unified Democracy Score and transparency by the Corruption Perception Index. Income inequality is measured by the Gini index of disposable income, after taxes and transfers. In addition, another measure of inequality, i.e., gender inequality, was approximated by the ratio of employment rate between women and men. Job opportunities are measured by employment rate, and the state's commitment to human development is approximated by social spending (on Health and Education) as a percentage of GDP (see Appendix A.1 for further details). Along the same lines, Panel 2 includes the following control variables: poverty, school leavers, gender equality (see below). The first variable is approximated by the number of people at risk of poverty or social exclusion as percentage of total population. The second is approximated by the percentage of the population aged between 18 and 24 years who are early leavers from education and training. In this case, with some stretch, we can consider the drop out from formal education as a symptom of disadvantage and poor social cohesion, and therefore as a proxy for social capital in the region. The third variable is a measure of gender inequality determined in a similar way to what was done for the national panel. These three indicators were introduced to measure the impact of instrumental freedoms on the processes analysed. Conversely, for the regional analysis, only one macro variable was included, i.e., the ratio of investment to GDP. The objective is to measure the role of investment in growth and innovation processes; in the case of the latter, through the element of technological innovation built into the new fixed capital.

The system in (1) has been run jointly on a balanced panel of 40 countries observed for 18 years (1995–2012) and a balanced panel of 266 European regions for 13 years (2000–2012) using 'three-stage least squares' (3SLS) method (Zellner, A. and Theil H., 1962). This is the most appropriate method for this analysis, making it easy to compare coefficients across regressions. Indeed, it allows us to estimate systems where some equations contain endogenous variables among the regressors, which are also dependent variables of other equations in the system. All the dependent variables are thus explicitly taken to be endogenous to the system and treated as correlated with the disturbances in the systems' equations; all other variables are instead treated as exogenous to the system and uncorrelated with the disturbances, thus used as instruments for the endogenous variables. This strategy leads to results in line with the scope of the analysis, which is to highlight feedback loops and simultaneous relations between the variables of main interest (see Appendix A.4 for details).

#### b. Spatial analysis

Since the spatial dimension is also relevant in determining the evolution of the circular relationships under study, a spatial approach has been also considered to account for potential spatial dependence, namely for the fact that income, innovation and human development values are likely to be dependent across units of observations due to spatial effects. For this scope, a spatial autoregressive (SAR) or spatial lag model has been tested on a balanced panel of 266 regions observed for 13 years (2000–2012). Basically, this model allows us to take into account the influence that income, innovation and human development achievements for a given region $i$ can have on the values of the same variables in adjacent regions. Hence, the second specification tested is as follows:

$$y = \rho W y + \beta X + \varepsilon \qquad (2)$$

where $y$ denotes the vector of the dependent variable (i.e., income, innovation or human development, respectively), $\rho$ is the spatial autoregressive parameter, $W$ is the spatial weight matrix, $\beta$ is the vector of the coefficients, $X$ is a matrix standing for all the regressors included and $\varepsilon$ is the vector of normally distributed, homoscedastic and uncorrelated errors.

Again, all the variables employed are defined in log form and several controls are included in X: poverty, school leavers, gender equality and fixed investment (see above). The spatial weighting matrix $(W)$, which synthetises the structure of spatial dependence, is a 266 by 266 matrix, where each entry is a measure of the spatial influence or spatial proximity between regions $i$ and $j$. This analysis has been based on the centroids distances[6] between each pair of spatial units, computed using the longitude and latitude coordinates for each region at NUTS-2 level.[7] The neighbours for a given observation are identified using the k-nearest neighbour's criterion. According to this procedure, the five nearest neighbours of each spatial unit are weighted by their inverse distance $i/d_{ij}$, where $d_{ij}$ is the distance (expressed in kilometres) between regions i and j (for $j \neq i$): this implies that larger values of $W^{n5}$ indicate that the regions are closer, and all but the five nearest neighbours receive weight equal to zero.

As for the estimation method, the approach based on Maximum Likelihood (ML) has been followed in order to get consistent estimates of the spatial parameter $\rho$ (see Lee and Yu, 2010; Elhorst, 2010).[8]

## 6.4 Empirical analysis: the results

### a. The virtuous circles

The main regression results are presented in the following tables. Table 6.1 and 6.2 below report the results from the 3SLS estimation[9] (specification 1) using respectively the sample of 40 countries (Panel 1) and the sample of 266 regions (Panel 2).

Both tables are divided into two sections: in the first the model is estimated only for the three central variables, while in the second control variables have been added to the previous three.

The 'virtuous circle' between income, innovation and human development clearly appears in the results. In all estimates the coefficients of the three variables are positive and significant. Taking a closer look at the left-hand side of the two tables, we can observe that in the regression run on countries, the coefficients of HD are more than proportional to both innovation and growth: a 1% increase in the human development index increases growth by 3% and innovation by 7.5%. In turn, ICI and EG have a positive impact on HD but on a much smaller scale. The regional sample (Panel 2) supports the hypothesis that virtuous circles occur between the three central dimensions though with different coefficients and degrees of intensity: at the regional level, economic growth has a more than proportional impact on innovation, while the impact of HD on innovation is less marked – 0.12% increase with every 1% variation.

Table 6.1 Three-stage least squares (3SLS) estimation results. Countries (Panel 1)

| | Dependent variables | | | | | |
|---|---|---|---|---|---|---|
| | Income | Innovation | Human Development | Income | Innovation | Human Development |
| **Explanatory variables** | | | | | | |
| Income | | 0.1798** (0.0861) | 0.1593*** (0.0057) | | 0.6343*** (0.0522) | 0.0785*** (0.0066) |
| Innovation | 0.0260** (0.0124) | | 0.0573*** (0.0023) | 0.2254*** (0.0194) | | 0.0887*** (0.0035) |
| Human Development | 3.0138*** (0.1087) | 7.4978*** (0.2971) | | 1.5735*** (0.1442) | 5.4256*** (0.2046) | |
| Democracy (first lag) | | | | 0.0209** (0.0087) | | |
| Income Inequality (first lag) | | | | | | -0.0147 (0.0090) |
| Gender Equality (first lag) | | | | | -0.1178 (0.1074) | 0.0414*** (0.0126) |
| Trasparency (first lag) | | | | 0.0423* (0.0256) | | |
| Employment (first lag) | | | | 0.2979*** (0.0846) | -0.3856*** (0.1354) | |
| Social expenditure (first lag) | | | | | | 0.0094* (0.0052) |
| Countries | included | included | included | included | included | included |
| Constant | 10.6762*** (0.0228) | -1.9835** (0.9168) | -1.6978*** (0.0611) | 9.3928*** (0.3547) | -5.3166*** (0.7180) | -0.8630*** (0.0734) |
| No. Obs. | 720 | 720 | 720 | 680 | 680 | 680 |
| Cross sections | 40 | 40 | 40 | 40 | 40 | 40 |
| R.2 | 0.9793 | 0.8849 | 0.9711 | 0.9835 | 0.9522 | 0.9810 |
| Chi2 | 35332.54*** | 6070.55*** | 27967.45*** | 41570.09*** | 15332.38*** | 38559.47*** |

One, two and three stars indicate significance respectively at 10%, 5% and 1%

Table 6.2 Three-stage least squares (3SLS) estimation results. Regions (Panel 2)

| | Dependent variables | | | | | |
|---|---|---|---|---|---|---|
| | Income | Innovation | Human Development | Income | Innovation | Human Development |
| **Explanatory variables** | | | | | | |
| Income | | 1.6055*** (0.0339) | 0.4645*** (0.0160) | | 1.1449*** (0.0417) | 0.2544*** (0.0082) |
| Innovation | 0.2796*** (0.0059) | | 0.0210*** (0.0071) | 0.1747*** (0.0064) | | 0.0240*** (0.0035) |
| Human Development | 0.4450*** (0.0153) | 0.1155*** (0.0392) | | 0.8226*** (0.0260) | 0.5991*** (0.0782) | |
| Poverty (first lag) | | | | −0.1063*** (0.0118) | −0.1978*** (0.0317) | |
| School leave (first lag) | | | | | −0.0330 (0.0348) | −0.1244*** (0.0067) |
| Gender Equality (first lag) | | | | | | 0.3475*** (0.0205) |
| Fixed investments (first lag) | | | | −0.0011 (0.0180) | −0.2912*** (0.0474) | |
| Countries | included | included | included | included | included | included |
| Constant | 10.8735*** (0.0235) | −18.2796*** (0.3532) | −4.9805*** (0.1709) | 11.0476*** (0.0660) | −11.9748*** (0.5107) | −2.4787*** (0.0909) |
| No. Obs. | 3458 | 3458 | 3458 | 3192 | 3192 | 3192 |
| Cross sections | 266 | 266 | 266 | 266 | 266 | 266 |
| R2 | 0.6866 | 0.7306 | 0.5511 | 0.7491 | 0.7608 | 0.8294 |
| Chi2 | 11508.16*** | 11999.44*** | 5171.40*** | 11857.17*** | 11412.27*** | 17142.09*** |

With the inclusion of the control variables the sign and the significance of the coefficients of the three dimensions do not change. Let us examine now the impact of these dimensions on the individual processes of growth, innovation and human development. In Panel 1, indices of democracy, transparency and employment have a significant, positive impact on *income*. Related to this, at the regional level we add the rate of poverty (Panel 2), which is negative (as expected) and significant. Taking some liberties in generalising from these regressions, it can be concluded that an economy grows if it innovates and invests in people, is democratic and transparent, offers job opportunities to its citizens and has a low risk of poverty. It is to be noted that in both panels human development has the highest impact on economic growth.

In the case of *innovation*, in addition to HD and EG, the control variables that prove to be significant are the employment rate in Panel 1, and poverty and fixed investment in Panel 2. However, both employment and investment have negative signs, which may mean that the innovation experienced in recent years has been achieved as a result of savings in physical and human resources, rather than by increasing them. Hence, the phase in which machinery, equipment and workers are replaced still dominates over the phase in which innovation benefits from their expansion.

Finally, *human development* is positively influenced, by not only income and innovation, but also by gender equality (in both panels) and social expenditure (Panel 1). School leave is also significant, and shows the expected sign (Panel 2). Gender equality therefore remains a key factor for the consolidation of human development. This is in line with the outcomes of the various studies described in Chapter 4. The positive impact of public spending in the education and health sectors on human development is also confirmed, again confirming other studies. (Gebregziabher and Niño-Zarazúa, 2014; Capriati, 2011). Income inequality has the expected sign but is not significant.

Finally, regressions including control variables do not result in a significantly improved[10] $R^2$ as compared to regressions run with only the three dimensions (the main variables), suggesting that most of the variance in the simultaneous relationship is explained by the main variables.

### b. Spatial analysis

Turning to the analysis carried out at the level of regions (Panel 2), where the issue of spatial dependence is addressed (Specification 2), the following Table 6.3 shows the coefficients estimates obtained by testing the SAR model, which takes into account spatial effects between regions by including the adopted weighting scheme ($W^{5n}$).[11] The next table, Table 6.4, reports the direct, indirect and total effect computations for the SAR model referred to the explanatory variables of main interest (i.e., income, innovation and human development).

As shown by Table 6.3, coefficients estimated using this method are mostly statistically significant and have the expected sign. Moreover, there is clear evidence of regional spatial spillovers (measured by the Spatial lag parameter).

Table 6.3 SAR (with spatial fixed effects), ML results (coefficients)

| Explanatory variables | Dependent variables | | | | | |
|---|---|---|---|---|---|---|
| | Income | | Innovation | | Human Development | |
| | (1) | (2) | (3) | (4) | (5) | (6) |
| Income$_{t-1}$ | | | 0.4278*** (0.0427) | | 0.4912*** (0.0318) | |
| Innovation$_{t-1}$ | 0.1637*** (0.0434) | | | | | 0.0974*** (0.0234) |
| Human Development$_{t-1}$ | | 0.1409*** (0.0527) | | 0.0880* (0.0487) | | |
| Poverty | -0.0099 (0.0537) | -0.0204 (0.0486) | -0.0751** (0.0427) | -0.1126* (0.0610) | -0.0114 (0.0321) | -0.0053 (0.0496) |
| School Leave | -0.1308*** (0.0229) | -0.1221*** (0.0234) | -0.0326 (0.0249) | -0.0466 (0.0377) | -0.0791*** (0.0156) | -0.1359*** (0.0172) |
| Gender Equality | 0.1606** (0.0639) | 0.1755** (0.0724) | 0.5789*** (0.0725) | 0.5830*** (0.1331) | 0.6152*** (0.0659) | 0.4273*** (0.0754) |
| Fixed Investments$_{t-1}$ | 0.1362*** (0.0251) | 0.1401*** (0.0250) | | 0.1120* (0.0584) | | |
| Spatial lag parameter | 6.7915*** (1.2313) | 6.6708*** (1.3300) | 0.9183*** (0.0888) | 1.0654*** (0.0923) | 1.1340*** (0.0959) | 6.3985*** (1.3414) |
| N Obs. | 3192 | 3192 | 3192 | 3192 | 3192 | 3192 |
| Cross sections | 266 | 266 | 266 | 266 | 266 | 266 |
| R-sq within | 0.2793 | 0.3370 | 0.3167 | 0.0559 | 0.6388 | 0.3371 |

Robust standard errors in brackets; * p < 0.1, ** p < 0.05, *** p < 0.01

Table 6.4 SAR (with spatial fixed effects), ML results (spatial effects)

| | Dependent variables | | | | | |
| --- | --- | --- | --- | --- | --- | --- |
| | Income | | Innovation | | Human Development | |
| | (1) | (2) | (3) | (4) | (5) | (6) |
| **Main explanatory variables** | | | | | | |
| *Direct effects* | | | | | | |
| Income$_{t-1}$ | 0.1729*** (0.0613) | | 0.4299*** (0.0363) | | 0.4978*** (0.0264) | |
| Innovation$_{t-1}$ | | | | 0.0882** (0.0417) | | 0.0921 (0.0739) |
| Human Development$_{t-1}$ | | 0.1412** (0.0583) | | | | |
| *Indirect effects* | | | | | | |
| Income$_{t-1}$ | | | 0.0249*** (0.0035) | | 0.0401*** (0.0061) | |
| Innovation$_{t-1}$ | 0.1209 (0.3504) | | | | | 0.0260 (0.2562) |
| Human Development$_{t-1}$ | | 0.0606 (0.1608) | | 0.0064** (0.0031) | | |
| *Total effects* | | | | | | |
| Income$_{t-1}$ | | | 0.4548*** (0.0381) | | 0.5379*** (0.0272) | |
| Innovation$_{t-1}$ | 0.2938 (0.4004) | | | | | 0.1182 (0.3272) |
| Human Development$_{t-1}$ | | 0.2018 (0.2039) | | 0.0946** (0.0446) | | |

Robust standard errors in brackets; * p < 0.1, ** p < 0.05, *** p < 0.01

Elaborating further, once spatial dependence among units in the dependent variable is taken into account, the existence of mutual causal linkages between income, innovation and human development achievements is fully supported, which is consistent with previous results. Alternative specifications for the SAR model also yield similar results regarding the parameter estimates of the variables of controls, which mostly show the correct sign and a highly significant influence on the dependent variable of interest. It is worth underlying that results for the spatial lag parameter display a highly significant (at 1% level) and positive spatial dependence in all specifications; the very large magnitude of the associated coefficients (ranging between 0.91 and 6.79) confirms the presence of strong positive interaction effects based on geographical proximity (i.e., spatial spillovers) among the observed regional units.

The estimated coefficients, however, cannot be interpreted (as in the case of non-spatial models) as marginal effects. For this purpose, one should use the direct and indirect effects' estimates of the independent variables (LeSage and Pace, 2009), which allow to disentangle the contribution to spatial dependence of each independent variable and thus to better appreciate the scale of intra-regional and inter-regional spillovers. To elaborate, direct effects of the explanatory variables are different from their coefficient estimates is because of the feedback effects that arise as a result of impacts passing through neighbouring regional units and back to the unit that has instigated the change. Indeed, since SAR models take into account spatial dependence among regional units in the dependent variable, intuitively, a change in an explanatory variable of a unit may affect the dependent variable on other observations and in this way, the dependent variable of the unit of reference itself, due to the spatial lag in the model. Therefore, direct effects estimates measure the impact of a changing independent variable on a dependent variable of a spatial unit ($x_{it} \rightarrow y_{it}$),[12] including the feedback effects (that is, passing through the neighbouring regions, $x_{it} \rightarrow y_{jt} \rightarrow y_{it}$).[13] Indirect effects estimates instead reflect how a change in the initial level of an independent variable of all adjacent regions would impact the dependent variable of the region under consideration ($x_{jt} \rightarrow y_{it}$).[14]

Hence, starting from columns 1 and 2 of Table 6.4, where *Income* is considered a dependent variable and Innovation and Human Development variables are included alternatively, positive and significant direct effects for both Innovation and Human Development (at 1 and 5% level respectively) have emerged, whereas there is no evidence of significant indirect effects. Since the direct effect of Innovation is 0.1729 and the relative coefficient estimate is instead equal to 0.1637 (see previous Table 6.3), the feedback effect of this variable (which equals to the difference between the direct effect and the parameter estimate) amounts to 0.0092. Similarly, the feedback effect referred to Human Development is 0.0003, thus relatively small, though still positive. This overall suggests that income levels in a given region are positively affected not only directly by enhanced innovation and human development in the same region but also by rising incomes in adjacent regions (measured by special coefficient, as in Table 6.3) and by the means of a (limited) feedback effect (i.e., passing through augmented income levels in neighbouring regions because of spatial income dependence among observations).

Turning to specifications 3 and 4, where *Innovation* is the dependent variable and Income and Human Development are alternatively included as main regressors, direct effects are also positive and significant, with the coefficient associated with Income turning out to be considerably higher in magnitude. Moreover, both variables show highly significant and positive indirect effects, although lower in magnitude compared to the direct effects. Hence, the innovative performance of an observed region turns out to be even more dependent on the relative performance of nearby regions: indeed, results overall show that it is not only enhanced Income and Human Development in a particular region that positively affect its innovation performance, but also being surrounded by other regions with improved innovation, rising income levels and enhanced human development. In this respect, it can be also noticed that the average total effects of a unitary increase in Income and Human Development in a region (given by the sum of direct and indirect effects) are also positive and highly significant: although these are only slightly higher in magnitude compared to correspondent coefficient estimates (see Table 6.3). On the whole, the data confirms that if regional spillovers are not considered, the overall effect of these variables on the region's own Innovation Index is likely to be underestimated.

Finally, columns 5 and 6, where *Human Development* is taken as a dependent variable, show highly significant and positive direct effects. This was observed only with respect to Income, which recorded a positive feedback effect, equal to 0.0066. This suggests that increasing income in a region as well as being surrounded by regions with high income levels positively affects the level of human development in the region of reference. As can be observed from the bottom of the table, in this case, the total effect is also positive and highly significant. Turning to the effect of Innovation on the outcome of interest, it appears not to be affected by spillover effects allowed by geographical proximity, as the direct, indirect and total effects estimates turn out to be all not statistically significant.

### Summing up

The analysis of empirical relationships conducted so far has essentially confirmed the theoretical assumptions of the previous chapters, allowing us to answer the questions that were posed at the beginning of this Chapter. First, the estimations indicate that there is a relationship of mutual reinforcement between the processes of human development, innovation and economic growth. The relationship between human development and innovation is particularly important: the data suggest that a certain level of human development is a precondition to trigger innovation and growth processes. Greater gender equality appears to also promote better conditions for the growth of people's capacity. A high impact of human development on income in both the international and the regional samples is highlighted. The analysis also suggests that in the past years there has been a substitution effect between innovation and factors of production (capital and labour).

The hypothesis that growth-generated resources, in particular those directed by governments towards education and health, are important to ensure long-term sustainable improvements in human development, is also confirmed.

Second, the regional analysis has further confirmed the existence of virtuous circles and highlighted the presence of spatial interrelationships, spillover and feedback effects that affect the three relationships. In particular, the three main processes analysed are all influenced by the fluctuations of the same variables in the neighbouring regions: the income (innovation, human development) of a region is strongly influenced by the income growth (innovation, human development) of the surrounding regions. Moreover, in the case of innovation, the impact of innovation growth on both income and human development of the neighbouring regions was significant; whereas for human development these indirect effects were significant only with regards to income growth. Overall, the analysis confirms the importance of geographic proximity in the evolution of the three processes.

## Notes

1  As in Chapter 5, two indices were added to the 'standard' ones (see A.2) in order to avoid correlation problems. The first (ICI★) does not include competence in the components of innovation. This measure was taken in order to analyse correlations and causal relations between this index and the human development index, which, as we have seen, includes competence among its components (as measured by expected years of schooling and average years of schooling). The second index that we have adapted in order to analyse correlation/causality is the index of human development, adjusted when related to per capita income. As referred to in Chapter 5, HDI★ is used when analysing the relationship between human development and per capita income. HDI★ does not include standard of living, measured in the international sample by GNI per capita and in the regional sample by GDP per capita.

2  These graphs were constructed by removing outliers: Luxembourg and Norway for the national samples and London, Brussels, Hamburg and Luxembourg for the regional samples. The data shown in the graphs are averages for the period.

3  By inserting a trend line, we go beyond a simple correlation analysis, arbitrarily assuming the presence of a causal relationship between the variables. Circular causation or endogenous relationships obtain: human development influences innovation, and as we have seen, innovation influences human development. As our scope is limited to the correlation between the variables analysed, only the most significant relationships have been selected. We will focus on causality later, using econometric analysis of panel data.

4  The only exception being the relationship between social expenditure and human development. See below.

5  Income, innovation and human development values are likely to be influenced by additional variables. As we pointed out in the introduction, however, the main focus here is to identify virtuous circles between variables and a preliminary check of the impact of instrumental freedoms on these relationships (see section 2.2). The equations have not made use of all of these control variables. The decision took into account the significance of relationships and of the collinearity problems between variables.

6  The word 'centroid' in the literature on geographic information systems indicates a weighted average of the vertices of a polygon that approximates the centre of the polygon (see Waller and Gotway, 2004, pp. 44–45).

7  These are provided by the dataset 'Nomenclature of Territorial Units for Statistics (NUTS) 2010 – European Commission, Eurostat/GISCO', which represents the regions for level 1, 2 and 3 of the Nomenclature of Territorial Units for Statistics (NUTS) for 2010

8  See Appendix A.4 for details.

9  Checks for robustness are also included in Appendix A.4.

10  With the exception of HD in the regional panel, whose $R^2$ goes from 0.55 to 0.83.

11  Note that, in these estimations, country fixed effects are included; moreover, to account for possible endogeneity due to circular causality, income, innovation, human development and fixed investment variables have been lagged by one period. The most correlated indicators are included in separate regressions and, again, the Human Development Index in specifications 2 and 5 is computed without the income dimension, whilst the Innovation Index in specifications 4 and 6 does not include education.

12  Measured by the regression coefficient of direct effects (Table 6.4, first section).

13  Measured by the difference between the regression coefficient of the direct estimates (Table 6.4, first section) and the coefficient of the main estimates (Table 6.3)

14  Measured by the regression coefficient of indirect effects (Table 6.4, second section)

## References

Capriati, M. 2011. Spesa Pubblica e sviluppo umano nelle regioni italiane (Public Expenditure and Human development in Italian Regions), *QA*, 2, 23–56.

Elhorst, J.P. 2010. Spatial Panel Data Models. In: Fischer, M.M. and Getis, A. (eds.), *Handbook of Applied Spatial Analysis*, Berlin, Springer, 377–407.

Gebregziabher, F. and Niño-Zarazúa, M. 2014. *Social Spending and Aggregate Welfare in Developing and Transition Economies*, WIDER Working Paper n. 82.

LaSage, J.P. and Pace, K.R. 2009. *Introduction to Spatial Econometrics*, London, New York, Taylor & Francis.

Lee, L.F. and Yu, J. 2010. Estimation of Spatial Autoregressive Panel Data Models With Fixed Effects, *Journal of Econometrics*, 154(2), 165–185.

Ranis, G. and Zhao, X. 2013. Technology and Human Development, *Journal of Human Development and Capabilities*, 14(4), 467–482.

UNDP (United Nations Development Programme) 2001. *Human Development Report 2001, Making New Technologies Work for Human Development*, Oxford, Oxford University Press.

Waller, L.A. and Gotway, C.A. 2004. *Applied Spatial Statistics for Public Health Data*, Wiley, Hoboken.

Zellner, A. and Theil, H. 1962. Three-Stage Least Squares: Simultaneous Estimation of Simultaneous Equations, *Econometrica*, 30(1), 54–78.

# Part III

# Policy

# 7 An introduction to policies

## 7.1 Policy matters

In the analysis this far, I have tried to discuss in more detail the relationships between human development, innovation and growth by drawing on the toolboxes of two major schools of thought, and provide empirical support to my claims. In both cases, sufficient evidence was found to suggest that these relationships are significant. The relationships between the three dimensions under study result in virtuous or vicious circles, thus promoting or inhibiting pathways of change. Activation of these processes depends on the policy choices that each country makes and the role of public institutions (see Figure 3.1). The latter may affect, in the first place, the variables which determine the pace of economic growth; second, the industrial policies and the proper functioning of the innovation systems; and third, the actual level of freedoms experienced by individuals through the current redistribution and welfare policies.

The empirical part of this study suggests that the interaction between innovation, human development and growth does not follow a unique strategy. There are countries, such as China, Korea and Estonia, which are able to grow well above the average in all three dimensions and appear to benefit from virtuous cycles of change. Other countries, such as Mexico, South Africa and India, seem to have become stuck in vicious circles that prevent their effective take-off. In turn, the countries of central-eastern Europe, such as Russia, Poland and Slovakia, have achieved high growth rates, but have low levels of innovation and human development. And still others, such as Switzerland, Denmark and Iceland, have focused on innovation and human development, experiencing growth rates lower than expected. In all these cases, the paths were largely the result of a diverse mix of industrial, macroeconomic, social and redistributive policies that have directed countries' economies.

The modalities of public intervention will therefore be the focus of this and the next two chapters. In this chapter, I will deal briefly with some theoretical issues in public policy, the role of non-market institutions and that of the state, with particular reference to policies on innovation and research. In Chapter 8 I will analyse innovation policies in light of CA's contribution. I will then discuss macroeconomic and redistribution policies in Chapter 9, in which I will discuss in detail their impact on human development and innovation.

## 7.2 Market failures

Addressing the issues of economic policy implies a consideration of the purpose and goals of a community and the means to achieve them. Considering purposes inevitably involves looking at ethical choices. What are the goals to be pursued by the policies that will be undertaken? How to select policies? How to set priorities? Which groups are at an advantage, and which are disadvantaged? All these questions involve ethical choices, but they are not always at the centre of economic debates. And when they are, the responses tend to oversimplify reality. In my opinion, the issues that concern the ethical assessment of policies and their effectiveness are an intrinsic part of the economic decisions and cannot thus be relegated to the field of philosophy or political science. (Richardson, 2015).

In addition, in democratic systems, it is necessary to reach an acceptable consensus that will enable the state to act. And as pointed out by Arrow (1951b), when consensus is the basis for social action, the market mechanism cannot be taken as a function of social welfare, because consent with respect to the actions of the state concerns moral obligations, while the market can only express practical imperatives.

The growth and innovation policies cannot escape this fundamental principle. If innovation is the essence of social and economic change, addressing the issue of *innovation policies* cannot but serve to clarify the purpose of these policies. One of the purposes normally associated with innovation is *the growth in competitiveness and increased well-being implicit in the availability of new technologies, as well as new and improved products* (Chaminade and Edquist, 2010; Edquist and Chaminade, 2006; Archibugi and Lundvall, 2002; Bajmòcy and Gèbert, 2014). Is this enough however, to justify a policy for innovation? The purpose of growth is taken as a value in itself, without any specifications on the quality of the latter and its distribution. Growth can occur through different processes and may follow goals that are not always ethically acceptable. Nazi Germany, for example, during the period immediately preceding the armed conflict was one of the few nations that emerged from the Great Depression having achieved and maintained high employment rates and growth (Overy, 1996; Braun, 1990). What resulted from that intense phase of economic growth is known to all. Therefore, it is important to seek satisfactory answers to questions such as: innovating for what? Innovating for whom? How to innovate? And for whose well-being?

So, what are the collective goals (and the goals of persons representing and acting on behalf of the community) that can be identified when it comes to innovation and growth? According to the standard theory, the point of departure for determining the appropriateness of an intervention by public institutions is the existence of *market failures*. In line with this approach, the highest level of social welfare is assured by a situation of perfect competition. The 'first theorem of the economy of welfare' (Arrow, 1951a; Debreu, 1959) states that 'if there is a state of perfect competition, this is also Pareto efficient'. That is to say that no allocation of resources would favour a consumer or a producer without disadvantaging another. This assumption is valid if a series of conditions allows the presence of perfect competition: a) no party can, with their behaviour, change the prevailing prices, i.e., there can be no non-competitive markets; b) the utility of each individual depends solely on the level of his/her consumption, i.e., no externalities exist; c) property ownership rights must be clearly defined, i.e., there can be no public or quasi-public goods; d) there must be market outlets for all existing goods, i.e., every good can be exchanged (the hypothesis of 'market completeness'); and e) information must be complete and symmetrical, all relevant facts must be known to every individual.

If one of these conditions, understood as benchmarks, is not respected, we then face the so-called 'market failures', an inefficient Pareto condition, in which the available resources are not used to their fullest and the highest possible social well-being is not achieved. In such a case, a state intervention is appropriate. According to this approach, the role of government is to intervene to 'fix market failures' and ensure the best use of the available resources; in this way, the state ensures that someone (or many) can improve their condition.

The market failure approach begins with identifying an ideal situation where the market is fully functional and tries to assess the deviations from this condition in order to justify state intervention. In this way, it implicitly assumes that public intervention should be the minimal, only including what is necessary to 'repair failures', and that any encroachment causes a distortion in the proper functioning of the market mechanisms. In addition, according to some authors (Tullock et al., 2002), the benefits of public intervention should be weighed against the presence of *government's failures* (generated by corrupt politicians, distortions induced by wrong choices, poor efficiency, etc.) finding a balance between advantages and disadvantages as a whole. Many criticisms of public intervention stem from the view that, despite the presence of inefficient markets, the disadvantages resulting from government failures outweigh the benefits of its intervention.

## 7.3 Criticism

The standard approach to market failures has received considerable criticism. First, it assumes *allocative efficiency and effectiveness* as its *ideal* objective (with respect to the objectives of maximum utility to the consumer and maximum profit for the entrepreneur) in the use of *given resources*. The highest social well-being is understood within a static context. As has been noted in several parts of this book, much of human progress comes from the ability of the economic system to evolve, creating situations that endogenously lead the market to depart from perfect competition, creating temporary profits and monopolies. Schumpeter (1936) dedicated the entire second part of his 'Theory of Economic Development' just to demonstrate that the theory of general economic equilibrium was not appropriate to explain the forces of change that guide capitalist development. The idea that public intervention is to be expected only in the case of market failure implies that public interventions are expected to contribute to a single goal, that is allocating current resources, but to neither increase these resources nor affect the availability of new products.

In addition, a crucial drawback of the standard approach is that any realistic analysis of the individual conditions listed above leads to the conclusion that they are almost never observed, and this leads us to agree with Cimoli et al. (2009a), that 'the whole world can be seen as a huge market failure' (p. 2).

Second, the traditional approach derives from the functioning of one institution, the market, as a valid code of conduct for other non-market institutions such as the state. Sen (1985) profoundly criticises this view in his publication *'The moral standing of the market'*, which stresses that, despite it being obvious that everyone appreciates the enormous advantages of the market, 'the value to an individual of a particular institution when society has been organised around that institution must be distinguished from how the society – and even that person – might have fared had the society been organised differently' (p. 1). An economic and social order, no matter how successful in certain relations (trade and production), does not exhaust the sphere of the possible alternative institutions and values. And with reference to the first theorem of well-being, Sen's point of view is even more radical: 'The ethical force of the direct theorem in establishing the case for the market mechanism may be seen to be quite limited. A Pareto optimum does, of course, have the valuable property that not all the parties can be made better-off (in terms of utility) in any alternative feasible state. But it is easily seen that a situation can be Pareto optimal but nevertheless highly objectionable – indeed, possibly disastrous. If the utility of the deprived cannot be raised without cutting into the utility of the rich, the situation can be Pareto optimal but truly awful' (p. 10). Without passing any judgment on the present conditions, there is no guarantee that perfectly competitive markets can be morally acceptable.

Which Pareto optimal situation, if any, can be considered good socially? According to Sen, it is difficult to answer this question without going beyond the welfarist approach. This challenge highlights an aspect of the market mechanism that is often overlooked: 'It is that the specification of the market mechanism is an essentially *incomplete specification of a social arrangement*. Even with the purest, perfectly competitive market mechanism, we are not in a position to understand precisely what will happen until we know something more about the rest of the social arrangements, in particular the distribution of endowments and resource ownership' (p. 13).

Some might argue that the distribution of resources, well-being and utility is not an ethically relevant question, but if a situation where a segment of the population lives in absolute or relative poverty is deemed worthy of being taken into consideration, the former issue cannot be overlooked and must be directly addressed. This can be tackled by using different views and different decision-making processes from those related to the free market.

This approach can lead, as we have seen in Chapters 2 and 3, to solutions that can go beyond mere market mechanisms, and achieve better results, as confirmed by the experience of some countries, which beyond the market mechanisms alone and with a strong involvement of the state, recorded outstanding results at the global level in terms of expanding the actual freedoms of their citizens (see Chapters 5 and 6).

Therefore, there is no ethical foundation in market mechanisms, but rather these mechanisms have to fit within a broader value framework. The capability approach would not be conceivable within the general economic equilibrium, as it focuses on people's achievements, who are understood not merely as producers and consumers of goods, but as human beings meant to live a dignified life. Such a scope, as we have seen, exceeds the welfarist approach. The capability approach provides, therefore, a theoretical and practical framework for the recognition of these values and the development of related policies.

## 7.4 System failures

This line of thought is complementary and makes the critique advanced by authors like Cimoli et al. (2009b), Mazzucato (2013), Nelson (2005) and Lundvall-Lorenz (2014) 'ethically grounded'. They are joined by most of the contributors to the neo-Schumpeterian literature, who have on one hand denounced the welfarist approach of market failures and on the other, shown special interest in the active role of the state in the attainment of public interest goals. Nelson (2005), for example, believes that following the reasoning of the Market Failure Theory, 'the only reason why government should provide for national security and protect citizens from crime is that markets cannot do this job well. Similarly, parents need to take care of their children because of market failure. As one reflect on it, the argument that we need government because market sometimes 'fail', seems rather strange, or incomplete. Can't one make a positive case for government, or families, for that matter, as a form that is appropriate, even needed, in its own right?' (P. 16).

Therefore, not only is the approach of 'market failures' inadequate to identify the role of the state, but as the entire conceptual apparatus of the general equilibrium of perfect competition is an *'incomplete specification of a social arrangement'*, there is a need to find the ethical justifications for public intervention beyond this limited outlook.

But if, as we have seen, market failures are not a good departure point for the identification of innovation policies, what is a valid alternative approach? What was the *innovation systems'* response to policy-setting problems for innovation? Which criterion is used to call upon public policies to take action in order to increase the innovative potential of a system? The answer provided by scholars of innovation systems emanates from *system failures*, i.e., 'the inability of a system of innovation to support the creation, absorption, retention, use and dissemination of economically useful knowledge through interactive learning or in-house R&D investments' (Lundvall et al., 2009, p. 360). This approach assumes that policies are set so as to intervene on specific *problems* (a terminology that the authors prefer to *failures*) related to a process within the national innovation system. The problems can be of two types: problems resulting from *components* or arising from *dynamics*.

The components-driven problems are related to the lack of knowledge, skills and capacity of the system organisations, to their poor interactions and weak institutional environment. Organisations may survive but they lack adequate skills to produce new knowledge and are unable to produce, over time, either technology or innovation; whereas the inability to interact produces network problems.

The dynamics-driven constraints refer to problems arising from changes in the technological paradigm and transition from one paradigm to another. These problems are related to the shortage of both the quantitative and qualitative skills needed to transition from a known paradigm to a new one.

Edquist (2002, p. 236) identifies three main categories of system failures based on the characteristics of innovation systems:

- inappropriate or missing organisations within the system of innovation;
- inappropriate or missing institutions; and
- inappropriate or missing interactions or links between these elements in the system of innovation.

System failures, too, mainly aim to understand 'the division of labour between private and public actors' (Chaminade and Edquist, 2010, p. 95); that is, up to which point the market can be left to itself, and when the government intervention can, and should, begin to influence the innovation process. 'That is, when, how and why should government intervene in the economy supporting certain innovative activities' (Chaminade and Edquist, 2010, p. 95).

Therefore, the intention is to intervene when the private sector fails to be effective, to address the deficiencies and inefficiencies of the system. According to this approach, innovation policies target 'the economic growth, productivity growth or increased employment and competitiveness' (p. 95). The objectives can also be of non-economic nature, such as cultural, social, environmental or military. In this case, however, the skills and choices are exclusively those of the policy maker.

Mazzucato (2013; Mazzucato-Penna, 2015, Mazzucato et al., 2015 Mazzucato and Wray, 2015) is critical of the approach of both market failures and system failures, so in her recent interventions she highlighted the need to define an eclectic horizon that includes 'Keynes' notion of socialisation of investments; Minsky's stage view of capitalism (his concept of money manager capitalism) and proposal for community development banks; Schumpeter's conceptualisation of economic development as a dynamic process; Polanyi's view of markets as shaped and created by the state; Neo-Schumpeterian studies on microeconomic dynamics and the concepts of technological trajectories and techno-economic paradigm shifts in evolutionary economics; mission-oriented policies in science and technology policy research; developmental network state in development economics; and Mazzucato's entrepreneurial state' (Mazzucato-Penna, 2015, p. 25). Through the combination of these concepts and schools of thought, the author builds a new theoretical framework for qualitatively different public investments that are more about market creating/shaping, than market fixing. This approach thus entrusts the state with identifying research objectives and creating markets necessary to drive innovation processes. In particular, the author entrusts the public development finance institutions with the important role of directing 'patient capital' to large-scale innovation programmes that do not find the necessary resources in the financial markets. But even in this line of thought, the modalities and basic decisions for public interventions remain in the background. The author suggests some innovative sectors and sectors that can have large environmental impact, but only in general terms, as areas of public interest worthy of a greater collective investment. Little is said about identifying alternatives (other areas of collective interest), motivation (which benefits? For whom?) and the objectives to be pursued (why?).

The prevailing direction of current industrial policies is simply pro-innovation, considering the choices of the goals and paths of innovation as a matter for businesses and the world of technology (Stiglitz and Lin, 2013; Cimoli et al., 2009). So far, the theories on innovation policy were largely depoliticised, demonstrating little interest in examining the appropriateness of their established objectives in the political sphere: rather they try to contribute uncritically to their actual implementation (Stirling, 2014). The innovation policy should, in order to make more effective choices, recognise in a more transparent manner the nature of the interests that are behind these innovation paths and clarify their purpose.

## 7.5 The informational basis of the innovation systems approach

Innovation policies operate in a context very different from that of the mere equilibrium of perfect competition. The focus of their analysis are the innovation systems, agents and relationships that form them. As we have seen, these approaches justify public intervention with failures (specific problems) of the system. But even in this case, as in the case of market failures, the task of the policy maker is merely to be a substitute: where the systems fail to function properly the state can 'assist' in their path of growth and innovation. The ultimate goal is ensuring growth and therefore this approach falls back into the welfarist approach, which, as we have seen previously, has little ethical foundation. What is the need for higher innovation, higher productivity growth and higher income? What are the differences in accessing the fruits of innovation? What are the consequences of transformation? Who benefits? What are the risks of transformation? The answers to these questions do not fall within the domain of innovation systems theory and probably would require a paradigm shift and a different *informational base* (Sen, 1992; Sen, 2011; Bajmòcy et al, 2014). According to Sen (1992), 'the informational basis of a judgment identifies the information on which the judgment is directly dependent and − no less importantly − asserts that the truth and falsehood of any other type of information cannot directly influence the correctness of the judgment' (p. 73). A change of the *informational basis* could then mean for innovation policies an extension of the set of objectives in technological change, going beyond the increase in GDP (or other related concepts such as productivity and employment). This would require the inclusion of further information[1] that would enable us to answer the above questions, as well as to identify technological choices nearest to collective needs. If we consider a broad and complex process, such as technological change, a means to address one single goal – growth – the information gathered to interpret this process is limited to a few data points (expenditure in R&D, patent application, education, etc.) related to research, technology, innovation and knowledge. In doing so, the informational basis becomes insufficient and the analysis of innovation limited.

As we have repeatedly pointed out, innovation is much more than just the introduction of 'a new way of doing things'; it involves a variety of elements beyond technology, such as the cultural, institutional and social spheres; and it enables new relationships within communities, within families and in the workplace. All these changes have profound impacts on human well-being. There is no guarantee, however, that the introduced innovation will necessarily result in positive effects: weapons of mass destruction, financial fraud, gambling, child pornography and new forms of torture are areas that generate and make extensive use of new technologies. Technological change does not benefit all parties to the same extent; indeed, it generates inequalities. A particular technology can contribute in different ways to various ways of doing and being of individuals and groups, depending on the individual and social conversion factors (Oosterlaken, 2015). The same technology can be perceived positively by a society or a group or as unacceptable by another. Therefore, the effects of innovation need a broader *informational basis* that goes beyond the welfarist approach. Increases in income, productivity, employment as well as a general 'technological advancement', do not tell the whole story. The information set that innovation policies focus on for the design, implementation and evaluation of interventions is too small when compared to the width of entities, relationships and contexts involved.

## 7.6 The role of the state and non-market institutions

Historical research has shown that all growth-related experiences have a foundation in an institutional setup, shared norms and well-financed public policies (e.g., Freeman, 2004, 2002; Mazzoleni and Nelson, 2007; Gerschenkron, 1962; Reinert, 2007). Indeed, the empirical evidence indicates that there is no single pursuit of economic growth that occurred in a context devoid of institutions and public policy, as described in most standard economics textbooks or prevailing economic theories. The most important institution is the state, the only organisation that is *universal* and the holder of the *power of coercion*, not granted to any other economic or social organisation (Stiglitz, 1989). Authors like Polanyi (1944) highlighted how this particular power has been exercised by national governments in *creating* markets, stressing that markets are the result of historical processes rather than a spontaneous form of economic organisation. The other important institution is the market where production relations take place and goods and services are exchanged. Between these two institutions, there is a wide range of institutions not belonging to either the market or the public sphere, thus not universal, with no coercive powers and no exclusive focus on exchange.

As evidenced by a large existing literature, *public policies* are the main ingredient in all development strategies, in particular in those countries that have shown greater catching-up capacity. Policies promoting the development of 'social capabilities' have played a central role in all experiences of growth (Abramovitz, 1986).[2] In these experiences the endogenous creation of new opportunities and capabilities is more important than the *ex-ante* availability of physical and human resources. An appropriate policy mix helped to unlock countries and project them on a new development path. This occurred in the past in countries like Germany, Italy, the United States and more recently Taiwan, Korea and China, and there is little reason to believe why this should not take place again now and in the future.

A number of *intermediate institutions* have also played a central role in the growth and development processes, and there are also theoretical reasons to believe that 'institutions and policies always matter' (Ocampo et al., 2007, Cimoli et al., 2009b). One of the limits of market failure approach is the distinction between the market and the institutions not related to it; this is a limitation because it assigns the state the (minimal) task of correcting the market and does not to consider the variety of individuals that affect the smooth functioning of the economic system as a whole. According to Cimoli et al. (2009a) 'non-market institutions (ranging from public agencies to professional associations, from trade unions to community structures) are at the core of the very constitution of the whole socio-economic fabric' (p. 22). These institutions play the important task of ensuring the running of many activities in which mere market exchange is either inadequate or impossible. In addition, these structures influence the behaviour of the actors in relation to other agents they associate with (competitors, suppliers, employees, civil servants, etc.) and thus play an important role, especially in the reduction of transaction costs. Even in a situation with characteristics typically closer to 'perfect competition', usually the context is part of a broader and denser set of non-market relationships. In such cases, the role of these competitive contexts cannot be evaluated solely on their ability to meet the conditions of allocative efficiency but also on their ability to create new networks of relationships and changes in organisational forms. It is in this sense that markets 'operate as (imperfect) mechanisms of selection' (Cimoli et al., 2009a, p. 22). Even at the level of the simple operation of individual markets, implementing the rules, interactions between economic agents and role of policies are core factors. However, as highlighted in Chapter 2, all the processes of scientific and technological knowledge generation, as well as the processes of imitation and adaptation of the existing technologies, involve a broad and diverse group of actors, ranging from private firms to public training and research institutions, from professional associations to trade unions, and from nonprofit organisations to consumers' associations.

This diverse exchange between heterogeneous and decentralised entities generates *coordination problems*. The task of coordinating such a network of relationships, typical of the environments in the operation of a modern economy, is highly dependent on *the quality of institutions*. As we have already seen in Chapter 3, the quality of institutions depends on the level of participation and democratic control of the citizens. In the following chapter, we will discuss the contribution of the capability approach to innovation policies. In doing so, we will consider the number and diversity of entities and the quality of institutions as core elements in the process of change.

## Notes

1 Some of which was used in Chapter 6 to investigate the interactions between the processes of growth and innovation and human development.
2 See Chapter 2.

## References

Abramovitz, M. 1986. Catching Up, Forging Ahead, and Falling Behind, *The Journal of Economic History*, 46(2), 385–406.

Archibugi, D. and Lundvall, B.A. (eds.) 2002. *The Globalizing Learning Economy*, Oxford, Oxford University Press.

Arrow, K. 1951a. An Extension of the Basic Theorems of Classical Welfare Economics. In: Neyman, J. (ed.), *Second Berkeley Symposium on Mathematical Statistics and Probability*, Berkeley, University of California Press, 507–532.

Arrow, K. 1951b. *Social Choices and Individual Values*, New York, Wiley and Sons.

Bajmócy, Z. and Gébert, J. 2014. The Outlines of Innovation Policy in the Capability Approach, *Technology in Society*, 38, 93–102.

Bajmócy, Z., Málovics, G. and Gébert, J. 2014. On the Informational Basis of Regional Innovation Policy: From Growth to Capabilities, *European Planning Studies*, 22(7), 1325–1341.

Braun, H. 1990. *The German Economy in the Twentieth Century*, London, New York, Routledge.

Chaminade, C. and Edquist, C. 2010. Rationales for Public Policy Intervention in the Innovation Process: A Systems of Innovation Approach. In: Kuhlman, S., Shapira, P. and Smits, R. (eds.), *Innovation Policy – Theory and Practice: An International Handbook*, London, UK, Edward Elgar Publishers, 95–119.

Cimoli, M., Dosi, G., Nelson, R.R. and Stiglitz, J.E. 2009a. Institutions and Policies in Developing Economies. In: Lundvall et al. 2009.

Cimoli, M., Dosi, G. and Stiglitz, J.E. 2009b. *Industrial Policy and Development: The Political Economy of Capabilities Accumulation*, Oxford, Oxford University Press.

Debreu, G. 1959. *Theory of Value: An Axiomatic Analysis of Economic Equilibrium*, New York, Wiley and Sons.

Edquist, C. 2002. Innovation Policy – A Systemic Approach. In: Archibugi, D. and Lundvall, B-Å. (eds.), *The Globalizing Learning Economy*. Oxford, UK, Oxford University Press, 219–238.

Edquist, C. and Chaminade, C. 2006. Industrial Policy From a Systems-of-Innovation Perspective, *European Investment Bank (EIB) Papers*, 11(1), 108–132.

Freeman, C. 2002. Continental, National and Sub-National Innovation Systems-Complementary and Economic Growth, *Research Policy*, 31, 191–211.

Freeman, C. 2004. Technological Infrastructure and International Competitiveness, *Industrial and Corporate Change*, 13(3), 541–569.

Gerschenkron, A. 1962. *Economic Backwardness in Historical Perspective*, Cambridge, MA, Harvard University Press.

Lundvall, B.A. and Lorenz, E. 2014. The Euro Crisis and the Failure of the Lisbon Strategy. In: Texeira, A.A.C., Silva, E.G. and Mamede, R.P. (eds.), *Structural Change, Competitiveness and Industrial Policy: Painful Lessons From the European Periphery*, London, New York, Routledge, 80–101.

Lundvall, B.A., Joseph, K.J., Chaminade, C. and Vang, J. 2009. *Handbook of Innovation System and Developing Countries: Building Domestic Capabilities in a Global setting*, Cheltenham, UK, Northampton, Edward Elgar Publishing Ltd.

Mazzoleni, R. and Nelson, R.R. 2007. Public Research Institutions and Economic Catch-Up, *Research Policy*, 36(10), 1512–1528.

Mazzucato, M. 2013. *The Entrepreneurial State: Debunking the Public vs. Private Myth in Risk and Innovation*, London, Anthem.

Mazzucato, M., Cimoli, M., Dosi, G., Stiglitz, J., Landesmann, M., Pianta, M., Walz, R. and Page, T. 2015. Forum: Which Industrial Policy Does Europe Need? *Intereconomics*, 50(3), 120–155.

Mazzucato, M. and Wray, L.R. 2015. *Financing the Capital Development of the Economy: A Keynes-Schumpeter-Minsky Synthesis*, Levy Economics Institute of Bard, Working Paper No. 837.

Mazzucato, M. and Penna, C.C.R. 2015. *Beyond Market Failures: The Market Creating and Shaping Roles of State Investment Banks*, Institute for New Economic Thinking, Working Paper No. 7.

Nelson, R.R. (ed.) 2005. *The Limits of Market Organization*, New York, Russell Sage Foundation.

Ocampo, J.A., Jomo, K.S. and Khan, S. (eds.) 2007. *Policy Matters: Economic and Social Policies to Sustain Equitable Development*, London, ZED.

Oosterlaken, I. 2015. *Technology and Human Development*, London and New York, Routledge.

Overy, R.J., 1996. *The Nazi Economic Recovery 1932–1938*, Second Edition, Cambridge, Cambridge University Press.

Polanyi, K. 1944. *The Great Transformation: The Political and Economic Origins of Our Time*, Boston, MA, Beacon Press.

Reinert, E.S. 2007. *How Rich Countries Got Rich . . . and Why Poor Countries Stay Poor*, London, Constable.

Richardson, H.S. 2015. Using Final Ends for the Sake of Better Policy-Making, *Journal of Human Development and Capabilities*, 16(2), 161–172.

Schumpeter, J.A. 1936. *The Theory of Economic Development: An Inquiry Into Profits, Capital, Credit, Interest, and the Business Cycle*, Cambridge, MA, Harvard University Press.

Sen, A. 1985. The Moral Standing of the Market, *Social Philosophy & Policy*, 2(2), 1–19.

Sen, A. 1992. *Inequality Reexamined*, Oxford University Press, Oxford.

Sen A. 2011, The Informational Basis of Social Choiceprotect. In: Kenneth J. Arrow, Amartya Sen and Kotaro Suzumura (eds.), *Handbook of Social Choice and Welfare*, Amsterdam, Elsevier, 2, 29–46.

Stiglitz, J.E. 1989. *The Economic Role of the State*, Oxford, Basil Blackwell.

Stiglitz, J. and Lin, Y. (eds.) 2013. *The Industrial Policy Revolution 1: The Role of Government Beyond Ideology*, Basingstoke, Palgrave Macmillan.

Stirling, A. 2014. Towards Innovation Democracy? Participation, Responsibility and Precaution in the Politics of Science and Technology. In: Annual Report of the Government Chief Scientific Adviser.

Tullock, G., Seldon, A. and Brady, G.L. 2002. *Government Failure: A Primer in Public Choice*, Washington, DC, Cato Institute.

# 8 Human development and policies for innovation

## 8.1 Introduction

What is the contribution of the capability approach to innovation policies?

As we have already seen, the informational basis on which innovation policies are formulated is grounded in the idea that technological potential is an input to the process (level of expenditure in R&D, number of researchers, level of education, infrastructure coverage, etc.) and that increasing the GDP (either in productivity or employment) is the goal. This effectively narrows down the scope of reflections in a field that, on the contrary, involves many actors, many interests and active processes that have an impact on society at large. In my view, innovation policies should broaden the framework of their informational basis and include goals that go beyond these limits. In doing so, they can benefit from the evaluation methodologies of programmes and policies adhering to the capability approach.

After more than two decades of widespread acceptance in the realm of human development and following the work of some large international organisations and NGOs, the capability approach has begun to find practical applications. These have so far mainly focused on the overall policy evaluation of countries in terms of human development, and the evaluation of small-scale development projects and policies to combat poverty and other conditions of deprivation; this allowed a certain experience gain and the ability to make comparisons between different methodologies (Alkire, 2002; Robeyns, 2006; Frediani et al., 2014; Panzironi and Gelber, 2012; Chiappero-Marinetti and Roche, 2009). In this chapter, I will outline the main ideas and suggestions emerging from applying the capability approach. Furthermore, I will seek to apply the ideas that guided human development projects to policies for innovation.

In order to approach the emerging problems and implications in an organised way, these ideas will be discussed as answers to six main questions: Why? Which capabilities? Who? How? What? Which implementation? In such a way, I will propose a 'sequence prototype' of actions, which, in my view, should be implemented to define industrial policies based on capabilities. Following this, some possible applications of a few policy instruments for innovation will be discussed, such as 'mission oriented' programmes, foresight exercises and technological assessments. Finally, a brief analysis of the innovation processes in developing countries will be undertaken.

Before going any further here are two warnings. The first concerns the object of assessment. With some oversimplification, it can be said that *policies* can consist of *programmes* and that these in turn can consist of *projects*. In this chapter I will interchangeably refer to programmes and projects; the difference between these two dimensions being mainly the size/complexity of the initiative. A programme mobilises more resources, is divided into several projects and involves multiple actors, and normally has a national or regional scope if not international. Projects on the other hand, usually refer to a more limited and better defined territorial/sectoral context and involve a more restricted number of actors. The stimuli that will be discussed below apply, in my view, to both dimensions. When the programme/project differences become relevant, these will be highlighted.

The second caveat relates to the use of a small explanatory device. To understand the issues that need to be addressed and above all to make it easier to appreciate some concepts that otherwise would be highly abstract, I will refer to a case in a (semi) unreal area (called 'Cotzyland'), hosting a large steel plant (called 'Sider') and facing great economic constraints. We assume that this area is located in a developing region and faces high unemployment rates. Furthermore, due to the operation of the plant over a few decades and the absence of adequate anti-pollution measures, the people of Cotzyland are suffering from serious respiratory diseases. The area's neoplastic disease rates are among the highest in Europe. The project under discussion is still unclear: should it aim at saving the plant or addressing the environment? Using this (semi) unreal case oversimplifies the challenges at stake, but I believe it will be helpful in displaying an array of actions and clarifying further the arguments.

## 8.2 Innovation projects and the capability approach

### a. Why?

What are the general objectives of a project? Typically, project goals are defined by the customary measures of welfare growth for a certain group of 'beneficiaries': more income, more employment, more efficiency, more competitiveness.

For the capability approach, the ultimate goal for any action mobilising human and material resources is not material wealth but to ensure that people live a life they feel is more dignified. Thus, defining what a more dignified life means for a community becomes crucial, though at the same time also relatively simple. Indeed, '[t] he fundamental insight of this approach is remarkably simple. It argues that the goal of both human development and poverty reduction should be to expand the capability that people have to enjoy 'valuable beings and doings'. They should have access to the positive resources they need in order to have these capabilities. And they should be able to make choices that matter to them' (Alkire, 2002, p. 2).

This first step in the decision-making process involves a fundamental political choice that affects all the other policies that follow. In standard innovation policies, as we have seen, the 'why' is implicit, i.e., technological progress, competitiveness, productivity, employment and growth, but this results in diverting the attention to an informational basis focusing mainly on inputs. The presence of adequate agents, well-functioning relationships and institutions guarantees the good use of the above inputs within the innovation systems. For the capability approach, access to resources is a means for obtaining a 'valued state of being and doing' rather than an end. This implies that the point of departure should be the expansion of capabilities, rather than imposing a sector, technology or innovation on a community or the economy at large.

An evaluation based on the capability approach begins with identifying the capabilities that the community intends to increase and/or favour. The limited or missing freedoms are then analysed, after which 'a new way of doing things' is developed, proposing a project of change that can contribute to the acquisition of a particular set of capabilities. In the real world, however, the artefact matters, the technology and the project precede the discussion and identification of the unfreedoms to be addressed. As claimed by Ferrero and Zapeda (2014), generally '[t]he logic models and the project approach focus on predefining an ideal "B" situation for all of the "beneficiaries" and prescribing how to achieve it. The process freedoms approach focuses on empowering people to collectively define, and autonomously choose from, a wider set of more flourishing "B" situations they value and have reason to value and that better contribute to the collective development vision of their communities' (p. 30).

The policy actions for innovation must therefore find their motivation in human dignity and human rights, rather than, as usually happens, interests of various pressure groups or market forces. The power relations that are determined within the social, political and cultural structures, which do not always concur, can tip the balance in favour of either approach. Ideas matter, and they are usually only implemented when they further interests. As we shall see, according to the capability approach, the critical point in the promotion of innovation is the decision-making process and the rules to be shared to implement it. The choice of approach (the why?), and the overall objective nevertheless remains fundamental to project implementation and decisions on its future evolution.

*The prevailing discussion in Cotzyland is focused on two alternatives: either to make the Sider establishment more efficient and improve its balance sheets (with the consequent choices in terms of financial arrangements, public funding, reduction of personnel, procurement policies, etc.) or to address the broader problems of the surrounding area and the plant's environmental sustainability. A decision needs to be made whether to give priority to efficiency or to the ability of people to live a healthier life. If the first policy is chosen, it would strongly be unidirectional (more public and private resources allocated to the plant) with a prominent top-down decision-making chain from ministries to local government to enterprise. If the second policy is pursued, it will be necessary to mobilise all stakeholders pertinent to the economic and living conditions of the area. In this case, the decision-making process will inevitably be participatory and democratic. A number of social pressure strategies directed to the local government (demonstrations, petitions, public appeals, etc.)*

*undertaken by citizens along with environmental and cultural associations, have led the decision makers to opt for the second option, i.e., the participatory one.*

### b. Who?

Thus, after having decided to adopt a capabilities-led process of project design, the specific content of the intervention can be defined. Here the questions 'who?' and 'how?' are more important than 'what?' Let's begin with analysing the 'who'.

The capability approach focuses on differences (personal, environmental, social) among individuals and groups, in order to better identify effective access to functionings[1] (see Chapter 2). People can differ because of personal characteristics (gender, age, health, etc.), environmental and contextual disparities (climate, levels of pollution, location, etc.) and social circumstances (class, group, profession, etc.). These differences are important because they affect the ability of individuals to convert resources into actual capabilities. For example, an electrification project of a village in a mountainous area may benefit a group, such as men, at the expense of another group, the women. This could happen because of the different abilities to convert the opportunity provided by the technology into actual life benefits (Fernandez-Baldor et al., 2014). In the case of men, the advantage may be due to higher market opportunities brought about by electrification; whereas in the case of women these benefits may not be realised due to lack of equipment that could be useful for their tasks, which are primarily non-market activities.

> *The plant in Cotzyland benefits the families of workers engaged in the plant by providing them with a secure income, but creates health hazards to all citizens (regardless of whether they are Sider employees or not). The most affected are families who live in poor neighbourhoods near the plant (and within this group, the children, breathing polluted air, are the most vulnerable and have no voice to protest). Families living in residential neighbourhoods far away from the plant are the least affected.*

A focus on diversity provides a window for development projects to direct their focus from the 'needs of the economy' or the physical structures to be achieved, to the weakest segment of the population in context in which the initiative is planned or managed, which is by far the most at risk.

An important implication of diversity is that it leads to the *design of a range of tools to respect the specificities of different groups.* This, as we shall see, has a strong influence on 'what' is to be planned. The project can therefore engage families in a small village (Fernandez-Baldor et al., 2014) or dwellers of urban centres under reconstruction (Oosterlaken, 2012) or focus on broader interventions impacting citizens at a regional or national level. In all these scenarios, projects need to identify and involve individuals who, for various reasons, have limited abilities to live in dignity.

What is the role of *actors in innovation systems*? They are part of the community and can play a role in all phases of the programme. Companies, workers, public and private research centres, training and university systems, development and technological agencies (the core that has been identified citing Lundvall in Chapter 2), all these actors must interact with individuals as well as cultural, environmental and social organisations. Within this dimension, the innovation system (regional, national, sectoral) can act in favour of a fair and socially acceptable change. Such systems should be characterised by a strong presence of public entities (research centres and universities, public investment banks) and be open to intermediary institutions representing collective interests and acting socially to defend the common good.

> *Coming back to Cotzyland, an approach appreciating the benefits of diversity and complexity would go beyond the ministry-local administration-business line and involve in the decision-making process workers' representatives and small business in the area; citizens, and particularly those from the neighbourhoods near the plant; environmental associations; health care facilities and environmental control agencies; educational and research system within the affected region; representatives of professions, kindergartens and schools (children being among the most threatened by the environmental conditions in the area).*

### c. How?

Let us discuss the 'how'. If there are no targets coming from the top, and diversity is seen as an asset, the only way to identify capabilities is through discussion between all parties involved and the application of the principles of deliberative democracy (see Chapters 2, 3 and 9). Deliberative democracy, as it is known (see Drèze and Sen, 2002), does not just take into account individual preferences aggregating them through a vote; on the contrary, it requires everyone to publicly justify their preferences and shape them by acquiring better knowledge of the issues at hand. Such a practice can be achieved through discussion and opinion exchange with others, as well as an expansion of the informational basis. Deliberative democracy assumes that decision-making is achieved through a learning process and not through a simple counting of preferences that could, in the absence of dialogue and information, be based on erroneous and inadequate foundations.

Whether the scope is a small investment in a village in a developing country or, as we shall see, a large 'mission-oriented' programme, the point of departure is always the same: open, transparent, informed and participatory debate between the people involved.

The modalities of the debate may therefore differ on the basis of size – whether that of a programme (more complex, multi-dimensional, multiple stakeholders) or that of a project (generally referring to a defined geographical area and a specific community). In a small village, individuals belonging to the village community will be involved; for major projects and programmes with broader impact, mainly the representatives of relevant interests will be involved, although the logic is the same, i.e., what are the capabilities of the people involved in the project/programme?

As it was noted earlier, the discussions must be transparent and informed. As much as possible, the asymmetries of knowledge should be addressed, and the conflicting interests that are present should be identified. In the case of programmes/major projects, aggregated analysis and specific studies on the concerned dimensions at the territorial, social, economic and environmental levels should not be excluded. To these must be associated qualitative analyses to identify, at a collective level, the dimensions of well-being to be addressed, as well as the collective objectives to be achieved in terms of improving the freedoms of individuals and communities.

In the case of small projects involving a well-defined community, the exchange is directed even further towards the qualitative dimension based on various participatory methods for the selection of relevant activities (Alkire, 2002; Biggeri et al., 2011; Biggeri and Ferrannini, 2014).

The methods to initiate the process of choice are different and depend on the specific situations. For Ferrero and Zepeda (2014), for example, the activities to be undertaken in the early stages of new development projects relate to: '(1) Mobilizing (start-up, taking the initiative); (2) Expanding participation capabilities; (3) Deliberating principles, values and vision; (4) Catalysing autonomy, partnerships; and (5) Learning (including evaluative activities), adapting, mutual accountability' (p. 42). These activities influence each other and aim at laying a base for collective learning, where common principles, values and long-term visions are defined to guide future actions towards positive change.

The decision-making process regarding the analysis of the situation and the choice of capabilities is therefore central to any development project for a number of reasons. First, participation *per se* is important since it facilitates, through the interrelation between individuals and groups, the process of collective learning and thus the expansion of the moral, technical and intellectual capacities of people. In this sense, there is room for an extension of the learning by interaction concept (Lundvall and Johnson, 1994), encompassing not only the technical aspects but also those which lead to greater awareness about collective change processes that impact the values of the community.

Second, managing a project from a capabilities perspective means: considering the people involved in the project as 'agents of change', rather than 'passive recipients'; focusing on achieving results that people give value to and not on objectives pre-defined by third parties and by 'development professionals'; following the principles of self-determination and empowerment to strengthen sustainability and accountability (see Chapter 3).

The emphasis has thus shifted from resources, ownership of assets, income and satisfaction of needs, to the capabilities and the real possibility of accessing functionings that people consider valuable. The process of defining the objectives and managing the project is a process which develops the ability to participate in decision-making that affects the structure of opportunities. In this sense, the development project for the capability approach is a collective learning process as well as a process of personal change that involves the ability to reflect, participate, decide and act (Nussbaum, 2011).

Actors and institutions involved in this process are trying to build collective experiences and new tools of intervention for a more ethical and participatory change. Participation alone is not sufficient though; it is also crucial to have an informational basis that broadens the capabilities in terms of understanding the issues under discussion (Dong, 2012).

> *A Health Committee was established in Cotzyland, formed by the actors listed above. During its first meeting, the committee appointed a chairperson and a secretary, defined an agenda of work and decided that the first phase should be devoted to a most extensive, transparent and pluralistic data gathering on socio-economic conditions, sanitation and environment in the area, on the economic and financial situation of the company, and on the private and public investments planned for the coming years.*

Enlarging the number of actors and creating a shared informational basis ensures that the intervention is not limited to the 'implementation' of an investment programme, but offers a solution to institutional, environmental and social challenges that affect the well-being of the concerned individuals.

The participatory approach entails a political dimension because, as we have seen, it triggers conflicts of interests, conflicting points of view and different visions of collective life. An approach based on learning and participation can question the work done and assumptions made by pre-existing institutions and their way of managing development programmes. Institutions must be involved in the learning process rather than simply managing pre-set inputs of financial, human and technological resources. According to Dreze and Sen (2002), it is important that the local deliberative process is *institutionalised*, with the aim of creating and strengthening democratic institutions, as a whole. According to the authors, this enables the process to go beyond the single project and to extend the individual and collective capacities to claim one's rights. In this way, the participatory approach is ensured not only in the initial step but also is kept alive, as we shall see, in the design phase, implementation and evaluation of the project/programme.

### d. Which capabilities?

After having made a political decision on the widening of the horizon in terms of general objectives (the 'why') and actors (the 'who'), and having defined a way to work collectively (the 'how'), the focus is directed on defining the relevant capabilities of the community.

The first challenge that arises is to answer the question: 'which are the capabilities that people have, to enjoy a valuable [for them] state of being and doing?' As we have seen (Chapter 2), the CA, especially as advocated by Sen, chooses not to answer clearly and definitively this question, considering it important that the choice is made by the community concerned. Giving a clear answer would go against the features of incompleteness and pluralism that are endorsed by the capability approach (Chapter 2). In the realisation of concrete projects, however, the need for a more operational guidance is naturally more pressing. Various authors addressed this kind of need (Alkire, 2002, Ch. 2; Fernandez-Baldor et al., 2014; Robeyns, 2006), proposing different methods which can be used as a starting point in the decision-making process of collective choice. Some experiences refer to the 10 'central human capabilities' indicated by Nussbaum (2011) as the initial stimulus for a discussion on the capabilities involved by the projects (Robeyns, 2006). For large projects, one could start from instrumental freedoms (Chapter 2), which I have used to identify the critical areas in the relationship between capabilities and innovation (see Chapter 3) and to lay down the empirical analysis (see Chapter 6). These are the only categories, deliberately broad, that are quoted by Sen in his work. They refer to political freedom, economic facilities, social opportunities, transparency, guarantees and protective security (see Chapter 2). They could be used as the basis for scrutinising the capabilities that have changed (for better and for worse) following the innovation process. In all cases, however, the approach must refer to *a collective process of participatory identification of capabilities that are significant to the community.*

*After a long series of meetings, detailed studies of health conditions and social and economic situation of the area, discussions by thematic commissions, and experts' reports, the Health Committee of Cotzyland decided that the most important values to be safeguarded for the community are as follows: 1. Ensure a healthy environment for all; 2. Ensure direct participation in decision-making process on matters affecting the community; and 3. Ensure a dignified life, job opportunities and the ability to procure the necessary means for all. The sequence of the fundamental values is not accidental. Priority is given to health and environment. The committee agreed and almost unanimously accepted that people's health goes beyond the availability of work and income. During a meeting a citizen questioned: 'What is the point of having a job and a wage if we then die of cancer and our children do not have clean air to breathe?' Democracy was identified as a second priority because industrial choices, which have had a great impact on the liveability of the area, have always bypassed the opinion of the citizens concerned. The rights to work and to a decent income were placed third. The historic conflict in the area between those who want to preserve the workplace at all costs and those who call for health for all was resolved in favour of the latter. Now the committee enters the second phase, i.e., choosing the solutions.*

### e. What?

Just like people, innovations are not all the same; and this is an important point of departure in the definition of innovation policies. According to Stirling (2014) innovation 'is not a single-trace race driven by a particular privileged field of science. Instead, it is about diversity, exploration and choice' (p. 9). Typically, the roads leading to a solution to a problem are numerous, thus choosing the preferred way is crucial and involves multiple parties and interests. In this sense, a shared and well-thought-out innovation can make an important contribution not only to growth and productivity, but also to many types of human flourishing and public goods (Stirling, 2014).

In addition, each innovation project is characterised by the existence of risk, uncertainty, ambiguity and ignorance (Stirling, 2014). The common way of approaching a knowledge gap is by undertaking risk analyses that suggest, on a probability basis, which risks may be considered 'acceptable'. These, however, may be incomplete and insufficient when the contexts in which the innovations will be applied are subject to rapid and complex changes. The distribution of the innovation-induced advantages and disadvantages is not always apparent and is subject to high degrees of ambiguity. The most disruptive element in the innovation choices, however, is ignorance. What did we know when, for example, we found ourselves having to deal with diseases like HIV/AIDS, the bovine spongiform encephalopathy (BSE) or damages to the ozone layer in the stratosphere from CFCs? Nothing. Similarly, we may ignore positive aspects – as in the case of laser applications, a phenomenon confined to laboratories and unused for a long time; or as it was the case with the Internet, which has certainly given rise to a number of applications which initially were totally unexpected.

Therefore, the claim that technological choices are 'objective' and 'technically measurable' is largely unfounded. This does not imply that these evaluations are futile – far from it – but they should be placed within a context of pluralistic and participatory evaluation, where possible alternatives can be identified and screened.

Within the scope of innovation, where risk, uncertainty, ambiguity and ignorance prevail, the alternatives should be selected following broader and transparent public discussions as well as thorough assessments of available proposals. Indeed, '[t]he central challenge in innovation policy is about helping to culture the most fruitful conditions across society as a whole, for seeding and selecting across many alternative possibilities and together nurturing the most potentially fruitful' (Stirling, 2014, p. 3).

An important contribution to these challenges of innovation comes from *the precautionary principle*. It is based on the idea that *scientific uncertainty is not a reason for inaction in preventing serious harm to human health or the environment*. The precautionary principle thus applies to potential hazards, about which there isn't yet proven knowledge, rather than known threats. This principle is grounded in the awareness that social choices in the field of innovation cannot simply depend on the calculation of technical risks without considering the values linked to the health of people and the environment in which they live. 'Precaution is also a guard against the error of treating absence of evidence of harm as evidence of absence of harm' (Stirling, 2014, p. 14).

Therefore, in a context of uncertainty, ignorance and ambiguity, an important question to ask is 'which innovation?' The answer to this question is not purely technical, but is fundamentally political. In fact, an important point of departure is the awareness that innovation is not a defined path along a single road leading into the future, but rather the interaction between interests fighting for the prevailing of possible solutions. The innovation policy should, in order to better direct choices, recognise in a more transparent way the nature of the interests that are driving the innovation paths. In fact, while technical alternatives can be subject to different levels of risk, uncertainty, ambiguity and ignorance, and thus not easily understandable by most and a source of uncertainty, the interest groups behind each alternative and their respective objectives are clearly identifiable. Thus, the first step toward an informed and transparent choice should be to make it clear, through the method of deliberative democracy (see above), what these interest groups are and which goals they pursue.

An important role in the clarification process is played by the relationship between 'experts' and 'non-experts'. The former must act with the task of clarifying the alternatives, as well as the advantages and disadvantages that each has on groups of individuals and the community (Abraham-Sheppard, 1997). The 'experts' have to clarify which interests they represent and must make it explicit that they do not play a neutral role. This means that even the most detailed aspects of innovation policy can legitimately be questioned by democracy (Sclove, 1995).

Normally, projects introducing change and innovation do not directly question the dimensions of politics and power, preferring to limit their analysis to the so-called technical dimensions of the project. The decision-making process, with its power struggles, conflicting interests and partnerships in both politics and business, is considered different and distant from the (alleged) technical nature of the project. The decision-making process will identify the priorities, while the technicians will take over from that point on and explain how to implement the objectives of the policy. This assumption has a limit, as it underestimates the importance of the decision-making process, so full of contrasting interests, for the effectiveness of the interventions. Conflicts of interests are already part of the process of change. The technical contribution is downgraded when taken to be dependent from this process, rather than being considered an integral part of it (Stirling, 2014). Information gathering on the technical and economic aspects is part of the problem analysis, but not the only nor the most important task. As stated earlier, when discussing the 'how', the interactions between 'experts' and 'non-experts' and between various interest groups are essential parts of the decision-making and collective learning process. Nowadays, the distinction between experts and non-experts is becoming increasingly blurred, especially in developed countries. Some studies on projects and decision making have highlighted the limits of expert knowledge and the virtues of 'lay knowledge' (Kleinman, 2005; Yearley, 2000). Instead of thinking in terms of experts and non-experts, it would be better to consider the different types of knowledge ranging from the theoretical to practical, which need to be engaged in a continuous and collaborative exchange. In the experimentation of such exchanges each can contribute his/her expertise: workers and teachers, engineers and social workers, computer and social scientists, users/customers and manufacturers among others.

By focusing only on technology rather than on people, an innovation project loses its potential for social transformation. The project is a tool to help people shape their lives and reduce inequalities.

*Five thematic working groups were put to work in our Cotzyland: the first was responsible for gathering and evaluating all the technical interventions implemented*

*in other steel industries around world to reduce their environmental impact; the*
*second was asked to evaluate the costs and technologies to decontaminate the areas*
*polluted by the activities of the plant; the third to check the tools to improve sanita-*
*tion and health in the area; the fourth to design communication tools via the web to*
*maintain a high level of citizens' participation in the choices of the project interven-*
*tions (e-democracy); and the fifth to assess the impact all of these innovations could*
*have on employment and income of the area.*

*After a careful evaluation of the impacts of all the proposed solutions by concerned*
*citizen groups, and the development of a cost-benefit analysis and other tools to make*
*an informed decision, the Cotzyland Health Committee decides, with the agreement*
*of the central and local administrations as well as enterprise, to launch an invest-*
*ment for the reclamation of the affected area, to support the technological solution*
*type 'A', widely used in similar plants in Japan, which can eliminate the polluting*
*emissions; launch an Internet information system for citizens focusing on the design*
*and implementation of the projects.*

### f. Which implementation?

The design phase and subsequent implementation and monitoring of the interventions should maintain the spirit of participation discussed earlier, and this
must also be guaranteed by the 'institutionalisation' of the decision-making process (see section c, above). All these steps should take risks, uncertainty, ambiguity and ignorance as central concepts characterising each project, and have been
previously discussed. The planning stage is the most critical and requires strong
collaboration between the 'technical experts' and the 'non-experts'. In this
phase, individual differences are very important. As previously stressed, addressing such differences compels designers to have differentiated solutions and
introduce innovations and changes that otherwise would not be identified due
to a tendency towards simplification. (Oosterlaken and Van den Hoven, 2012)

The implementation phase should avoid excessive use of standard methods derived from company management. The conventional planning tools, in
fact, try to capture on timetables the process of change by trying to detail
the planned activities by associating rigid implementation schedule to each of
them. The process of 'innovation respectful of human capabilities', described
so far, does not have efficiency as the sole guiding criterion, but rather focuses
on respect for the individual, which implies that an inevitably high degree of
flexibility and unpredictability is embraced. Change over time almost never
occurs in a linear fashion: the results from one component of the project can
become inputs to another or they may take unexpected paths; some phases may
take longer than others, and so on (Hirschman 1967; Fernandez-Baldor et al.,
2014). There is hardly one definite and linear sequence of actions to be implemented within a development plan, especially if the implementation is open to
interaction with the community. Results themselves may change as part of the
implementation process, through unexpected outcomes and paths. It is hard to
bring a process of change that is always both social and economic, within very
rigid patterns.

It is precisely because of this inevitable variability in the innovation project, that monitoring activities, i.e., the on-going checking of project performance, have to be put in place to reach decisions that will enhance changes that aim to expand the capabilities of citizens and solve problems that limit the realisation of the identified objectives.

The design, implementation, and monitoring of innovation projects must be accompanied by a constant attention for the growth of the agency of individuals and community. An active role of the community guarantees the long-term sustainability of a project and its effectiveness (Ferrero and Zepeda, 2014).

> *The Health Committee of Cotzyland continues to operate after the choice of the technological and design alternatives is made. For the design phase, the organisation of meetings becomes tighter and the relationship with technical personnel becomes more important. The latter are systematically challenged to address the smallest details to ensure that no one is left without the health and environmental security that the community decided to guarantee to all citizens. In the implementation and monitoring phases, the committee organised itself around working groups that carry out inspections in the areas of reclaimed land and check the development of new 'clean' technologies. The same working groups hold monthly meetings to monitor project implementation, analysing the emerging problems and assessing the possibility of introducing changes to the proposed programmes.*

## 8.3  Mission-oriented innovation programmes and the capability approach

Over the past three decades, despite overall technological progress, both in developed and developing countries, the number of unsolved collective problems concerning, *inter alia*, environment, health, social arrangements, demography and infrastructure remains high. Although technology in itself cannot solve all the problems that need to be addressed, it nevertheless has an important role to play in achieving solutions. In many of these cases, the solution to problems cannot come from the market because the required investments in R&D are very high and present a high risk. In such cases, the rationale for action goes beyond the logic of market failures and requires the state to define an overall goal and allocate financial, human and technological resources with the intent to achieve it. Thus, the state does not have a 'repair the market' role but is expected to act in response to far-reaching problems that otherwise, in the absence of collective action, would remain unsolved. This type of intervention is commonly defined as 'mission-oriented research programs'.

Two important examples of this type of programme are the Apollo Mission and the Manhattan project. The first is a programme launched at a joint session of Congress, on 25 May 1961, by President John F. Kennedy, who declared that it was a national target to 'land a man on the moon' before the end of the decade. This was achieved on 20 July 1969. The Manhattan Project, on the other hand, had the less-noble goal of producing a particularly devastating military weapon: the atomic bomb. The project begun in 1939, engaging 120,000 people in its final stage with a total cost of US$2 billion at the time (corresponding to US$28 billion in 2008) and with the deployment of the nuclear device on 6 and 9 August 1945 on the cities of Hiroshima and Nagasaki, that caused around 140,000 deaths.

These two great mission-oriented programmes demonstrate that it is possible to reach, within a defined period of time, important public objectives by mobilising substantial resources and intensifying efforts in research and development. The *ex-post* analysis of these interventions also highlighted that they generated over time a significant impact on the entire innovation system. Another important lesson learned from these big programmes is that huge investments in new knowledge have impacts and repercussions that also benefit private companies.

In recent years, the logic of large programmes has also been used to achieve objectives in health, education, agriculture, energy and climate change[2] (Foray et al., 2012). The most important differences between the Apollo Mission and the Manhattan project, on one hand, and the investments in social programmes, on the other, can be summarised by the following characteristics: the first were centralised, radical and closed, while the second were decentralised, incremental and open in nature.

The objective of the Apollo and Manhattan programmes was to develop a particular technology, thus once their technological goal was achieved, this signalled the end of the programme. The technological set up and the purpose of the programme had a defined and very clear timetable. After having bombed Hiroshima and Nagasaki and explored the moon several times, the programmes had achieved their objectives. From that moment onward, the typical problems of maintenance/adaptation of technology became the main concerns. On the contrary, the objectives and the timeframe for the realisation of social goals are less definable in advance; they can be achieved through more technological interventions and therefore require a longer time period. In many cases (such as environment and natural resources) the solution should be addressed at the global level, preferably with the involvement of international organisations. Further objectives could be better pursued at the global level, but in many cases the divergence of national interests does not facilitate the process. With other initiatives, the direct involvement of national governments and local communities can suffice to address the problems.

In addition, large programmes were headed by government agencies specifically created for their implementation. These structures were provided with the necessary financial and human resources to implement these programmes. Current challenges, on the other hand, require the involvement of several parties, both public and private, many of which are not able to contribute financially to the implementation of the projects, although each of these actors has an important role in identifying the technologies to be developed. In large programmes the funding had only one source: the government; in social programmes funding can come from the public sector but – according to Nelson (2011) – it cannot come from the public sector alone, as private financial effort will prove necessary, especially in the stages of technological development and adoption of innovations.

In large projects, the government is the only donor, the main purchaser and user of the product; while in social projects, as we have seen, there could be a number of donors and a wider user base. Unlike centralised programmes, social programmes could face problems concerning involvement, because of the number and diversity of participating parties. Therefore, the articulated innovation objectives in themselves are complex, with highly decentralised processes (Nelson, 2011). Finally, another important difference is that, unlike the Manhattan and Apollo programmes, the technologies of social programmes are mainly incremental and have to compete with existing ones owned mostly by large enterprises and by very strong interest groups (Nelson, 2011).

With reference to the major 'mission-oriented' programmes, it is not uncommon to ask the question 'If we can land a man on the moon, why can't we solve the problems of the ghetto?' (Nelson, 1974, p. 376). Reference is often made to the Apollo programme and to the social contradictions still witnessed in developed countries, in particular in the most advanced country in the world, the US, where the first objective was achieved with relative ease while the second still poses difficulties. If, by concentrating substantial public resources, such important and complex goals have been achieved, why not adopt the same approach to address issues of collective interest such as the reduction of atmospheric pollution, the elimination of global poverty, education for all, protection for all against common diseases, etc.? Are we sure that resources in terms of knowledge, technology, finance, human capital, organisation necessary to achieve collective goals are more extensive than those used to achieve military objectives and that of space exploration?

These questions have already been partially answered. It is generally believed that (Nelson, 2011; Foray et al., 2012) the model of the large American innovation projects (Manhattan and Apollo) is not adequate for achieving collective goals. In fact, these two types of projects have, as we have seen, important differences: the nature of their mission, the type of R&D that is supported, the institutional characteristics of the persons involved, and the main beneficiaries.

For Nelson (2011), however, the real problem is the lack of knowledge required to solve social problems. He gives the example of education and notes how few improvements have been made in this sector in recent decades. This is in spite of the general agreement on the importance of education in the social development of a country, and on the type of interventions that would be useful to improve the effectiveness of the educational processes. According to Nelson, the real limitation to political action lies in the lack of knowledge of adequate technical solutions. 'There is little evidence supporting the proposition that simply investing more in education would have large positive effect' (p. 681). The same could be said about fighting drug trafficking and global warming. In all of these cases, the real limitation to defining effective policies is the lack of an adequate understanding of the problems themselves. It thus remains to be understood why in certain fields knowledge is particularly well developed, while in the social fields this is not, and consequently, what actions are to be taken to overcome this lack of knowledge. According to this critical school of thought, a high social impact mission is more difficult to undertake due to a lower tech content ('core', as defined by Nelson, 2011) that allows us to understand when it is reached. In addition, it is considered difficult to come up with an innovation system oriented towards knowhow of a more social nature. Even if such an orientation were possible, it remains a challenging task to redesign the innovation systems to orient the technological progress towards these goals. Moreover, the institutions and policies that work well in one context may not work in another.

In my view, the large 'mission-oriented' programmes can become an interesting testing ground for the integration of the capabilities approach and technological change. Obviously, I am referring to interventions that have non-military[3] purposes. In these cases, the objectives focus on the creation of public goods or the solution of social or environmental problems, and their characteristics recalled above – decentralisation, expansion and openness – render them extremely interesting. It is precisely because these programmes address 'major public goals' that they could be implemented according to the principles listed above: starting from capabilities rather than artefacts; agency; pluralism and diversity of individuals, interests and solutions; transparency, more fluidity and information exchange within expert/non-expert relationships; non-linear implementation and monitoring processes, that are open to the unexpected and to deviations from the path; extensive evaluation of projects that does not stop with welfare and technological improvements, but also involves the expansion of opportunities for different stakeholders.

In my view, the weaknesses of social programmes, as identified by Nelson – i.e., unawareness of needs, difficulties in identifying core technologies and the arduous reorientation of innovation systems – represent opportunities for a different approach. An unawareness of needs requires a paradigm shift, starting with the capabilities of people rather than what is assumed/perceived to be their needs. The absence of a technological core calls for an approach based on technological pluralism and experimentation, as previously described. The reorientation of the innovation systems is not the result of a policy directive, but an effect of a process of change itself, a process of institutional learning supported by the interaction of all parties involved. As we have seen, the 'who' and the 'how' are more decisive than the 'what'.

Every social project has its specific characteristics and possible technological needs that depend on the context in which they are implemented. For example, the projects that have more direct impact on production, such as those related to agriculture and energy, differ substantially in terms of issues and stakeholders from those that aim to benefit the society, such as those focusing on environment, health and training (Foray et al., 2012). This presents a challenge for *the innovation systems* that must deal with projects with a social dimension, in which starting from the capabilities and defining technologies requires a more complex course. Therefore, what is identified by some authors as a limitation becomes a challenge for the innovation systems. In these cases, the purpose of the 'mission-oriented' programmes is not the generation of technological innovation that results in a series of 'artefacts', but rather a path that sees converging changes affect society, institutions, individuals and organisations.

An important role, in this context, can be taken up by *public investment banks*. According to some authors (Mazzucato and Penna, 2015), these players can provide a supporting role to both development and innovation: countercyclical, developmental, venture capitalist role, and challenge-led. All roles that go beyond the pure function of 'adjusting the markets', targeting instead to the creation of the latter by providing the means to achieve several objectives at the macroeconomic and microeconomic level. It is also interesting to reflect on the possibility of establishing *community development banks* (Minsky, 1993). These would be charged with providing financial resources to invest based on competence and social context, favouring the inclusion of those who would otherwise be excluded from the economic process.

In connection to the strengthening of the innovation and development funding initiatives as those mentioned above, Atkinson (2015) suggests the establishment of a *sovereign Wealth Fund* with the aim of increasing the net worth of the state with investments in companies and assets. Similar funds already exist in some countries; the most famous (and richest) are in those countries that enjoy large oil revenues: Kuwait, Norway, Saudi Arabia, Alaska and Qatar, although they are also present in China, Singapore and France. These funds can acquire shares in companies and real estate. Their establishment and expansion may be related to another problem raised by Mazzucato (2013): if most of the technological innovations that are normally introduced by private companies arise directly or indirectly from the public investment in R&D, why shouldn't the State (and therefore the entire community) benefit from at least some of the benefits (profits) that are accumulated by private firms? A chapter from a book written by Mazzucato is adequately entitled 'Socialization of risk and privatization of rewards: can the entrepreneurial state eat its cake too?' Mazzucato's proposal is to support public funds through the payment of royalties on research generated by public funds and used by companies, returns on loans and government warranties beyond a certain profit threshold, as well as share in companies that use the results from such research. Something similar exists in countries such as Finland, where the state maintains a share in companies that have taken advantage of state resources to launch their research and innovation processes.

The idea proposed by Mazzucato and Penna (2015) that the State Investment Banks (SIB) can take over the governance of some research and innovation programmes requires answers to some questions. If research and technological innovation processes depend on the use of public resources and the choices made by the state, what is the purpose of these choices? Who are the parties involved? And above all, what is the contribution that these programmes can make to increase the capabilities of individuals? How are priorities established in terms of stakeholders and aims? How are the results controlled?

These banks might be better placed within the institutions that are generated in the process of evaluation and control described above. Every 'mission oriented' innovation programme should be governed according to the principle of deliberative democracy and should be supported by a public investment bank. This would allow a more democratic governance of the policies, and enhance the opportunity to interact with more stakeholders and thus work out the best use of financial resources. In the absence of democratic control, these resources risk being 'captured' by particular interests.

## 8.4 Foresight and technological assessment

### *a. Technological foresight exercises*

Another area of possible and fruitful interaction between innovation policies and the capabilities approach is related to Foresight exercises. These can be defined as 'a systematic, participatory, future intelligence gathering and medium-to-long term vision building aimed at present day decisions and mobilizing joint actions' (Georghiou et al., 2008, p 11).

Technological foresight is a process that attempts to look at the long-term developments in science, technology, economy and society, aiming at identifying strategic research areas and emerging technologies that are most likely to generate economic and social benefits. The purpose of these exercises is to provide a broader understanding of the forces shaping the future in order to influence business decisions as well as the formulation of planning policies and decision-making.

Technological foresight consists in a body of systematic studies conducted by different parties and a debate on the future development of certain technologies or technological developments that normally involves experts, companies and policy makers. Foresight exercises have been undertaken on a regular basis in many countries around the world for the past forty years, mainly at the national, but also at the regional level (Foren, 2002). The method that is most commonly used is the Delphi method, which involves experts working on the specific technology or sector, but also includes debates, analyses and studies involving a large number of social and economic actors. This occurs also because particular emphasis is placed on the building of social networks and interactions between stakeholders. The formal results of these exercises are the presentation of scenarios and medium- to long-term plans on the development and the effects of technological applications. However, an equally important but more informal result is the building of a shared vision between the parties participating in such exercise (this happens as a result of the networking process that is stimulated by the exercise itself). This shared vision between enterprises, technology experts and social and political associations becomes a common ground for the definition of policy actions and economic as well as social behaviours.

Foresight can be considered as a policy tool for innovation because, following the logic of system failures, the agents (companies, public agencies, etc.) are inclined to behave in a rigid and incorrect way, reducing their opportunity to foster links and interrelations, thereby reducing the potential for innovation and forecast of any technological changes. As a result of foresight, businesses can access information on markets and new technologies more effectively than what they usually obtain from the daily market activity or partners in the innovation system. They can benefit from new networks, new ideas and new areas of intervention that, due to historical factors, may simply not emerge.

The main focus of these exercises has so far been the improvement of national competitiveness, the definition of priorities and the development of strategic objectives for various areas of research and technology. Its potential could be directed to the social, political, infrastructural and environmental sectors, embracing a greater openness to issues that go beyond immediate economic impacts. 'One of the main lessons of foresight exercises to date is that science and technology issues are inextricably linked with a wider range of social factors – and vice versa. Social forces shape the development and use of science and technology and the social implications associated with this' (Georghiou et al., 2008, p. 12).

The core of foresight is therefore to share ideas of possible technological futures. The way to achieve it is to identify the trend of long-term opportunities and threats that these futures present. In my view, these exercises do not envisage a future that needs to be changed but rather see the future as a scenario for which one must be prepared. It also aims to limit as much as possible the uncertainty previously discussed, and formulate an idea of 'what will be.' The information that is presented to a company and a policy maker is essentially a warning of what could be a possible scenario in order to induce them to make the necessary decisions to take advantage of the opportunities or mitigate risks. As a tool for innovation policy, the foresight moves following the logic of market/system failures and offers solutions that companies alone would not attain, to achieve the objective of greater efficiency.

The question is – can an idea of the future be shared without sharing the ultimate goals of the community and the changes that are taking place? What capabilities need to be improved for a more equitable society? What are the priorities that need to be addressed by the change? Who will benefit and who will be penalised by the change? Can the capabilities expand with the change? If not, what are the policies that must be implemented to prevent the deterioration of people's achievements? All of these issues go beyond the understanding, more or less shared, of economic and technological trends to which we must adapt by anticipating them, and involve a greater degree of insight into goals and ethical choices.

These exercises could also endorse a different framework, starting from clear normative assumptions and from a participatory and shared way of identifying central capabilities, to then ground on those medium- and long-term analyses of the social, economic, technological and environmental context.

### b. Technological assessment

The *Technology Assessment* (TA) seeks to assess the social, economic and environmental impact of technologies (Sclove, 2010; Ely et al. 2011; UNDP 2010). The first such exercise was launched in 1972 by the US government and conducted by a special unit, the Office of Technological Assessment, between the '70s and

'80s. During those years, this was also replicated in many OECD countries with the aim of providing a neutral assessment of the impact of technologies (in particular those that at the time were the most disputed, such as nuclear power) and addressing the technological policy choices of governments. After the first experiences, however, it became clear that TA was anything but objective and neutral. In fact, the feedback on the technologies could not be separated from value judgments about social goals underlying the analysed technological process. The TA was based on often-implicit judgments and assumptions concerning the nature of problems that required an evaluation, the purpose of the evaluation, the type of effects to evaluate, the most appropriate methods to be used, the criterion against which the effects had to be assessed and the interpretation of results (Ely et al. 2011). The evaluations focused on the technical feasibility and the economic effects, while neglecting to explore the social and ethical implications of technology. The underlying problem of this first generation of evaluation exercises was that they were carried out by stakeholders who were directly involved in the financing and commercial use of the new technology (mainly companies and academics), and this led to biases in the impact assessment.

On the basis of the criticism of these early experiences, over the last two decades, a new generation of TA has emerged. One example is the 'Danish participatory TA', which involves not only businesses and academics but also trade unions, NGOs, journalists and ordinary people. 'Technology Assessment (TA) is a set of practices that attempt to anticipate and analyse the broader social, environmental, and economic implications of technological projects, and to investigate the consequences of the options available to decision-makers. Technology Assessment attempts to anticipate impacts and feedbacks in order to reduce the human and social costs incurred in social learning about technology purely through trial and error' (Ely et al. 2011;, pg.11). 'One that is more transnational, networked, virtual and flexible than its predecessors, and crucially that combines citizen participation and decision-makers participation with traditional subject-matter-based expertise' (p. 18). In this new generation of TA, the methods used are largely participatory and aim at using these exercises for sharing and collective learning (Ely et al. 2011; Sclove, 2010).

This second wave of TA is strongly in tune with what we have described as an innovation policy based on capabilities. As it has been often mentioned before, and as the criticism on the first type of TA has pointed out, technological choices involve the ethical sphere, an aspect that should be made explicit and should be placed in the hands of the people. If one starts from democratically identified choices and priorities and not on the technological solutions, the latter may be subject to changes, as in case of the Citizens' Jury on Genetically Modified Organism (GMOs) in Karnataka, India, who contested the use of Bt cotton in small farms, a genetically modified variety produced by Monsanto (Ely et al. 2011). This body composed of citizens, politicians and experts challenged the sustainability of the product and proposed natural, 'non-GMO' alternatives compatible with the needs of the farmers. Their use has proven successful and beneficial to the area's economy.

## 8.5 Innovation and capabilities in developing countries

### a. Why is it important to promote a mix of innovation and capabilities in developing countries?

In the traditional approach, the line between development and non-development is delineated by the availability of resources (physical, technological, cognitive). Developing countries, communities and individuals are in this condition, ultimately, because of an inadequate level/lack of resources. The resulting development policy holds that to achieve the desired change the community needs to increase the resources at its disposal.

But as we have seen, the promotion of capabilities depends only partly on resources, and it is also affected by the effective capacity of a system to promote a set of instrumental freedoms that can enable individuals to participate actively in the social and economic life of their community. This active participation is the engine of change and growth, not vice versa. Growth alone without an expansion of capabilities is not sustainable in the long run. In the absence of policies that broaden participation of those who can have access to an active life (agency), growth will lead to inequality, poor dissemination of knowledge and dominance by powerful groups that use the state to protect their own interests. Looking at these problems from the perspective of the capability approach, the differences between developed and developing countries become more nuanced and less clear. There are many countries enjoying a high per capita income and at the same time restricting the fundamental rights of groups and categories of people (such as women, the poor, ethnic and religious groups, the youth, etc.). On the other hand, countries that invest a good portion of their limited resources in education, health and the agency of their citizens are also common.

Simultaneously, if, as we have extensively argued, the process of technological innovation is the very essence of economic and social change, it must then be a priority of any government that wants to improve the conditions of the citizens of their country. The innovation policies are important in all countries at all levels of development. First, because innovation (understood in its broadest sense) and learning are the key engines of growth; and without growth, society will never implement the structural changes it needs to progress. Second, because innovation can help to settle or mitigate in an independent way some of the problems (concerning health, environment, urban planning, etc.) that are unlikely to be solved merely by the flow of capital and expertise available on an international market which is far from being fully functional.

What has emerged so far from the exploration carried out in this book is that striving for both an extension of capabilities and building/strengthening of innovation systems is a conceivable and virtuous path. In the empirical part, we have seen how this in fact is the path chosen by some booming countries in recent decades: Korea and China in the lead. This has also been the strategy pursued in the past by many countries of Central and Northern Europe, in particular the Scandinavian countries (Miettinen, 2013; Lundvall, 2002; Castells and Himanen, 2002), as well as the path taken in original ways by Kerala, an inland state of India (Parayil, 2000; Subrahmanian and Abdul Azeez, 2000). This is not the only way, but it is the one that seems most respectful of people and the most economically and socially sustainable. Pursuing the elimination of unfreedoms that limit individuals and prevent them from living a life that is worth living is an end, but as we have seen, it is also a means to create the right conditions for social and economic change and technological innovation. At the same time, technological change is the only way to ensure the growth of the means necessary to the well-being and the expansion of opportunities of individuals.

The extreme heterogeneity in the historical, geographical, cultural and economic characteristics, however, makes it impossible to identify policies applicable in all countries. Each country has a specific socio-economic and institutional context, and it would be wrong to recommend the same recipes that proved to be effective in developed countries. There is no 'one size fits all' strategy or a 'magic bullet' for development (Cimoli et al., 2009).

Depending on its stage of development and its historical and geographical context, a country should attempt nonetheless to reach the highest possible achievements in the areas that we have mentioned on several occasions, that is: improving democratic participation; building an environment of transparency and trust; reaching an acceptable level of health and education for all; providing forms of protection against the risks of illness, old age and unemployment; as well as employment opportunities and ways to escape from poverty traps. Each country should direct its resources, according to the democratically defined priorities, to these areas of emancipation and freedom. This can be supported by a democratic process of selection of areas of technological change which would best support the extension of capabilities. This step too depends on the context and the developmental level of the country. For countries taking their first steps towards the start of this process, the *inclusive innovation* discussed in Chapter 3 can provide a point of departure. In particularly difficult contexts, it might be important to focus on technologies that are outside the circuit of international markets, but are highly valuable for the growth of the community and for building an initial base and widespread technological expertise. At more advanced stages, it may be possible to introduce strategies similar to those of Korea (see below) where the state plays a prominent role in the construction of national innovation systems and directs public resources to support the advancement of innovative companies.

The state always plays a crucial role in any development strategy. A precondition for the proper functioning of these, and other, policies is that it is not captured by any particular interest groups directing resources to purposes that are not favourable to development (see Chapter 3). For example, the prevailing interpretations of the different paths pursued by some Latin American and South-East Asian countries agree that the former have been penalised by the pressure exerted by 'regressive' rent-seekers (Khan-Blankenburg, 2009; Acemoglu and Robinson, 2012) on policy and on the functioning of the state. The distribution of political power among interest groups, public administrators and politicians has been a decisive factor in achieving different results (more positive in Asian countries than Latin America), despite substantially similar policies based on a central role of the state, and a focus on rapid acquisition of technology and an accelerated economic development. A possible reason for this outcome is 'a weak and risk adverse indigenous industrial class and a domination by foreign capital that operates in its own rather than Latin America's interest' (Khan-Blankenburg, 2009, p. 373).

The state intervention must at the same time create the right conditions to launch innovative activities that are deemed useful for local communities, in accordance with the participatory process mentioned in this chapter. There isn't a before and after. Based on a country's resources, interventions and investments should spring from the realisation that there is no growth without innovation, there is no innovation without capabilities and there are no capabilities without growth. And since there is no 'magic bullet' for development, the sequence of steps and the policy mix should be based on the principle of cautious experimentation (Lundvall et al., 2009).

### b. Attracting investments

As we have seen, innovation should be understood as the dissemination of something that is new in a given context, not in an absolute sense. Therefore, the innovation process can be of interest to any country regardless of its level of development. Developed countries will move mostly on the technological frontier, while developing countries will be able to use the available technology to adapt it to their needs or choose to explore independent paths of innovation starting from the knowledge available.

One way to access technology is to welcome foreign investment. This model has been tried by many developing countries but has not always produced the same results. Results depend on the management style of governments and on the forms of access to technology (Foreign Direct Investment – FDI, purchasing of fixed assets, licensing, venture capital agreements, etc.).

The mode of acquisition and management of technologies greatly influences the development of technological capabilities within a country. Historically the most widely used form of technology transfer has been the FDI, but developing countries have managed this flow in very different ways. On the basis of different approaches to FDI, two groups of countries can be distinguished (Amsden, 2001, 1992). The first, called *the independents*, minimally relied on FDI and focused on strengthening local enterprises, the building of a research base, internal technical expertise and various instruments of industrial policy aimed at creating national champions. A good example of this approach is Korea that made a limited use of FDI and even when the country allowed Multinational Companies (MNCs) to invest on its territory, adopted a series of control measures that enabled Korea to maximise the technological skill transfer benefiting the local economy. The second group, called *the integrationists*, consists of two sub-groups. *Active integrationists* rely on the spill-over from MNCs to access new technologies and implement policies promoting high value-added activities.

A good example of this sub-group are Brazil and Taiwan, whose strategies aimed at attracting foreign capital have sought to maximise the benefits for domestic enterprises through a series of targeted policies. The main tools used to maximise the benefits from FDI were: the commitment to buy from local businesses and a certain amount of nationally produced goods and services, as well as the obligation to transfer skills and technology to local suppliers. The second sub-group can be named *passive integrationists*. These countries do not select the type of FDI but rather try to attract it through various types of benefits: reduction of labour costs, settlement costs and tax advantages. A successful case of such strategy is Singapore, which focused almost exclusively on attracting foreign investments and pursued a number of industrial policy initiatives aimed at satisfying the needs of MNCs.

Strategies for attracting FDI have all highlighted that the acquisition of technologies through this means is far from obvious. Simple direct investment by itself is not enough. An important success factor in any strategy is the ability to invest in education, technical training and national R&D. This additional effort is the only way to create learning processes and achieve endogenous technological growth in the long run.

In this regard, the case of South Korea is interesting. In the mid-'60s this country had a per capita income similar to that of Somalia (Reinert, 2009). From the second half of that decade, the government began to encourage improvements in the field of technology in various ways. First, tax exemptions were introduced for technology imports, technological consultancies and expenses for patent royalties. A public fund was then created to finance R&D and technological innovations; at the same time, public research laboratories were launched and private research was generously funded. In addition, since the '60s Korea promoted a series of policies aiming at making the country independent from foreign technology. The most intense effort was observed in education at all levels: as early as the late '70s Korea reached a similar education level as that of many developed countries (Kim, 1997; Di Maio, 2008; Amsden, 1992, 2001). A distinctive feature of Korea in the early stages of its development was the attention given to avoid losing highly qualified youth (brain drain). To this end, the country placed the qualified personnel that had not yet found a job in private enterprises within the state apparatus and in activities related to research funded by the state (Kim, 1993). A second effort focused on increasing the technical capacity to adapt and imitate the innovations acquired from abroad. In this direction, the system protecting intellectual property of small innovations (utility model) was strongly encouraged (Kim et al., 2012; Capriati, 2013). Unlike the protection of inventions by patents, the protection of utility models was more suited to the early stages of development of the country. This is because innovation does occur in developing countries, but it is incremental, adaptive and imitative, unlike in developed countries where the prevailing innovations are on the technological frontier. The protection of small inventions can stimulate a strong process of learning by doing, while its absence may reduce the incentive to engage in the development of incremental innovations (Capriati, 2013). This protection system for small innovations enabled Korea to accumulate the capacity for technical learning, the basis for most radical inno- vations and 'new to the world' big businesses observed in recent years (Kim et al., 2012; Lee and Kim, 1993).

These experiences therefore suggest that one of the critical elements in growth and development strategies is to define viable objectives and tailor interventions to maintain a balance between economic investment and invest- ment in human development. As part of these strategies, focusing on growing internal expertise and directing intensive investments in the fields of health, environment, infrastructure and education remain central, also in so far as new markets and new technological solutions can be nurtured in these sectors.

### c. *Excessive openness to international trade penalises the accumulation of knowledge in developing countries*

The idea that developing countries can greatly benefit from opening their markets is widespread. It is based on the belief that substantial benefits can be derived from greater opportunities for distribution of their products (export) and greater access to more, better and cheaper goods (imports). These benefits are believed to ground the consolidation of the productive base and in this way, increase incomes and foster well-being in the country. This idea has emerged in recent decades and led to the opening of many large markets of developing countries and the reduction of many restrictions to international trade (reduc- tion of tariffs, quantitative limits, technical and quality standards). This phase of extreme intensification of trade has been accompanied by a new institutional framework that led to the establishment of free trade areas (EU, NAFTA, etc.); the signing of bilateral and multilateral agreements and the creation in 1995 of the WTO (World Trade Organisation) (Stiglitz, 2012).

The assumptions underlying the doctrine of free trade can be traced back to Smith, who fought against the mercantilist policies, and Ricardo, who devel- oped the theory of comparative advantage. It has recently been refined by neo- liberal economists and has provided the basis for the policies referred to above (Reinert, 2007b, 2009).

Recent studies have shown that in the absence of even one of the basic conditions of perfectly competitive markets (which is normally observed in developing countries), free trade is not desirable (Thirlwall and Pacheco-López, 2008) and that in a learning economy long-term growth and well-being can be improved through measures limiting international trade (Stiglitz and Green- wald, 2014) and protecting local industries in which learning processes can be stimulated. In recent times, the critical voices against those assumptions have become numerous, increasingly supporting trade restriction measures (Cimoli et al., 2009).

The idea that greater openness can in itself improve the conditions of devel- oping countries is both counterintuitive and contrary to historical experience (Reinert, 2007b). If the only real engines of a country's growth are knowl- edge and innovation, policies should aim at increasing the processes that facili- tate learning, which are almost entirely concretely realised in the workplace.

On-the-job learning obviously needs time to materialise, hence, if policies increase the probability of job loss and do not protect existing employment, they will never stimulate the processes needed to broaden well-being and employment. In fact, in most cases the *premature* opening of the markets in a developing economy kills the existing fragile manufacturing activities, making it impossible to consolidate the learning processes (Reinert, 2003, 2007a, 2007b, 2009). The fact that liberalisation does not in itself ensure growth has been confirmed by the existence of huge disparities observed also within developed countries and within different regions of countries that have long been united. For Reinert (2007a) '[f]rom the unification of Italy in the nineteenth century to the integration of Mongolia and Peru in the 1990s, historical experience shows that free trade between nations of very different levels of development tends to destroy the most efficient industries in the least efficient countries' (p. 202). The premature competitive pressure on the economies of developing countries has impacted wages. These have fallen because companies subject to competition needed to reduce their costs, as they are not yet able to rely on the growth of technological potential. This strategy however, has deleterious macroeconomic effects: it leads to the curtailment of an important component of the demand – consumption – and, in this way, also to a reduction of production capacity and employment opportunities.

The *timing* of the opening of an economy is thus very important: putting an infant industry under competitive pressure at a stage when it is building its foundations in terms of knowledge and internal and external relations to production activities can be dangerous and can condemn the economy to de-industrialisation and the reduction of its growth potential. Persisting, in the case of the developed economies, with an attitude of market closure may, on the contrary, prevent capitalising on opportunities for growth through exports. Therefore, in this case, as in others when dealing with industrial policy issues (see above), the measure and timing of interventions are crucial (Reinert, 2007a).

## Notes

1 As explained in Chapter 2, functionings refer to the achievements, such as being able to have a good health, be adequately nourished or have an adequate shelter.
2 Although in countries like the United States, Britain, France and many others, the expenditure on R&D in the military is by far greater than those in non-military applications
3 Perhaps, in the future, it will also be possible to endorse this approach for military projects.

## References

Abraham, J. and Sheppard, J. 1997. Democracy, Technocracy, and the Secret State of Medicines Control: Expert and Nonexpert Perspectives, *Science Technology & Human Values*, 22(2), 139–167.
Acemoglu, A. and Robinson, J. 2012. *Why Nations Fail. The Origins of Power, Prosperity, and Poverty*, New York, Crown Publishers.
Alkire, S. 2002. *Valuing Freedoms: Sen's Capability Approach and Poverty Reduction*, Oxford, Oxford University Press.

Amsden, A. 1992. *Asia's Next Giant: South Korea and Late Industrialization*, New York and Oxford: Oxford University Press.

Amsden, A. 2001. *The Rise of the Rest: Challenges to the West from Late Industrializing Economies*, Oxford, Oxford University Press.

Amsden, A. 2009. Nationality of Firm Ownership in Developing Countries: Who Should 'Crowd Out' Whom in Imperfect Markets? In: Cimoli et al. 2009, 409–423.

Atkinson, A.B. 2015. *Inequality: What Can Be Done?* Cambridge, MA, London, UK, Harvard University Press.

Biggeri, M. and Ferrannini, A. 2014. Opportunity Gap Analysis: Procedures and Methods for Applying the Capability Approach in Development Initiatives, *Journal of Human Development and Capabilities*, 15(1), 60–78.

Biggeri, M., Ferrannini, A. and Mauro, V. 2011. *L'analisi dello sviluppo umano e sostenibile a livello locale*, Dossier UmanamENTE, Firenze.

Capriati, M. 2013. Gli indicatori di innovazione a livello territoriale. In: *L'Industria* n. 1, 55–86.

Castells, M. and Himanen, P. 2002. *The Information Society and the Welfare State: The Finnish Model*, Oxford, Oxford University Press.

Chiappero-Marinetti, E. and Roche, J.M. 2009. Operationalization of the capability approach, from theory to practice: a review of techniques and empirical applications, in Chiappero-Martinetti E. (ed.), *Debating global society: reach and limits of the capability approach*, Fondazione Feltrinelli, Feltrinellil Editore, Milano, pp. 157–201.

Cimoli, M., Dosi, G. and Stiglitz, J.E. (eds.) 2009. *Industrial Policy and Development: The Political Economy of Capabilities Accumulation*, Oxford, Oxford University Press.

Di Maio, M. 2008. Industrial Policies in Developing Countries: History and Perspectives. Working Papers, N° 48, Macerata, University of Macerata.

Dong, A. 2012. Beyond Participation: A Capabilities Approach to Urban Development in Sydney. In: Panzironi and Gelber, 2012.

Drèze, J. and Sen, A. 2002. *India: Development and Participation*, Oxford, Oxford University Press.

Ely, A., Van Zwanenberg, P. and Stirling, A. 2011. New Models of Technology Assessment for Development, Working Paper, STEP Centre.

Fernández-Baldor, Á., Boni, A., Lillo, P. and Hueso, A. 2014. Are Technological Projects Reducing Social Inequalities and Improving People's Well-Being? A Capability Approach Analysis of Renewable Energy-Based Electrification Projects in Cajamarca, Peru, *Journal of Human Development and Capabilities*, 15(1), 13–27.

Ferrero Y de Loma-Osorio, G. and Zepeda, C.S. 2014. Rethinking Development Management Methodology: Towards a "Process Freedoms Approach", *Journal of Human Development and Capabilities*, 15(1), 28–46.

Foray, D., Mowery, D.C. and Nelson, R.R. 2012. Public R&D and Social Challenges: What Lessons From Mission R&D Programs? *Research Policy*, 41, 1697–1702.

Foren Network. 2002. *A Practical Guide to Regional Foresight*, European Commission Research Directorate General.

Frediani, A.A., Boni, A. and Gasper, D. 2014. Approaching Development Projects From a Human Development and Capability Perspective, *Journal of Human Development and Capabilities*, 15(1), 1–12.

Georghiou, L., Harper, J.C., Keenan, M. and Popper, R. (eds.) 2008. *The Handbook of Technology Foresight. Concept and Practice.* Cheltenham, UK; Northampton, MA, Edward Elgar.

Hirschman, A. O. 1967. *Development Project Observed*, Washington, D.C., USA, The Brooking Institution.

Khan, M. and Blankenburg, S. 2009. The Political Economy of Industrial Policy in Asia and Latin America. In: Cimoli et al. 2009, 336–377.

Kim, L. 1993. National System of Industrial Innovation: Dynamics of Capability Building in Korea. In: Nelson, R.R. (ed.), *National Systems of Innovation: A Comparative Analysis*, Oxford, Oxford University Press, 357–83.

Kim, L. 1997. *Imitation to Innovation: The Dynamics of Korea's Technological Learning*, Boston, MA, Harvard Business School Press.

Kim, Y.K., Lee, K., Park, W.G. and Choo, K. 2012. Appropriate Intellectual Property Protection and Economic Growth in Countries at Different Levels of Development, *Research Policy*, 41, 358–375.

Kleinman, D.J. 2005. *Science and Technology in Society; From Biotechnology to the Internet*, Malden, MA: Blackwell Publishing.

Lee, K. and Kim, Y.K. 1993. IPR and Technological Catch-Up in Korea. In: Odagiri, H., Goto, A., Sunami, A. and Nelson, R.R. (eds.), *Intellectual Property Right, Development, and Catch-Up: An International Comparative Study*, Oxford, Oxford University Press.

Lundvall, B.A. 2002. *Innovation, Growth and Social Cohesion: The Danish Model*, Cheltenham, UK, Northampton, MA, Edward Elgar.

Lundvall, B.A. and Johnson, B. 1994. The Learning Economy, *Journal of Industry Studies*, 1, 23–42.

Lundvall, B.A., Joseph, K.J., Chaminade, C. and Vang, J. 2009. *Handbook of Innovation System and Developing Countries: Building Domestic Capabilities in a Global setting*, Cheltenham, UK, Northampton, Edward Elgar Publishing Ltd.

Mazzucato, M. 2013. *The Entrepreneurial State: Debunking the Public vs. Private Myth in Risk and Innovation*, London, Anthem.

Mazzucato, M. and Penna, C.C.R. 2015. *Beyond Market Failures: The Market Creating and Shaping Roles of State Investment Banks*, Institute for New Economic Thinking, Working Paper No. 7.

Miettinen, R. 2013. *Innovation, Human Capabilities, and Democracy: Towards an Enabling Welfare State*, Oxford, New York, Oxford University Press.

Minsky, H.P. 1993. *Community Development Banks: An Idea in Search of Substance*. Hyman, P. Minsky Archive, Paper 278.

Nelson, R. R. 1974. Intellectualizing about the Moon-Ghetto Metaphor: A Study of the Current Malaise of Rational Analysis of Social Problems, *Policy Sciences*, 5, 376–414.

Nelson, R.R. 2011. The Moon and the Ghetto Revisited, *Science and Public Policy*, 38(9), 681–690.

Nussbaum, Martha, C. 2011. *Creating Capabilities: The Human Development Approach*, Cambridge, MA, London, UK, Harvard University Press.

Ocampo, J.A., Jomo, K.S. and Khan, S. (eds.) 2007. *Policy Matters: Economic and Social Policies to Sustain Equitable Development*, London, ZED.

Oosterlaken, I. and van den Hoven, J. 2012. *The Capability Approach, Technology and Design*, Berlin, Springer.

Panzironi, F. and Gelber, K. (eds.) 2012. *The Capability Approach: Development Practice and Public Policy in the Asia-Pacific Region*, London and New York, Routledge.

Parayil, G. (ed.) 2000. *Kerala: The Development Experience. Reflection on Sustainability and Replicability*, London and New York, Zed Books.

Reinert, E.S. 2003. Increasing Poverty in a Globalised World: Marshall Plans and Morgenthau Plans as Mechanism of Polarisation of World Incomes. In: Chang, H. (ed.), *Rethinking Development Economics*, London, Athen, 453–478.

Reinert, E.S. 2007a. Development and Social Goals: Balancing Aid and Development to Prevent 'Welfare Colonialism'. In: Ocampo et al. 2007, 193–221.

Reinert, E.S. 2007b. *How Rich Countries Got Rich . . . and Why Poor Countries Stay Poor*, London, Constable.

Reinert, E.S. 2009. Emulation Versus Comparative Advantage: Competing and Complementary Principles in the History of Economic Policy. In: Cimoli et al. 2009, 79–106.

Robeyns, I. 2006. The Capability Approach in Practice, *The Journal of Political Philosophy*, 14(3), 351–376.

Sclove, R. 1995. *Democracy and Technology*, New York, Guildford Press.

Sclove, R. 2010. *Reinventing Technology Assessment: A 21st Century Model*, Washington, DC, Science and Technology Innovation Program, Woodrow Wilson International Center for Scholars.

STEPS Centre. 2010. *Innovation, Sustainability, Development: A New Manifesto*, Brighton, University of Sussex.

Stiglitz, J.E. 2012. *The Price of Inequality*, New York, London, W.W. Norton and Company.

Stiglitz, J.E. and Greenwald, B.C. 2014. *Creating a Learning Society*, New York, Columbia University Press.

Stirling, A. 2014. Towards Innovation Democracy? Participation, Responsibility and Precaution in the Politics of Science and Technology, in Annual Report of the Government Chief Scientific Adviser.

Subrahmanian, K.K. and Abdul Azeez, E. 2000. *Industrial Growth in Kerala: Trends and Explanations*, Centre for Development Studies, Thiruvananthapuram, India.

Thirlwall, A.P. and Pacheco-López, P. 2008. *Trade Liberalisation and The Poverty of Nations*, Cheltenham, Edward Elgar.

UNDP (United Nations Development Programme) 2010. *Human Development Report 2010: The Real Wealth of Nations: Pathways to Human Development*, New York, UNDP.

Yearley, S. 2000. Making Systematic Sense at Public Discontents With Expert Knowledge: Two Analytical Approaches and 2 Case Studies, *Public Understanding of Science*, 9, 105–122.

# 9 Macroeconomic policies for human development and innovation

Each macroeconomic policy affects the distribution of resources between individuals, social groups, sectors and regions. Governments play a key role in directing the economy, encouraging innovation and promoting people's well-being, both with regards to what they do and what they don't. They can choose to tax income rather than consumption, tax real assets rather than financial ones; they may spend resources on health, education and infrastructure rather than public works that benefit only contractors or weapons; they may choose to intervene or not to intervene in the currency market and trade with foreign countries. The ways in which the state influences the economy are many, and analysing all of them to grasp their impacts on human development and innovation is not possible in this book.

As I indicated in the first part of the book, some interconnections are nevertheless relevant to development strategies. First, macroeconomic policies affect the economic cycle and therefore people's incomes and their employment opportunities; second, they guarantee an adequate access to basic services such as health, education and protection from risks. Furthermore, they can be modulated as to promote or hinder a reasonably equal distribution of income among citizens. In this chapter, we will analyse *the stabilisation policies of the cycle* and in particular, the importance they have on employment, learning and innovation (Section 9.1). We will then take a closer look at how public policies affect *instrumental freedoms* that have been discussed in the first part of the book (Section 9.2), and then finish with some guidance regarding *taxation* (Section 9.3).

## 9.1 Stabilisation policies

Macroeconomic stabilisation policies allow countries and regions to maintain employment and income at levels consistent with economic factors that a nation or region is endowed with. In this way, these policies can avert bankruptcies and layoffs affecting enterprises and workers. This allows the learning and innovation processes that are the engine of change to flourish, led by active workers. The first important link between macroeconomic policies, human development and innovation therefore is the link between *the business cycle and employment*. Avoiding high unemployment means both guaranteeing income, and therefore maintaining the means necessary to achieve pre-set life projects, and avoiding interruptions in on-the-job learning, and thus preventing a waste of knowledge. Let us analyse this relationship by starting to look at employment.

### a. Employment

Why is employment central to the processes of innovation and human development?

To answer this question, I will start by quoting a work by A. Sen (1975) entitled 'Employment, Technology and Development' in which the author begins his argument by listing three aspects of employment:

1    *the income aspect*, employment gives an income to the employed;
2    *the production aspect*: employment yields an output;
3    *the recognition aspect*, employment gives a person the recognition of being engaged in something worth his while. (p. 5)

The income and production aspects are the most discussed and refined in the economic analysis. The third aspect is discussed more within the field of sociology but has an important role for human development.

My framework, however, sees the three aspects of work as equally crucial for the functioning of the interrelationships between innovation, human development and growth. Let us examine the reasons why.

The first aspect, that of *income*, has a role both on the micro and the macro levels. For the individual worker, the income received is an important instrument of control over material resources that allow him/her to live a dignified life, and represents (or should represent) the recognition of his/her skills/ knowledge/commitment in doing the jobs. An adequate income, therefore, impacts both the efficiency of workers and their material well-being (ILO, 2013). For the economy as a whole, the income earned by workers generates consumption, which is the main component of aggregate demand. According to the Keynesian analysis, the countercyclical policies must aim primarily at setting into motion the income-expenditure mechanism by increasing aggregate demand and employment. Again, adequate incomes have positive effects on the overall economy, lower incomes tend to undermine its sustainability.

The ability of the economy to grow depends in turn on the innovation forces and technological change. In this context, the work and the workers, in their double function of users and producers, are at the core of the learning by doing, using and interacting processes. Therefore, the second aspect of the *work as 'input'* (or perhaps as *'the actor of production'*) is at the root of change and learning and innovation processes. Without workers who learn and develop routines (Nelson and Winter, 1982), organisational processes and interactions (Holm and Lorenz, 2015; Leoni R., 2012; Lundvall and Lorenz, 2010), that act and share institutions, the very substance of change would be impossible.

The third aspect, that of *recognition*, is more related to human development. Provocatively, Sen (1975) wondered 'Is employment a benefit or a cost?' (P. 81).

Considering work to embody only the first two aspects (i.e., income and production) would in fact be a sterile and 'schizophrenic' exercise: work is helpful because it allows workers to receive an income, but it is a cost that must be faced to organise production. In a judgment based on society as a whole, which of the two aspects prevails? To answer this question, focusing only on production and income is not enough. It is important to also consider work recognition. In fact, compensation asked for work does not make occupation merely a cost. Similarly, it cannot be viewed positively only in so far as it allows access to important means of support or is at the centre of the learning process. Work must also be considered valuable for a number of reasons that make it important in itself. These factors include: personal dignity that is established by participating in a production activity in collaboration with others; the ability to use one's knowledge and skill, sensitivity and creativity; as well as recognition from one's community as a person able to play a useful role. In fact, with reference to the recognition aspect, work increases the individual's self-esteem and the esteem that others have towards the individuals who work. Looking at the occupation from this angle, an answer can be given to the previous provocative question by Sen, and it can be understood how important it is, economically, socially and humanly speaking, to set full employment as a priority.

But this broad view must take into consideration that 'each economic system seems to produce its own values, its own illusions, its own ideology' (Sen, 1975, p. 39). Thus, 'unemployment is a state of being without fruitful work and the perception of fruitfulness of work is, to a large extent, a result of social conditioning' (p. 40). Much depends also on social status; representatives of upper classes, for example, can consider paid work not suited to their social position; for those who have only their job to survive, the lack of work is not only lack of income but also a form of marginalisation and dishonour. In societies where women do not have a significant role in the formal labour market and are entrusted exclusively to manage the family, the work done in this position has no market relevance, although in effect it is both important and strenuous.

Within this realm, there is also the case of people who have an income but do not actually consider themselves employed because what they do is a fall-back, i.e., a job that is underpaid and performed only due to the absence of alternatives. This phenomenon is widespread (and fast growing) in contemporary economies and calls into question the idea of work that prevailed in these societies until a few decades ago. According to the three analysed dimensions, these are jobs insufficiently paid to ensure the necessary means to a decent life; allow cost advantages to employers but offer few learning opportunities in the workplace; and fail in the task of recognising a worker's social role and dignity.

Today, the idea that a working labour market, like other markets, should make the adjustment of the equilibrium wage easier, is very much alive; we must ensure that this measure tracks supply and demand with maximum flexibility. As a result, the prevailing idea is that the real cause of unemployment is the rigidity of wages. The policy recipe that follows involves the elimination of minimum levels of pay, overcoming forms of monopsony on the labour supply front (weakening of trade unions), the individualisation of contractual relationships and the dismantling of rules and protections in labour market.

In fact, adequate wages and learning processes, collaborative ways of organising work and innovation, social recognition and personal gratification are phenomena linked to each other (Bassanini and Ernst, 2002; Lorenz and Valeyre, 2005; Lorenz, 2015). A labour market that is mainly precarious and unbalanced in favour of the entrepreneur, with few staff unions, with ample freedom of dismissal and low wages, will hardly generate the learning processes and organisational structures benefiting innovation (Lundvall and Lorenz,2006, 2010, 2014). Underpaid workers, employed in activities that they do not deem appropriate to their aspirations, will not feel gratified, and this will reduce the opportunities to interact in the innovation systems, and will inhibit the proper functioning of the institutions. In these cases, the work is treated as 'cost' to be minimised, rather than as 'investment' to implement. Remuneration does not reward skills and does not produce emulation and stimulation to improve collectively and personally, but only frustration and low motivation (Lorenz and Valeyre, 2005).

There is also another, equally important, aspect of the matter, which affects the balance of power between social groups: a well-paid job and working arrangements encourage participatory learning and *agency* of individuals as well as their awareness as collective individuals. This awareness can come in various organised forms (trade unions are the most important and the most 'traditional', but not the only one) and give voice to typically under-represented individuals (Atkinson, 2015, see proposal 2, on the subject). This shift of power relations can facilitate choices characterised by greater equity: progressive taxation; higher taxation of assets, inheritance and donations tax, reduction of indirect taxation; increased spending in education and health; greater social spending and interventions to fight poverty. These policies have a major impact on instrumental freedoms, on the reduction of inequality and the virtuous circles which I have discussed in this book.

Therefore, work, as analysed in its three aspects, plays an important role in policies favourable to human development, innovation and growth. Hence, maintaining a high level of employment should be one of the central objectives of the stabilisation policies of the economic cycle. This idea, however, although in some ways it seems to be stating the obvious, did not have many supporters in recent years.

### b. The economic cycle and restrictive policies

Since the late '70s, economic policies that prioritise stabilising prices, wage flexibility and balanced government budget have been established in most countries, considering in reality employment a secondary factor among set targets (Krugman, 2012, Stiglitz, 2016). These policies have been widely applied and are still widely accepted by economists and governments of many countries, central banks and international organisations. The basic idea is that the task of an economic policy is to ensure some 'structural' conditions, and once those are defined, the maximum social welfare is assured by the free operation of markets.

These policies have been implemented within an international context characterised by a high freedom of movement of capital and goods (Stiglitz, 2003). This resulted in a strong limitation of autonomy in economic policy decisions, especially those that are expansionary and pro-growth in the case of developing countries and regions, and a reduction in wages, especially for medium- and low-skilled jobs in the case of developed countries (Ivanova, 2017).

Wage flexibility is an outcome of economic policy choices but is also the cause of an amplification of negative economic cycles. In the event of unemployment, wages are reduced in nominal terms and this, according to the Keynesian approach, leads to a reduction in aggregate demand and a further push into unemployment. Even though prices are reduced to the same extent, which means that the real wages remain unchanged, an amplification effect may arise from the fact that the indebted entities – families, enterprises, state – must repay debts in nominal terms, the extent of which remains greater than the perceived income. This may cause chain bankruptcies with losses both in terms of human capital and organisational and entrepreneurial skills. Governments see the relative and absolute scale of its debt and deficit widening and face this eventuality by reducing spending, especially in the social field: unemployment benefits are reduced or the range of beneficiaries is reduced; the pension system goes from being determined on the basis of the definition of benefits to being determined on the basis of contributions; public health services are reduced and a significant proportion of these are paid on the basis of premiums; public education is reduced and increases in the fees for enrolment are introduced (Stiglitz, 2012a, 2012b).

The ultimate rationale of all of these interventions with respect to public spending is that *the protection of social risks is gradually reduced*, leaving more scope for private protection (Stiglitz, 2012a). Therefore, this leads to a greater role for private insurance for health and pension coverage and for the introduction of vouchers to choose between private and public school (which, with lower funding becomes 'less competitive' compared to the private one). This results in the inability of the weaker sections of the population to afford access to private forms of risk insurance, thus suffering mostly from the consequences of these policies. With respect to the macroeconomic dynamics, the reduction in spending results in a further reduction in aggregate demand, an aggravation of the economic cycle and a subsequent rise in unemployment. The set of orthodox macroeconomic policies reduces also the potential of *automatic stabilisers*: the reduction of the progressiveness of the tax system mainly through lower tax rates on higher incomes and the decreasing taxation on assets and on capital gains; pension moving to a contributory system; the reduction of social protection forms and contributions to families. All this has made the economy more vulnerable to shocks and, for the most vulnerable citizens, the effects of recessions have become more burdensome (Stiglitz, 2012b; Krugman, 2012).

Structurally restrictive fiscal policies have been associated with the extreme *financialisation of the economy*. The latter has taken shape as a result of two major processes that also began at the end of the '70s, and that led to the financial crisis of 2007: deregulation of the financial sector and liberalisation of capital movements (Jarsulic, 2013; Kotz, 2014 Epstein, 2015;Vercelli, 2013). Deregulation has produced a hypertrophy of the financial sector both because practices with higher risk factor were not limited, and because the recurrent cases of rescue in recent decades has created a sense of security within the financial entities, encouraging them to introduce more risky investments. In addition to this, we have experienced the transformation of the banking sector. In recent decades, banks have become increasingly dependent on short-term financing and began focusing more on investing on their own in the financial market and increasing services to customers. As a result, this created a push towards more speculative financial activities and an inability by the banks to provide patient capital that is necessary for development (Mazzucato, 2013; Lazonik and Mazzucato, 2013). One of the most important effects of this financial liberalisation is that it has greatly reduced the degree of freedom of macroeconomic policies. The expansionary policies based on reducing interest rates and/or increasing public spending underwent many limitations because, following the liberalisation of capital movements, these manoeuvres could now influence rapid capital outflows and speculative trading on the exchange rate, causing harmful effects on the entire economy. Countries with a greater need for capital have been forced to implement pro-cyclical policies with the aim of attracting capital to their country: in times of recession in order to attract capital, they need to maintain a high rate of interest and a strong currency, the opposite of what is needed for an economic recovery. Furthermore, the flow of capital is particularly sensitive to inflation levels, and this forces governments to favour inflation targeting at the expense of policies that prioritise job creation and stimulate aggregate demand. The extreme mobility of capital in search of profitable investments also stimulates wage restraint policies. Entrepreneurs threaten to invest elsewhere, i.e., in countries with low labour costs, and this demands more caution from workers when demanding wages and in some cases, even a reduction in pay in order to become competitive with workers in countries with lower labour costs. All this in turn causes a reduction in demand and a reduction in tax revenue, exacerbating the deficit and prompting governments to further reduce spending. What occurs in these cases is a sort of 'austerity trap'.

### c. The effects of cycle instability and of restrictive policies on innovation

For some authors (Krugman, 2013; Stiglitz, 2012a), the economic crisis that was experienced in the United States in late 2007 is the result of the *extreme volatility of the economic cycle*, caused by the emergence in recent years of the aforementioned economic policies. This has had a negative impact on the levels of unemployment in many countries and especially on the living conditions of the most vulnerable population. Furthermore, it has also impacted the learning and innovation processes.

### Demand

The initial impact of the instability of the cycle accompanied by restrictive policies is observed in the decline of the stimulus to invest and develop new products and new processes, originating from a growing and not stagnant demand. Other factors being equal, a growing market favours the introduction of innovations (according to the traditional school of thought, from Smith to Young, Verdoon, Kaldor and Myrdal) and reduces the perception of risk inherent in starting a new enterprise. A stagnant and unstable demand induces adverse effects of uncertainty and an aversion to business risk. In this regard, the state can either take up a direct role to stimulate, through public procurement, the sectors in which the externalities generated by knowledge are higher (typically in manufacturing industries and technological services) or an indirect role by investing in infrastructure, materials and intangibles, that can facilitate the introduction and dissemination of technological innovations.

### The learning processes

Economic policies that expose countries to a high instability have negative effects on learning and innovation (Stiglitz and Greenwald, 2014). The generation of knowledge that triggers increases in productivity and fosters innovation is undoubtedly cumulative. This feature depends on the existence of permanent organisations and people who are continuously involved in this process and make the flow of knowledge possible (Nelson and Winter, 1982). Stability and continuity benefit the learning processes. Recessions, on the other hand, are situations in which companies and institutions, where the learning processes occur, die, and with them, the knowledge accumulated until then[1] also dies. An economic recovery does not guarantee the return of companies and institutions with the same capacity. What has been destroyed as a result of a recession is lost and can hardly be recovered.

In this respect, it is good to distinguish between the process of 'creative destruction' generated by the introduction of innovations and the effects of macroeconomic instability. In fact, '[w]hile there may be some virtues in the process of "creative destruction" that is associated with innovation, the destruction that occurs in the process of cyclical fluctuations is not offset by any creation, and the anticipation of future volatility dampens investment in learning and R&D' (Stiglitz and Greenwald, 2015, p. 98). A macroeconomic policy that keeps the product and employment growth reasonably stable is the best ally of the accumulation of knowledge processes.

### Increased marginalisation and social exclusion

Among the workers who are negatively affected by the impacts of the economic downturn, the highest burden is carried by the *least qualified*. This occurs because the companies that need to reduce staff choose in the first instance to lay off the least-qualified personnel and retain the most-qualified employees (for as long as they can), both because more investment was channelled into their training and because it is more expensive to replace them. Long periods of unemployment cause further impoverishment of the human capital of the already low-skilled workers. Such loss has negative effects on the economy's resilience and leads to a further deterioration of the capabilities of individuals.

In situations of persistent economic crisis, the phenomenon of *discouragement among workers* adds to the jobs losses. Discouraged workers are the unemployed, especially women and young people, who, discouraged by the situation of the labour market, stop looking for work. They judge, in fact, that it is not realistic to find employment at a time when their husbands, elder brothers or parents lose theirs. These workers mainly fall back on abnormal extensions of training (in the case of young people) or the care of the family (the case of women). They find themselves facing a situation without prospects. In such conditions there is less optimism, less desire to work or invest in oneself and in one's community, the necessary ingredients for any social and economic change.

Rising unemployment and the reduction of social protection lead to increased inequalities and a gap between *the haves and the have nots (the affluent and the marginalised segments of the population)*. This is also accompanied by a progressive shrinking of the middle class. This gap has important consequences. First, it will limit the ability to increase one's knowledge. Access to higher levels of education will be more and more exclusive, and fewer and fewer persons will be able to train in the best universities. Second, it will limit access to better health care and protection from risks to those segments of population who will be able to pay for these services. In general, the capacity to learn will be restricted to a privileged circle, not always corresponding to the best individuals. This will reduce the number of potential innovators, best managers, best policy makers and those forming the bedrock of innovation systems. Limited access to higher levels of knowledge and health impacts the innovation potential. Small and closed systems find it difficult to survive in the long run as they cannot benefit from the necessary turnover.

The growth of marginalised segments of the population reduces another important factor: the relational/social capital; this undermines participation in public affairs and in communities, and also undermines the agency of subjects; it reduces the possibility of building innovation systems powered by the learning through interaction processes and participation.

### Risk privatisation

Insurance markets are far from being perfect, and even in the most advanced economies many risks cannot be insured by the markets. Indeed, when a risk has an appropriate insurance coverage, the contracts involve high transaction costs. To overcome these limitations (failures) of insurance markets, many countries developed *social security* covering various risks as in the case of illness, old age, unemployment and death. In recent decades, the extreme instability of the economic cycles together with policies aimed at reducing public spending, are increasing the sense of insecurity of individuals. In fact, public forms of insurance are shrinking, giving way to the privatisation of risks. In a system in which information asymmetries prevail and subjects are by nature averse to risk, this privatisation reduces the propensity for business and innovation (Stiglitz, 2012a).

For example, a young man who has a good idea will have more qualms about risking to implement it if he knows that in case of a possible failure he will not find an adequate system of protection. On the other hand, he will have more incentives to take risks if he knows that, in case of failure the state will guarantee him a minimum income, a contribution for housing, healthcare, training courses to upgrade his expertise, etc. If such protections are, as it occurs in several countries, only partially guaranteed, or if an individual is an employee in a public or private organisation, then that person will have an incentive to find a job as a hired employee, allowing him to access these protections instead of risking to start his/her own initiative.

### d. Expansionary policies for full employment and stabilisation of the business cycle

For these reasons, macroeconomic policies should set full employment at the core of their objectives. As it is known, a decrease or increase in GDP has an impact on unemployment: negative cycles tend to be accompanied by phases of increased unemployment rate, positive cycles tend to reduce unemployment and bring the economy closer to full employment. An economic policy that has as its main objective making use of its workforce to its fullest potential should aim at stabilising the economy, trying to bring aggregate demand in line with this target. This is the only policy available to stimulate innovation and ensure a dignified standard of public services to the population. This leads, in the case of recession, to interventions of an expansionary nature on the monetary and fiscal front. The monetary policy, however, is effective only in the short run to cool the economy in case of inflationary flare-ups, but ineffective to foster growth in recessionary situations. This is because, due to stagnant demand and low profit opportunities, companies are reluctant to invest even in the face of very low interest rates. In these cases, an increase in public expenditure is the most effective remedy.

> *The State will have to exercise a guiding influence on the propensity to consume partly through its scheme of taxation, partly by fixing the rate of interest, and partly, perhaps, in other ways. Furthermore, it seems unlikely that the influence of banking policy on rate of interest will be sufficient by itself to determine an optimum rate of investment. I conceive, therefore, that a somewhat comprehensive socialisation of investment will prove the only means of securing an approximation to full employment; though this need not exclude all manner of compromises and of devices by which public authority will co-operate with private initiative. But beyond this no obvious case is made out for a system of State Socialism which could embrace most of the economic life of the community. It is not the ownership of the instruments of production which is important for State to assume. If the State is able to determine the aggregate amount of resources devoted to augmenting the instruments and the basic rate of reward to those who own them, it will have accomplished all that is necessary. Moreover, the necessary measures of socialization can be introduced gradually and without a break in the general tradition of society.*
>
> (Keynes, 1936, 377–8)

Keynes thus suggested that it was up to the state to do what companies alone could not do. He was assigning the state a central role, in particular with respect to funding public works for roads, railways, houses. Today we could add land use, green energy, knowledge and training, broadband, rehabilitation of the suburbs to this list of responsibilities. Such public investments have the capacity to *directly* increase demand (which does not occur, as it is known, with the reduction of taxes and/or increase in transfers to households), *directly* engage a large number of people who are out of work and *distribute income*, which would help to further increase demand.

This, in a nutshell, is the essence of the Keynesian economic policy that found consensus among academics and leaders of the developed world between the '40s and the '70s of the last century and that allowed high growth levels, low inflation and full employment. But in recent decades, other policies, those referred to earlier, have prevailed.

Yet an alternative route appears to be more sensible and capable of bringing benefits to the entire system. Today, more than in other phases of the world economy, thanks to the convergent action in expanding the money supply by major central banks of the developed world, interest rates are extraordinarily low. This advantage is not able to stimulate private investments until the economic recovery will convince companies that the demand is sufficiently strong to require additional investment. As it is known, however, even when the signs of recovery are sufficiently encouraging, companies will not make new investments and will not hire new workers until they put to work all the underutilised resources of capital and labour. Therefore, the only entity that can take advantage of extremely low interest rates is the state. In many countries, because of under-investment in public investments over the past decades, the margins for intervention are extensive and in some cases action is even urgent: environment, land, urban planning, hydro-geological balance, infrastructure, research and education as well as health; many countries lag behind in many of these areas, but they could catch up with large investment plans (Mazzucato, 2015; Mazzucato-Wray, 2015). These investments would give impetus to the demand both in the short and medium term, increasing income, employment and investment, and thus also tax revenues.

Expansionary macroeconomic policies would be a possible solution to the problem of unemployment even in the most indebted countries. Normally, what is prescribed to such countries is the austerity measures as the only way to reduce the debt/GDP ratio. This prescription emerges from the parallel between good family management and good administration of the public budget. It argues that, just as for a family that borrows, its debt to a third party (usually a bank) cannot go beyond a certain limit; the state too has a limit to its debt, beyond which it threatens a collapse. There is no common view as to what this limit should be (Reinhart-Rogoff, 2009), although in some cases, as in the Monetary Union, it has been set and applied. This association between good management of family income and the state budget overlooks, of course, the fact that the prescriptions for the macro economy cannot always be derived from individual behaviour. The sum of individual behaviours can lead to paradoxes (the best known is that of savings). The state also issues currency, something that the family cannot do, and above all, the social and economic value of state investment exceeds the cost of capital employed and therefore cannot be decided only on the basis of financial considerations. The idea that assimilates the behaviour of a 'good family man' with those of the state, however, has taken hold, especially in Europe, and has brought governments to reduce public spending in case of deficits and high debt. This prescription is particularly dangerous in recession. In fact, when the economy slows down a gap between the expenditures (growing, because of the social spending needed to help needy families) and revenues (decreasing, due to income reduction) is automatically created. In these situations, the response is to deal with the deficit by reducing public spending (and/or increasing tax revenues). This response obviously aggravates the recession and, in this way, the debt of the state.

With well-targeted expansionary policies in the medium term, the debt/GDP ratio can be reduced in three ways by: (a) increasing the denominator of the ratio; (b) increasing tax revenues, following an increase in incomes; and (c) reducing spending on subsidies for the unemployed and assistance to low-income groups, i.e., that part of the public transfers, which increases in cases of economic crisis. Furthermore, each fiscal intervention (such as greater progressivity of taxation, taxes on capital and on capital gains, inheritance and gift tax, lower taxes on consumption) shifts the tax burden from low incomes, with high propensity to consume, to high incomes with low propensity to consume, broadens the potential multiplier effect of expansionary policies and in this way, the production and employment.

Another way of reducing the debt burden is by stimulating inflation. Because of the recession associated with pro-cyclical fiscal policies, the economy of developed countries shows instead a dangerous tendency towards deflation, occurring despite the expansionary monetary policies pursued speedily by the Federal Reserve, the Bank of Japan and belatedly, the European Central Bank (ECB). An inflation rate of around 4% (Krugman, 2012) could act as a stimulus to the activities of enterprises and help ease the debt burden, both private and public. Achieving this goal, however, would require the restoration or the development of income indexing systems, since the income will otherwise be subject to a dangerous loss of purchasing power.

## 9.2 Policies for instrumental freedom

### a. Macroeconomics and human development

The dialogue between macroeconomics and human development has always been difficult (Nayyar, 2012). This is because macroeconomic targets do not include the typical HD targets; furthermore, being more concerned with the accomplishments and freedoms of individuals, human development is less interested in the mechanisms of macroeconomics, while recognising the importance of the impact these policies have. This may be the consequence of the time horizons in the two schools of thought: in the case of the macro economy, the emphasis is on the short term, whereas in the case of HD transformations occur over a long term. All these differences, though, arise from the different foci of the two approaches: macroeconomics is interested in the means (income, consumption, investment, etc.), while HD focuses on the objectives of the individuals' well-being (Nayyar, 2012).

As elaborated in this work, the absence of clear long-term objectives (or the assertion of incorrect goals) misguides the short-term policies in a manner that is contrary to the well-being of people and to the economic and social mechanisms of change; therefore, the inclusion of an ethical dimension within macroeconomic policies, and the inclusion of short-term mechanisms in the capability approach, can lead to interesting results.

One interesting area of focus concerns inequality, which, as we have seen, affects not only the so-called developing countries, but also the developed ones. Inequality is most often interpreted as the result of two phenomena characterising our era: globalisation and technological change (Atkinson, 2015; Franzini and Pianta, 2016). These are two unstoppable forces which the economies and policies must address, and which, by their nature, lead to a gap between the haves and the have nots. As I have argued so far, inequality seems rather to be the result of economic policies that, for at least the past thirty years, have altered the availability of opportunities between groups of citizens, deepening the differences in well-being (Piketty, 2014; Stiglitz, 2012a; Atkinson, 2015; World Bank, 2006). Confirmation of this interpretation can be derived from the empirical part in Chapters 5 and 6, where we observed that the same economic phase, characterised by globalisation and technological change, had different impacts on countries with similar level of wealth: leading to more inequality in countries such as Italy, Great Britain and France, and less inequality in countries such as Sweden, Denmark and Finland.[2] The distribution of the costs and benefits of change depends on political decisions that are made within countries; policies may either deepen or mitigate the differences.

As we have seen when discussing the capability approach's take on inequality (Sen, 1992), this has several dimensions within which it can be assessed. Gender, ethnicity, social group, parental education and the level of income of individual families can all be causes for differences in capabilities between people, beyond individual responsibilities. Policies need to overcome these differences in order to ensure a life of dignity and create tangible conditions for supporting free choice to all individuals. Differences in income resulting from merit and motivation of individuals may be acceptable, provided they are not biased by differences in other dimensions. Policies that do not address the issues of inequality, or which merely conceal them below formal equality (such as equality of access to education or the labour market), are not acceptable.

Also for this reason, a policy promoting capabilities cannot follow a single path; it must be understood as a set of coordinated policies in various areas, from macro-economic policies to market regulation, from social to industrial policies, from education to health care.

As we saw in Chapter 2, five areas can be identified in which institutions must intervene to ensure citizens the greatest possible access to freedom of choice. These are: political freedom, transparency guaranties, protective security, social opportunities and economic facilities. In the following sections, we will revisit these instrumental freedoms to highlight some useful considerations for policies aiming to boost human development.

### b. Political freedoms

Political freedoms and the role of democracy have already been discussed in Chapter 3. What we want to emphasise is that, in the absence of radical changes in the performance of democratic processes, it is hard to direct economic policies to support human development. A change can occur through the widest possible dissemination of the method of *deliberative democracy*, i.e., of a 'government by debate' (Drèze and Sen, 2002), which goes beyond the more traditional one that sees democracy as essentially based on *public votes*. The core of deliberative democracy is the exchange of views between citizens and the discussion of different topics to gain knowledge about public problems and to then be able to decide on them in a conscious and informed manner. In this method, differences of opinion are an asset not an obstacle (Fishkin, 2011; Ocampo et al., 2007; Crocker, 2006).

Another course of change may relate to political actors. Public policies should be understood as a set of collective actions in the interest of the public, rather than exclusive actions of the state. Correspondingly, the 'public domain' should be conceived as the meeting point of collective interest rather than being a synonym for state activities. In other words, the public domain belongs to the society and not to the state, which is the main but not the only means that the society can exploit to achieve collective goals. Following this approach, it becomes important to create a strong institutional structure – *high institutional density* – with the active participation of multiple social actors and adequate civic responsibility – *high democratic density* (Ocampo, 2007).

A third important element for change is to embrace the notion that *democracy is diversity*. There are different models of capitalism and different balances between state and market. Institutional development requires an active learning process, which gives different results in various countries. The idea that there should be one single model or path of development applicable to all countries is not only ahistorical, but also harmful and contrary to the concept of democracy. Supporting democracy means understanding that democracy generates a diversity of solutions to the problems of people who depend on their history and their culture.

One of the features of the recent phase of development has instead been the drastic *reduction of forms of direct and participatory democracy* and restriction of political choices to a small circle of financial and industrial oligarchies (Duggan, 2003; Formisano, 2015; Stiglitz, 2015, 2012). The problem that occurs in many countries is that when high levels of inequality occur in democracies, policies too, as we have argued previously (Chapter 3), tend to be unbalanced, and the combination of unbalanced policies and uneven economy can be destructive for maintaining the social fabric (Piketty, 2013).

Inequality, as we have seen, is both the cause and the effect of orthodox macroeconomic policies. The proportion of the population that holds a significant part of the income and assets of an economy is also highly influential in the political sphere. Those who have more have an enormous influence on political decisions; and this influence is exercised through various means: control over the media, pressure on political decisions through the lobbying of interests; funding of candidates for the election campaigns, appointing politicians who are at the end of their mandate as big company leaders (sliding doors). Through these instruments, the ever-shrinking number of wealthy people directs policy choices in their favour, securing thus resources to further strengthen their positions through, for example, weaker antitrust laws, privatisation of public assets, tax breaks, etc. At this point a vicious circle is set in motion, 'if societies with greater inequality adopt weaker measures of social protection and less progressive income tax structures, and act as if they face tighter fiscal constraints, then an economic shock will result in more adverse effects on inequality, weakening further the political weight of the poor, weakening further social protections, reducing tax progressivity, and tightening further fiscal constraints' (Stiglitz, 2012, p. 13).

The subject is very broad, and the quoted works can be studied more closely for further details. For the themes covered in this book, however, deliberative democracy plays a decisive role in the following ways:

- the identification of the most important capabilities, well-being targets and societal goals at local, national and international levels;
- the distributive choices implicit in economic policy both from the expenditure and revenue point of view (see below)
- the choice of the purposes and methods of implementing changes and innovations, particularly in the analysis of future trends (foresight); impact assessments of technology (technological assessment), in the identification of large mission-oriented programmes; and the evaluation and management of individual programmes/projects of innovation (see Chapter 8).

In these contexts (and others), democracy is a tool for making collective choices in the most appropriate way and at the same time, a moment of institutional and collective learning as well as an effective means of controlling the concrete implementation of policies, programmes and projects. However, democracy is directly connected in these cases to the concept of equality, understood as the freedom guaranteed to all individuals to fully develop their potential so as to participate actively in the life of their community.

### c. *Transparency guarantees*

Advancing practices of deliberative democracy and the resulting institutional change promote the enhancement of *transparency guarantees*. Forms of political control of public administration by the people may limit episodes of corruption and the influence of personal interests in the management of public affairs. The generalisation of 'government by debate' can ensure the widest possible and most pluralistic dissemination of information, triggering thus increased awareness and, consequently, increasing the levels of mutual trust and strengthening structures of living together (see Chapter 2) as well as institutions that facilitate the processes of change, rather than limiting them (see Chapter 3).

Conversely, conditions of extreme social and economic precariousness, the insecurity of an unstable job and the individualisation of working paths favour a disintegration of collective identities and of the structures of living together. This reduces the transparency of community relationships and induces the search for 'shortcuts' (ranging from behaviour outside the rules to participating in criminal activities) to ensure survival. The disintegration of the social fabric has as its counterpart the emergence of 'regressive coalitions' that deny the values of civil society and in this way, any prospect for economic and social change.

### d. Protective security

Considering the social protection system as a safety net for the less fortunate, i.e., those who fail to enter the 'virtuous' mechanism of production and market distribution, is tantamount to assigning to social policies a role of follower to other. Social security, in this case too, is intended as a reparation of 'market failures'. Social policy, on the other hand, is a vital tool for social cohesion, and thus its design must be based on something more than economic rationality (Esping-Andersen et al., 2002; Morel et al., 2012). It must be broad and should aim at implementing the principles of universality and solidarity in itself, regardless of the operation of the market – living in good health, accessing all levels of education, being protected from the risks of illness and unemployment and at the end of the working capacity, having the opportunity to earn an income that ensures a dignified life. In all these cases the common denominator is a set of rights to be guaranteed to all members of a community, which by their nature cannot be regulated by the market but which must be publicly managed and delivered.

Such a choice, as it has been discussed at length in this book, and as it can be understood from the recent literature on the relationship between economic equality and growth (Ostry et al., 2014; WB, 2006), does not preclude efficiency in any way. In fact, welfare models constitute an important link between social policies on one hand and learning processes and innovation on the other (Lundall and Lorenz, 2010; Bassanini and Ernst, 2002). There is an overlap between countries that are characterised by a low dispersion of wages and high degree of coordination in negotiation of salaries, on the one hand, and countries that intensively use forms of business organisation based on learning, on the other (Lorentz and Valeyre 2005). This means that strong unions and strong social cohesion lead to or follow organisational strategies based on an intensive use of knowledge. In contrast, the individualisation of the contractual relationship and the consequent wage dispersion encourages strategies of containment of costs and price competition, which do not have innovation and knowledge at their core (Lorenz, 2015).

In addition, some studies conclude that these different institutional arrangements in Europe have mediated in different ways the distribution of productivity gains associated with increasing investments in knowledge (Cappelen, 2006). In deregulated labour markets of Anglo-Saxon countries, emphasis has been placed on the private appropriation of gains, resulting in an increase in inequality. In continental Europe and the Scandinavian countries, a relatively more regulated labour market and a higher propensity for collaboration between the public and private sectors have resulted in a lower degree of inequality (Bassanini and Ernst, 2002). This confirms 'that innovation dynamics are tightly connected to the characteristics of the socio-political system and, in particular, to the mechanisms whereby the benefits and costs of change are redistributed' (Cappelen, 2006, p. 5).

An uneven distribution can create a negative attitude to change among those who mainly sustain the costs, and if there is a high degree of insecurity among individuals, they will tend to resist change. This is one of the reasons why social cohesion is crucial to the economy of learning. 'Not only do people work and learn differently under different welfare regimes. The welfare they experience from specific modes of working and learning reflects such differences' (Lorentz and Lundall 2006, p. 412).

What should be the main interventions to promote a social security system aimed at making people's lives worth living, and at the same time capable of reducing the impact of risk in choosing changes? Again, we are in a very broad field, and we recommend exploring the cited literature for further details. The recent debate on these issues, however, has brought forth a number of important proposals that are appropriate to recall.

### e. Pensions

There has been a general trend in industrialised countries to reduce the real value of the minimum pension guaranteed by the state in case of absence or insufficiency of pensions arising from contributions during the working life. This penalises the elderly, the weakest segment of the population that can only rely on a state pension to maintain a decent standard of living. In these cases, a significant raise in minimum pensions and the restoration of the central role of the state minimum pension would be desirable. Naturally, this increase depends on the situations of the individual countries and is desirable particularly in the absence of a minimum citizen's income (see below). Its amount could take the latter as a reference point.

Within the current pension schemes in most countries, private pension funds play a central role in collecting savings for retirement plans of individuals. These funds, by their nature, have to manage these savings according to 'a long-term' perspective with a view to ensuring that after a few decades, a fixed sum proportionate to the savings paid and income accrued will be paid for a few years (decades hopefully). However, the management of these funds is not in the hands of those who contribute these savings but rather those who manage them professionally, fund managers (Atkinson, 2015). The latter, because of the competitive mechanisms in the financial market, focus greatly on 'short-term returns', and tend to invest in stocks of large companies. The autonomy of the fund managers thus creates a dangerous twofold impact: first, it makes the investment of many investors less secure and sustainable in the long term; second, it pushes the companies which hold these shares to favour even more a short-term vision.[3] The pension fund thus becomes a shareholder, who wants to get returns on its investment, straightaway. This, however, pushes the management of the companies to neglect the long-term perspective which promotes learning and innovation (Lazonik and O'sullivan, 2000 Lazonik and Mazzucato, 2013). Thus, an increase in state pensions and, more generally, a better security condition in the non-working phase of life, could also have the effect of reducing the speculative pressure on the economic system of pension funds. This would reduce the negative influence on businesses caused by the demand for short-term profits and might foster innovation and growth.

### *f. Unemployment*

The risk of unemployment has dramatically changed in recent decades. Until the '70s, this risk was connected to either temporary or definitive crisis of businesses that led to a suspension of work. The job losses that resulted from the crises were compensated by the recovery that created new job opportunities. The waiting periods were covered by various forms of unemployment benefits. Today, occasions of interruption of employment for an individual are more numerous and 'structural', rather than occasional in the course of his/her working life. Therefore, the traditional forms of unemployment risk protection, primarily based on insurance-based unemployment protection (the employee pays part of his salary to finance the risk of suspension from work) are no longer sufficient. A form of *guarantee for all those seeking work* becomes necessary as people may spend a long time waiting to find a job. Just as it is necessary to step up active labour market policy measures to facilitate the entry of workers in companies (Auer et al., 2008).

### *g. Universal income/minimum income/citizen's income/participation income*

This should be a complementary tool to the social insurance system in place. It entails safeguarding for all citizens an amount of resources derived from general taxation with the objective of ensuring a decent standard of living for all, regardless of their position in the labour market. Atkinson's (2015) proposal aims at overcoming the fragmentation of ad hoc subsidies in developed countries (such as family allowances) and making this tool universal and taxable. This would allow those who have very low incomes, so low that it does not reach the level at which the minimum tax rate is applied, to receive the full transfer, while for those who have higher income, this contribution would be taxed at the level of their marginal tax rate. This would of course require a revision of the structure of income tax rates (see below) and above all an increase in the marginal tax rate for those in higher income brackets, which have been reduced in recent decades in all countries. In such a way, for example, with a maximum tax rate of 65% those earning very high incomes would receive only 35% of the universal income.

### h.  Social opportunities – education

Education is key to both the processes of learning and innovation as well as to increasing individuals' human capabilities. Being able to fully develop one's skills and actively participate in society is a universal right recognised at the international level and in most constitutions.[4] Access to education at all levels must therefore be secured for all. The only way to ensure the fundamental freedom to learn for all is by having it organised by the state and making it always free of charge. Access to education, which depends on market rules (competition, prices, various forms of access costs, etc.), is inherently discriminatory and prevents the true universality of this fundamental right. Market rules effectively differentiate the quality of supply and the effectiveness of the service in favour of those with higher incomes. The family income would be decisive in the choice of 'the most qualified' institutions and differences in opportunities would remain unchanged, reducing social mobility (Franzini and Pianta, 2016).

Many authors have highlighted the importance of education in the early years of schooling and even at the pre-school level for the learning process and the social inclusion of youth (Sabel et al., 2011). Education in the early years of school, as well as preschool, should be inspired by a non-competitive approach to learning, aiming at individualising as much as possible the teaching process, taking into account the individual, family and social differences of the students. Such reflections on the role of education enable us to uncover another meaning of human capabilities, which concerns the capabilities of individuals, how they emerge and develop and how they can be systematically improved. These problems are typically the subject of developmental psychology and educational sciences (Miettinen, 2013) and share many points in common with the capability approach and the innovation issues.

### i.  Social opportunities – health

Physical and mental health, thus the treatment of disease, health care and decent hygienic conditions, a healthy environment in which to be born, grow up and live one's lives, is another fundamental right of every person. Health is both a constitutive part of people's well-being and a prerequisite for accessing a life that is worth living (Bloom and Cunning, 2003). Nonetheless, these activities cannot in any way be subject to market rules (Arrow, 1963; Ruger, 2015) according to which health services have a cost that is determined on the basis of supply and demand. Moreover, health is a sector in which information asymmetries – adverse selection, moral hazard and incomplete markets – are particularly evident and crucial in the provision of services (Greenwald and Stiglitz, 1986). In these cases, treatment is available only for those having an adequate income.[5] However, health is priceless (WHO, 2013).

Moreover, health strongly interrelates with other important issues addressed in this book. Let us mention a few.

Differing levels of access to services ensuring an acceptable quality of life can result in critical inequalities across work paths that are difficult to overcome (Chakraborty and Chakraborti, 2015). In fact, people's health is strongly linked to the environmental and cultural context in which people live as well as their *education*: a good level of education enhances one's ability to take care of oneself. Furthermore, investments in medical expertise influence the ability to make adequate health care available. In the absence of appropriate interventions in education, training and services, these inequalities are perpetuated. The health sector is also a source and recipient of important *innovations* within the pharmacological sector and various biomedical equipment (WHO, 2013). At the same time, investing in health has a strong and proven impact on growth and development (Wagstaff, 2001; Deaton, 2013). In fact, health, education and technologies closely interact and can trigger virtuous circles that are crucial for population growth and increased well-being (Pogge, 2012). People's health thus plays a central role in the activation of virtuous circles.

The methods of financing, the geographical distribution of health facilities and the use of qualified personnel require the selection of health policies that promote equity in protecting this basic right. Obviously, the choices that are made are different depending on the geographical, historical, economic and social contexts in which they exist. However, it can be stated that free of charge access to health services must be guaranteed to all citizens; the state, in its various forms, has to ensure the infrastructure and adequate staff at all territorial levels; the state must commit to solve all environmental, cultural, technological and education-related problems that influence the level of people's health and the ability to arrange appropriate services.

### *j. Economic facilities – income inequalities*

The economic facilities include everything related to the production and distribution of income (see Chapter 2). The latter of these two aspects plays a central role. Chapters 2 and 3 extensively discussed the issue of inequality and the problems it poses to the ability to live in a society that puts people at the core of its agenda and stimulates change. We have also examined the impact of state interventions on the distribution of opportunities among the citizens to live a life worth living. In this section, we will touch upon some policies, on the expenditure side, that can prevent the emergence and intensification of income inequality.

The first problem concerns *the guarantee of employment for everyone*, and the identification by law (or by agreement between the legal entities) of *a minimum wage*.

Following the changes in the labour market and the wide diffusion of new forms of work, Atkinson (2015) calls for the need to reformulate the overall employment goals in terms of minimising involuntary unemployment. In fact, many workers who are officially considered to be employed even though they are engaged either only for a few hours per month or in under-remunerated activities in the absence of alternatives, cannot be considered as employed to all effects and purposes (Brandolini and Viviano, 2012). Most of such engagements are non-voluntary jobs that cannot be considered in the same way as stable and adequately remunerated occupations (ILO, 1997). Forms of involuntary underemployment should instead be treated as forms of unemployment. The measurement of involuntary unemployment should be updated to the new conditions of the labour market, comprising all those precarious, under-remunerated and occasional jobs that are undertaken not by choice but because of compelling economic conditions. Furthermore, a minimum level of involuntary unemployment should be identified, as is the case of inflation targeting, at a very low rate, of for example 2%. To achieve these goals, the governments must adopt measures of macroeconomic and labour policies, going as far as offering the unemployed a public employment at a minimum wage, as part of works for public utility. Atkinson's (2015) proposal is for workers to have a job at a public or a recognised non-profit institution, for a minimum of, for example, 35 hours per week at a minimum wage (see below). This type of public intervention has been widely used in the past and is, contrary to popular belief, still far-reaching across the world (Atkinson, 2015 p. 144–146).

Linked to the previous intervention, however, is the need to identify *a minimum wage level*. As we have seen, the highest levels of income have grown faster in recent decades, while lower levels have slipped even lower. In the latter case, the decline has gone beyond a socially acceptable salary level (ILO, 2013). This has resulted in the increase of the so-called working poor, i.e., people who, while working, get a salary insufficient to ensure a dignified life for themselves and their family. As we have seen, this phenomenon is the result of a widespread weakening of trade union representatives which has inversely strengthened the negotiation power of firms in wage setting. Therefore, *an action in favour of the consolidation of the trade unions legislation* would be desirable. In 1933, in the middle of the Great Depression F. D. Roosevelt pushed through the National Labor Relations Act with the intent to further strengthen the rights of workers to organise themselves in unions, start collective negotiations and strike. The legislative action was based on the realisation that the weakness of workers, inequalities in incomes and low wages were some of the causes of the Great Depression, and thus higher salaries and greater protection of trade union rights were encouraged.

In addition to the strengthening of trade unions, another important tool introduced to prevent the wages from falling below the threshold of dignity is the establishment by law of *a minimum wage*. According to the traditional approach, the existence of a minimum wage would prevent the labour market from achieving the equilibrium between supply and demand leading to the unemployment of mainly low-skilled workers. Empirical experience, however, does not indicate the existence of any correlation between the introduction of the minimum wage and the level of employment. In Germany, for example, the progressive introduction in 2015 of a minimum wage equivalent to 62% of the median wage has been accompanied by an increase in employment. In many countries, the minimum wage is ensured by law, while in others it is defined by national labour contracts, but is legally enforceable for all. A key aspect is the level at which the minimum wage is set. A level that can be considered acceptable would be equal to two-thirds of the median wage of a country; this in fact is the threshold of the 'low wage' applied in OECD publications and by other institutions (Salverda et al., 2000; Gregory et al., 2000).

### k. Does investment in human development have a negative macroeconomic impact?

According to some authors (Amsden, 2010; Nyyar, 2012; Hartmann, 2013), an investment in human development, unaccompanied by sufficient economic growth, can cause adverse macroeconomic effects. These could result due to investments in people's health and education culminating in an oversupply of skilled workers. For investment in human development a 'Say's law' (according to which supply creates its own demand) would not operate (Amsden, 2010). This would result in increased unemployment of trained personnel who are also in good health. For these authors, investing in human development would also result in a higher level of productivity by employed workers, which in turn, with constant production, would reduce even further the demand for labour, increasing unemployment. Another reason for thinking that investing in human development would lead to negative results concerns, according to these authors, developed countries. Investment in human development would raise public expenditure, which beyond a certain point, would become untenable because of budgetary constraints (Nayyar, 2012).

Of these criticisms, we share the basic idea that human development cannot be considered outside the process of growth, which, as we have seen, is important for sustaining long-term policies for human development. Two aspects of these observations, though, are not convincing: they assume a narrow definition of human development and do not take into due account the dynamics of change.

Let us start with the first aspect. The *concept of human development is used in a very restrictive way*, practically coinciding with that of human capital. Chapters 2 and 3 have argued that human development cannot be reduced just to the three dimensions of income-health-education, as it is much broader. The need by UNDP to develop an index able to compare countries at very different levels of development, led to the restriction of focus on these three factors, although the scope of the capability approach is much wider.

The choice of a restricted concept leads to misleading conclusions, the most important of which is to suggest that basic education and longevity problems are virtually solved in developed countries and that each additional investment translates into a potential waste. Believing that developed countries have no difficulties with regards to capabilities means neglecting the unfreedoms that still persist in these countries manifesting – including inequality, exclusion, high rates of poverty and lack of democratic participation. The expansion of capabilities in the broadest sense *is to be pursued for itself* both in developing and developed countries, regardless of compatibility in terms of demand and supply (in terms of labour and goods). Taking about the equilibrium of markets means weakening the innovative strength of human development. Moreover, to simplify further, an educated and healthy individual who cannot immediately find a job lives better than a person who, besides being unemployed, is also uneducated and in bad health.

On the second point, it can be observed that social spending for human development has *multiplier effects* that may contribute to the increase of income and employment opportunities. In this book, I have tried to argue in favour of a harmony between the processes of innovation, growth and human development. For example, expenditure for mission-oriented programmes (see Chapter 8) directed to solving collective problems in education, health, social exclusion, safety, and the environment can create additional aggregate demand and expand the opportunities for work. The experience of South-East Asia and some northern European countries provides us with arguments that support this hypothesis.

Moreover, these critics emphasise *the role of labour-saving technologies* neglecting that innovation is a broad process that can also cover collective unfulfilled needs and in this way open new areas and new markets. In this context, *the increase in productivity* is an essential element of transformation of an economic system. The launching of activities with increasing returns and the corresponding reduction of economic sectors with diminishing returns allows the increase in wages, thus positively influencing the domestic demand of a country. Without the gradual strengthening of sectors with increasing returns, the transformation of an economy could hardly be realised (Reinert, 2007).

As it has been discussed throughout the book, reasonably convergent policies in terms of human development, innovation and growth may combine to deliver an interesting development strategy. The entry point of our argument is that a commitment to increasing the capabilities of people is a prerequisite for any innovation or growth policy. Investing in people and their freedom is the most promising way to achieve sustainable development. Furthermore, in line with a long tradition of studies, it has been stressed that innovation is the real engine of growth in the long run and that only a reasonable rate of growth can generate the necessary resources to further enhance human development. The interaction between these processes can be understood only by assuming a dynamic point of view.

Policies to increase the capabilities of individuals have, according to this approach, both *a value in themselves* and as *an instrumental value* because in their absence innovation and growth are not sustainable over the long term. The hypothesis of this book is that, although the empirical evidence suggests that there isn't a before and an after, without an adequate investment in human development, it is not possible to start any process of a just and lasting change.

## 9.3 Revenues, some recent proposals

### a. Income taxes

If we consider the group of developed countries, we find that the sharp decline in the rate of the top marginal income tax observed from 1970 until the first decade of the twenty-first century is closely linked to the rapid rise in the share of the upper percentile in the composition of national income during the same period. Concretely, there is an almost perfect correlation between the two phenomena: the countries that have lowered most the top rate are also those where higher incomes – in particular the high bonuses of the top business executives – have increased more; conversely, countries that have lowered less the top rate are also those where high incomes grew much more moderately (Atkinson, 2015; Piketty, 2014).

Over the past three decades, the progressivity of the income tax rates has gradually reduced. In the UK in 1979 before the Thatcher administration, the marginal tax rate on the highest incomes was 83%, in the United States until 1963 it was 91%, dropping to 70% until 1980. Today, in the UK it is at 45%, whereas in the US it is at 35%. Reducing the progressivity of income tax affected practically all industrialised countries, although to a lesser extent compared to the two Anglo-Saxon countries (Atkinson, 2015). A policy that is suggested by many is the return to a steeper structure of tax rates on income aiming at reducing the rates for lower incomes and increasing higher rates. A reasonable maximum rate on which there is a general agreement by scholars of inequality (Atkinson, 2015; Franzini and Pianta, 2016; Piketty, 2014) would be 65%, a lower rate, as we have seen, than those of the '60s and '70s, but adequately higher than those currently prevailing, which have led to a strong increase in the income shares of the richest segment of the population (Atkinson, 2015).

### b. Taxation of capital

As we have seen, over the last forty years the burden of wealth on the national income has increased sharply, triggering a vicious circle that is feeding the phenomenon that Meade called with a great foresight in 1963 the 'Brave New Capitalist's Paradise'. This increase in the great wealth was also sustained by the reduction and, in many cases, elimination of taxes on wealth (capital and financial) and those relating to the change of ownership in the case of inheritance or donation. An important way to stop this phenomenon is by introducing or raising taxes on wealth. Piketty (2014), for example, proposes the introduction of a global progressive tax on capital as per the following structure: no taxation up to one million euro, a 1% tax on properties between 1 and 5 million; and a 2% tax on properties worth over 5 million euro. He estimates that structurally applying a similar tax on wealth in European countries would yield revenue equal to 2% of Europe's GDP. The assets are considered in full, including property-related and financial as well as enterprises net of debt. An important feature of this tax is that, given the current high level of integration of financial markets, it would be applied at the international or at least European level.

### c. Inheritance and gift taxes

As indicated by Piketty in his book cited several times, inheritance has once again become a crucial factor for the concentration of wealth. The declining population and the increase in rich families with fewer children limit the process of large estate redistribution. A proposal made by Atkinson considers taxing inheritances and donations received over the life span, treating them as capital income and taxing it at the rates of income tax. In this way, the tax would be progressive (according to the rates curve) and would be calculated cumulatively over the life of the beneficiary. The transferring party cannot obtain any tax advantage.

For example, if a person receives a donation of 50,000 Euros and the minimum threshold for the application of the tax is 60,000 Euros, if the person does not have any other income, no tax should be paid. If the following year the person receives another donation of 70,000 Euros, this will be added to the amount from the previous year, reaching the total value of 120,000 Euros. Let us say that the first rate of income tax is of 20%, the share of income above the threshold of 60,000 Euros would generate a revenue of 12,000 Euros. An advantage of this proposal is that those who have a low income and receive a gift/inheritance, pay a limited tax, whereas those who have high incomes would face a higher curtailment of the transferred assets (up to a hypothetical maximum of 65%). For an inheritance received once, it is possible to distribute the amounts over a period of ten years, in order to avoid excessive curtailment of the inheritance.

## Notes

1　Contrary to what we normally think, it is not always the least efficient firms to die during a crisis, but the most indebted ones (Stiglitz and Greenwald, 2014).
2　See also the recent study by McKinsey (2016) entitled 'Poorer than their parents? A new perspective on income inequality'.
3　A problem that has been previously signaled; see section 9.1.
4　The right to education is recognised, for example, by the United Nations Declaration of the Rights of the Child.
5　In some African countries the recent elimination of some fees, introduced in the late '80s, for access to health services has greatly increased access to basic health services (UNDP, 2010, pp. 34–35).

## References

Amsden, A. 2010. Say's Law, Poverty Persistence, and Employment Neglect, *Journal of Human Development and Capabilities*, 11(1), 57–66.

Arrow, K.J. 1963. Uncertainty and Welfare Economics of Medical Care. *The American Economic Review*, 53(5), 941–973.

Atkinson, A.B. 2015. *Inequality: What Can Be Done?* Cambridge MA; London, UK, Harvard University Press.

Auer, P., Efendioğlu, Ü. and Leschke, J. 2008. *Active Labour Market Policies Around the World Coping With the Consequences of Globalization*, Second edition, Geneva, ILO.

Bassanini, A. and Ernst, E. 2002. Labour Market Regulation, Industrial Relations and Technological Regime, *Industrial and Corporate Change*, 11(3), 3912–426.

Bloom, D. and Canning, D. 2003. The Health and Poverty of Nations: From Theory to Practice, *Journal of Human Development*, 4(1), 47–71.

Brandolini, A. and Viviano, E. 2012. Extensive versus intensive margin: Changing perspective on the employment rate. Conference on Comparative EU Statistics on Income and Living conditions (EU-SILC), Wien, December.

Cappelen, A. 2006. Differences in Learning and Inequality. In: Lorenz and Lundvall 2006, 80–105.

Chakraborty, R. and Chakraborti, C. 2015. India, Health Inequities, and a Fair Healthcare Provision: A Perspective From Health Capability, *Journal of Human Development and Capabilities*, 16(4), 567–580.

Crocker, D.A. 2006. *Deliberative Participation in Local Development*, Paper presented at 2006 International Conference of the Human Development and Capability Association, Groningen, Netherlands.

Deaton, A. 2013. *The Great Escape: Health, Wealth, and the Origins of Inequality*, Princeton, NJ, Princeton University Press.

Drèze, J. and Sen, A. 2002. *India: Development and Participation*, Oxford, Oxford University Press.

Duggan, L. 2003. *The Twilight of Equality: Neoliberalism, Cultural Politics, and the Attack on Democracy*, Boston, Beacon Press.

Epstein, G. 2015. *Financialization: There's Something Happening Here*, Political Economy Research Institute, University of Massachusetts Amherst working paper series, n. 394.

Esping-Andersen, G., Gallie, D. and Hemerijk, A. 2002. *Why We Need a New Welfare State*, Oxford, Oxford University Press.

Fishkin, J.S. 2011. *When the People Speak: Deliberative Democracy and Public Consultation*, Oxford, Oxford University Press.

Formisano, R.P. 2015. *Plutocracy in America: How Increasing Inequality Destroys the Middle Class and Exploits the Poor*, Baltimore, Johns Hopkins University Press.

Franzini, M. and Pianta, M. 2016. *Explaining Inequality*, London and New York, Routledge.

Greenwald, B.C. and Stiglitz, J.E. 1986. Externalities in Economies With Imperfect Information and Incomplete Markets, *Quarterly Journal of Economics*, May, 229–264.

Gregory, M., W. Salverda, and Bazen, S. (eds.) 2000. *Labour Market Inequalities: Problems and Policies of Low-Wage Employment in International Perspective*, Oxford, Oxford University Press.

Hartmann, D. 2013. *Economic Complexity and Human Development: How Economic Diversification and Social Networks Affect Human Agency and Welfare*, London, New York, Routledge.

Holm, J.R. and Lorenz, E. 2015. Has "Discretionary Learning" Declined During the Lisbon Agenda? A Cross-Sectional and Longitudinal Study of Work Organization in European Nations, *Industrial and Corporate Change*, 24(6), 1179–1214.

International Labour Organisation (ILO) 1997. Part-Time Work: Solution or Trap? *International Labour Review*, 136, 557–578.

International Labour Organisation (ILO) 2013. *Global Wage Report 2012/13 Wages and Equitable Growth*. Geneva, ILO.

Ivanova, M.N. 2017. Profit Growth in Boom and Bust: The Great Recession and the Great Depression in Comparative Perspective, *Industrial and Corporate Change*, 26(1), 1–20.

Jarsulic, M. 2013. The Origin of the US Financial Crisis of 2007: How a House-Price Bubble, A Credit Bubble and Regulatory Failure Caused the Greatest Economic Disaster Since the Great Depression. In: Wolfson, M.H. and Epstein, G.A. (eds.), *The Handbook of the Political Economy of Financial Crises*, Oxford, Oxford University Press, 21–46.

Keynes, J.M. 1936. *The General Theory of Employment, Interest and Money*, London, Palgrave Macmillan.

Kotz, D.M. 2014. *The Rise and Fall of Neoliberal Capitalism*, Cambridge, Harvard University Press.

Krugman, P. 2012. *End This Depression Now!* New York, W.W. Norton & Company.

Lazonick, W. and Mazzucato, M. 2013. The Risk-Reward Nexus in the Innovation-Inequality Relationship: Who Takes the Risks? Who Gets the Rewards? *Industrial and Corporate Change*, 22(4), 1093–1128.

Lazonick, W. and O'Sullivan, M. 2000. Maximizing Shareholder Value: A New Ideology for Corporate Governance, *Economy and Society*, 29(10), 13–35.

Leoni, R. 2012. Workplace Design, Complementarities Among Work Practices and the Formation of Competencies: Evidence From Italian Employees, *Industrial & Labor Relations Review*, 2, 316–349.

Lorenz, E. 2015. Work Organisation, Forms of Employee Learning and Labour Market Structure: Accounting for International Differences in Workplace Innovation, *Journal of the Knowledge Economy*, 6, 437–466.

Lorenz, E. and Valeyre, A 2005. Organisational Innovation, Human Resource Management and Labour Market Structure: A Comparison of the EU-15, *Journal of Industrial Relations*, 47(4), 424–442.

Lorenz, E. and Lundvall, B.A. (eds.). 2006. *How Europe's Economies Learn: Coordinating Competing Models*, Oxford, Oxford University Press.

Lundvall, B.Å. and Lorenz, E. 2006. Welfare and Learning in Europe – How to Revitalize the Lisbon Process and Break the Stalemate. In: Lorenz and Lundvall 2006, 411–431.

Lundvall, B.Å. and Lorenz, E. 2010. Accounting for Creativity in the European Union: A Multi-Level Analysis of Individual Competence, Labour Market Structure, and Systems of Education and Training, *Cambridge Journal of Economics*, 2, 269–294.

Lundvall, B.Å. and Lorenz, E. 2014. The Euro Crisis and the Failure of the Lisbon Strategy. In: Texeira, A.A.C., Silva, E.G. and Mamede, R.P. (eds.), *Structural Change, Competitiveness and Industrial Policy: Painful Lessons From the European Periphery*, London, New York, Routledge, 80–101.

Mazzucato, M. 2013. *The Entrepreneurial State: Debunking the Public vs. Private Myth in Risk and Innovation*, London, Anthem.

Mazzucato, M. 2015. Innovation, the State and Patient Capital, *The Political Quarterly*, 86(Supplement S1), 98–118.

Mazzucato, M. and Wray, L.R. 2015. *Financing the Capital Development of the Economy: A Keynes-Schumpeter-Minsky Synthesis*, Levy Economics Institute of Bard, Working Paper No. 837.

McKinsey and Company 2016. *Poorer than their parents? A new perspective on income inequality*, McKinsey Global Institute.

Miettinen, R. 2013. Innovation, Human Capabilities, and Democracy: Towards an Enabling Welfare State, Oxford, New York, Oxford University Press.

Morel, N., Palier, B. and Palme, J. 2012. *Towards A Social Investment Welfare State? Ideas, Policies and Challenges*, Bristol, The Policy Press.

Nayyar, D. 2012. Macroeconomics and Human Development, *Journal of Human Development and Capabilities*, 13(1), 7–30.

Nelson, R.R. and Winter, S.G. 1982. *An Evolutionary Theory of Economic Change*, Cambridge, MA; London, UK, The Belknap Press of Harvard University Press.

Ocampo, J.A. 2007. Markets, social cohesion and democracy. In: Ocampo et al. 2007, 1–31.

Ocampo, J.A., Jomo, K.S. and Khan, S. (eds.) 2007. *Policy Matters. Economic and Social Policies to Sustain Equitable Development*, London, ZED.

Ostry, J.D., Berg, A. and Tsangarides, C.G. 2014. *Redistribution, Inequality, and Growth*, IMF Staff Discussion Note, n. 14/02.

Piketty, T. 2014. *Capital in the Twenty-First Century*, Cambridge, MA, London, UK, Harvard University Press.

Pogge, T. 2012. The Health Impact Fund: Enhancing Justice and Efficiency in Global Health, *Journal of Human Development and Capabilities*, 13(4), 537–559.

Reinert, E.S. 2007. *How Rich Countries Got Rich . . . and Why Poor Countries Stay Poor*, London, Constable.

Reinhart, C.M. and Rogoff, K.S. 2009. *This Time Is Different: Eight Centuries of Financial Folly*, Princeton and Oxford, Princeton University press.

Ruger, J.P. 2015. Health Economics and Ethics and the Health Capability Paradigm, *Journal of Human Development and Capabilities*, 16(4), 581–599.

Sabel, C., Miettinen, R., Kristensen, P.-H. and Hautamäki, J. 2011. *Individualized Service Production in the New Welfare State: Lessons From the Special Education in Finland*, Sitra Studies 62, Helsinki, Sitra.

Salverda, W., Lucifora C. and Nolan, B. (eds.) 2000. *Policy measures for low-wage employment in Europe*, Edward Elgar, Cheltenham, UK, Northampton, MA, USA.

Sen, A. 1975. *Employment, Technology and Development*, Oxford, Oxford University Press.

Sen, A. 1992. *Inequality Reexamined*, Oxford, Oxford University Press.

Stiglitz, J.E. 2003. *Globalization and Its Discontents*, New York, W.W. Norton & Company.

Stiglitz, J.E. 2012a. *The Price of Inequality*, New York, W.W. Norton and Company.

Stiglitz, J.E. 2012b. Macroeconomic Fluctuations, Inequality, and Human Development, *Journal of Human Development and Capabilities*, 13(1), 31–58.

Stiglitz, J.E. 2015. *The Great Divide: Unequal Societies and What We Can Do About Them*. New York, W.W. Norton & Company.

Stiglitz, J.E. 2016. *The Euro: How a Common Currency Threatens the Future of Europe*, New York, W.W. Norton & Company.

Stiglitz, J.E. and Greenwald, B.C. 2014. *Creating a Learning Society*, New York, Columbia University Press.

UNDP (United Nations Development Programme) 2010. *Human Development Report 2010: The Real Wealth of Nations: Pathways to Human Development*, New York, UNDP.

Vercelli, Alessandro. 2013. Financialization in a Long-Run Perspective; An Evolutionary Approach, *International Journal of Political Economy*, 42(4), Winter, 19–46.

Wagstaff, Adam. 2001. *Poverty and Health*, Commission on Macroeconomics and Health Working Paper Series, Paper No. WG1 5, March.

WHO (World Health Organisation) 2013. The World Health Report 2013: Research for Universal Health Coverage, Geneva, WHO.

World Bank. 2006. *World Development Report 2006*. Equity and Development, Washington, DC.

# 10 Conclusions

## a. More capabilities for more innovation

Many factors that affect the expansion of human capabilities seem to directly impact the functioning of innovation processes. Improving the structures of living together encourages the sharing of rules and institutions and ensures a social climate that is favourable to change. Greater social protection can enhance the sense of individual and collective safety and entice people to take risks and innovate, thus creating a more dynamic economy. Equality therefore, plays a crucial role in the link between human development and innovation. A more inclusive society may intensify and improve learning by using, by interacting and by doing, which are at the heart of innovation. On the contrary, exclusion and excessive disparities in the freedoms of individuals result in the formation of closed systems consisting of privileged groups who hesitate to support social and economic change. Excessive inequality also affects the functioning of institutions and can facilitate their 'capture' by interest groups with greater economic power. These may adversely affect the use of public resources for research and innovation drawing them away from collective goals.

## b. More innovation for increased growth and better human development

Innovation, too, contributes directly and indirectly to the expansion of capabilities. Directly, by equipping people with new technologies and new ways of living a better life and expanding their available opportunities. Indirectly, through innovation's contribution to growth and increased employment opportunities. Growth, in turn, stimulates the increase of resources that policy makers can allocate to health, education and security of citizens, in order to further expand their capabilities. Only an economy that is changing and growing can ensure sustainability in the process of inclusion and expansion of freedoms. More generally, the interpretation of change in line with the broader approach of innovation systems is useful to link efficiency and equity. This, unlike in other approaches, pays more attention to individuals' education, the role of institutions and social capital as well as the relationship between users and producers of innovations. Interpreting the innovation process in such a way means thinking about innovation as a process that puts people at the centre.

## c. Virtuous circles

The idea that the innovation processes can benefit from giving greater attention to freedom, and that innovation can foster processes of change and economic growth necessary for the expansion of capabilities, led me to hypothesise the existence of *virtuous circles* between innovation, human development and economic growth. Each of these dimensions influences and is affected by others. The intensity and direction of these relationships are not deterministic or automatic. They depend on policies. Public decision-making, in its various forms, has the option of choosing whether to prioritise one or more of these dimensions.

The empirical analysis has shown, in fact, that some countries, such as Korea, Estonia and China, have invested in a virtuous way in the three dimensions of innovation, economic growth and human development in the past two decades. Others, like Japan, France, Belgium, Mexico and South Africa, on the other hand, seem to have fallen into a spiral of difficulties, achieving limited progress on all three fronts. Between these two extremes, other strategies have emerged – countries such as the USA, Sweden and Russia, have focused on growth more than on innovation and human development; and countries like Denmark, Norway, New Zealand and Israel have invested more in human development and/or innovation, despite lower levels of growth.

The analysis of European regions has also highlighted interesting differences. Long-term dynamics showed intensified processes of growth along the east-central axis of the continent, with a lower degree of dynamism in the western and southern regions. The regional map on innovative excellence includes a large part of central and northern regions of the continent, indicating a lag in the southern and the majority of the eastern regions. The dynamism of recent years has affected the majority of these regions (notably, with the exception of the Scandinavian regions), and the inclusion of others, especially in France, Great Britain, Ireland and Spain can also be observed. Human development in European regions, as represented by this index, seems to follow its own long-term trend, not influenced by the events of conjuncture of the economic cycle. In this case, the differences between regions are much smaller, compared to the other two indices, and are decreasing progressively. The regions that have experienced the highest increase in the levels of human development are mainly in Eastern Europe, but also in northern Spain, Greece, England and Ireland.

A confirmation of the importance of the relationship between innovation, human development and growth also comes from the tests run using some simple econometric models. The results show a mutually reinforcing relationship between the three processes. The relationship between human development and innovation is particularly strong: the data suggest that a certain level of human development is a precondition to initiate the innovation and growth processes. It also shows a high influence of human development on income, both in the international and regional samples. The analysis at the regional level provided additional confirmation of the existence of *virtuous circles*, and also highlighted the importance of spatial effects, both in terms of spill over and feedback, in influencing these relations. Overall, the analysis confirms the importance of geographical proximity in the evolution of the three processes.

## d. Which policies?

The capability approach, and in particular the criticism that Sen makes on welfarism, allows us to go beyond the idea that both market and system failures are a sound foundation for innovation policies. After more than two decades of widespread acceptance of the human development approach and thanks to the activities of some large international organisations and NGOs, the capability approach began to find practical applications. These applications have allowed a certain accumulation of experience and the ability to compare different methodologies. A paradigm based on the expansion of freedoms seems to also apply to policies for innovation. In policies driven by the capability approach the *why, who* and *how* are more important than the *what*, and the duly institutionalised democratic participation of citizens, plays a central role. The capability approach can be a useful aid in the definition of the ethical dimension of the innovation process. In fact, the informational basis of innovation systems is limited to concepts related to competitiveness, efficiency and economic growth. This restricts its potential, as the innovation process goes beyond the efficiency of an economic system, involving people's lives, their freedom and their choices. Some of the areas of application of the capability approach in the field of innovation policies include specific innovation projects, large mission-oriented programmes, as well as technological assessment exercises and long-term forecasting.

In order to maximise the potential of a virtuous link between human development and innovation, macroeconomic and welfare policies need to be consistent with the previously identified objectives. The key element to give due attention to is employment. More employment, that is of a better quality and is better remunerated, is a precondition for learning processes, human development and growth. Employees are at the centre of interactions that sustain innovation: thus, considering them only as a production cost greatly limits the growth capacity of enterprises. Employment provides access to the means to live a decent life but it is also, and above all, a means of social recognition of a role and position in the community. Finally, more employment and better-paid jobs are preconditions for a high demand, which is essential for macroeconomic equilibrium and growth. It is thus important to restore maximum employment as an objective within the set of government goals. The instability of the economic cycle, the liberalisation of capital markets and the endorsement of restrictive policies have represented and still represent a threat both for the social fabric of many countries and for their innovation potential. In fact, the uncertainty of the economy is neither conducive to the long-term investment that is necessary for technological change, nor does it direct capital toward the patient use that is needed for applied research and innovation.

Finally, the instrumental freedoms of individuals must be guaranteed if a dynamic and just society is to be built. The state must develop its own spending policies seeking to ensure free health, access to all educational levels and protection from sickness, unemployment and old age for all citizens. These policies should be associated with more fair and more progressive tax systems than those that have been established in recent decades, by taxing more high incomes, as well as real and financial capital, and taxing less basic consumption, low and average incomes.

# Appendices

## A.1. Sources and database building

The national database (Panel 1) is built for 40 countries (see Table A.1): 34 are OECD[1] member states, and six are emerging countries with rapidly expanding economies (known as BRICS). The sources used to build this database are shown in Table A.2, the main being UNDP, the World Bank and OECD. The timeframe of the study covers the period between 1995 and 2012. As discussed in Chapter 4, analyses of the innovation-growth nexus favoured developed countries, while studies on the growth-human development focused on developing countries. Having to also consider in our analysis the innovation dimension, the sample was selected to allow the gathering of sufficient data on innovation as well as human development and growth. Therefore, the sample group includes mainly developed countries, along with six fast-growing countries (China, Brazil, India, Indonesia, South Africa and Russia) and three middle-income countries – Turkey, Chile and Mexico. The latter nine countries will be considered as emerging countries. The sample also includes (besides Russia) other six economies in transition (the Czech Republic, Estonia, Hungary, Poland, Slovakia and Slovenia). The list of the analysed data for both the building of the indices and the empirical analysis in Chapter 6, is presented in Table A.2.

The Unified Democracy Score is a composite index that incorporates information from 10 measures of democracy.

The Corruption Perception Index was developed in 1995 by Transparency International as a composite indicator that measures perceptions of corruption in the public sector. It does so by aggregating different sources of corruption-related data that are produced by a variety of independent and well known institutions, such as the World Bank, the World Justice Project, the African Development Bank, the Economist Intelligence Unit and others. A high index indicates a low level of corruption (or high level of transparency) and vice versa.

The regional database (Panel 2) includes data from 266 regions (see Table A.3): all regions are found within the 27 member states that formed the European Union in 2012 (the last year of the data studied), except for the four overseas territories of France. The source for the entire data set is Eurostat, and Table A.4

*Table A.1* Countries included in the sample

|   | CODE | COUNTRY |
|---|------|---------|
| 1 | **AU** | Australia |
| 2 | **AT** | Austria |
| 3 | **BE** | Belgium |
| 4 | **BR** | Brazil |
| 5 | **CA** | Canada |
| 6 | **CL** | Chile |
| 7 | **CN** | China |
| 8 | **CZ** | Czech Republic |
| 9 | **DK** | Denmark |
| 10 | **EE** | Estonia |
| 11 | **FI** | Finland |
| 12 | **FR** | France |
| 13 | **DE** | Germany |
| 14 | **EL** | Greece |
| 15 | **HU** | Hungary |
| 16 | **IS** | Iceland |
| 17 | **IN** | India |
| 18 | **ID** | Indonesia |
| 19 | **IE** | Ireland |
| 20 | **IL** | Israel |
| 21 | **IT** | Italy |
| 22 | **JP** | Japan |
| 23 | **KR** | Korea (Republic of) |
| 24 | **LU** | Luxembourg |
| 25 | **MX** | Mexico |
| 26 | **NL** | Netherlands |
| 27 | **NZ** | New Zealand |
| 28 | **NO** | Norway |
| 29 | **PL** | Poland |
| 30 | **PT** | Portugal |
| 31 | **RU** | Russian Federation |
| 32 | **SK** | Slovakia |
| 33 | **SI** | Slovenia |
| 34 | **ZA** | South Africa |
| 35 | **ES** | Spain |
| 36 | **SE** | Sweden |
| 37 | **CH** | Switzerland |
| 38 | **TR** | Turkey |
| 39 | **UK** | United Kingdom |
| 40 | **US** | United States |

lists the indicators used in the analysis. The reporting period covers the years 2000–2012.

It is important to note that the two levels of data collection complement each other: in the case of national data, the quality of indicators is ensured by a better availability of data, which is an advantage. However, the disadvantage

*Table A.2* List of data and sources used for country panel

| | | |
|---|---|---|
| 1 | Patent application filed under PCT | OECD |
| 2 | GERD as a percentage of gdp, percentage | OECD |
| 3 | Scientific and technical journal articles/POP | World Bank |
| 4 | Electric power consumption (kWh per capita) | World Bank |
| 5 | Fixed telephone subscriptions (per 100 people) | World Bank |
| 6 | Mobile cellular subscriptions (per 100 people) | World Bank |
| 7 | Fixed (wired) broadband subscriptions (per 100 people) | World Bank |
| 8 | Internet users (per 100 people) | World Bank |
| 9 | Time series of Expected Years of Schooling | UNESCO Institute for Statistics |
| 10 | Time series of Mean Years of Schooling | Barro and Lee (2013), UNESCO Institute for Statistics |
| 11 | School enrollment, tertiary (% gross) | World Bank |
| 12 | Time series of Life expectancy | World Population Prospect, The 2012 Revision |
| 13 | Time Series of GNI pc (2011 PPP constant) | World Bank |
| 14 | Gross fixed capital formation (% of GDP) | World Bank |
| 15 | Employment to population ratio, 15+, total (%) (modeled ILO estimate) | World Bank |
| 16 | General government final consumption expenditure (% of GDP) | World Bank |
| 17 | Government expenditure on education and health, total (% of GDP) | World Bank |
| 18 | Gini (at disposable income, post taxes and transfers), Total population, Current definition | OECD |
| 19 | Employment to population ratio, 15+, female/male ratio (%) (modeled ILO estimate) | World Bank |
| 20 | UNIFIED DEMOCRACY SCORE | Pemstein, Meserve, Melton (2010); www.unified-democracy-scores.org/ |
| 21 | CORRUPTION PERCEPTION INDEX | Trasparency international; www.transparency.org/ |

lies in the lower number of observations, a problem that was partly addressed by considering a wide timeframe, a period of 18 years. On the other hand, it is more difficult to build very long series from the regional database; in addition, data quality is compromised as a result of limited availability of data, although a larger number of observations is available.

## A.2. Construction of the indices

The analysis undertaken in Chapters 5 and 6 was conducted using some synthetic indices developed from the merger of several partial indicators. The most important are the Human Development Index (HDI) and the Innovation Capacity Index (ICI). At the national level a standard methodology was utilised for both indicators, whereas at the regional level the methodology was adapted, due to the different availability of data.

Table A.3 List of European regions included in the sample, NUTS-2, 2010

| Code | Name | Code | Name | Code | Name | Code | Name | Code | Name |
|---|---|---|---|---|---|---|---|---|---|
| BE10 | Région de Bruxelles-Capitale/Brussels Hoofdstedelijk Gewest | DEA1 | Düsseldorf | FR23 | Haute-Normandie | NL12 | Friesland (NL) | SK01 | Bratislavský kraj |
| BE21 | Prov. Antwerpen | DEA2 | Köln | FR24 | Centre | NL13 | Drenthe | SK02 | Západné Slovensko |
| BE22 | Prov. Limburg (BE) | DEA3 | Münster | FR25 | Basse-Normandie | NL21 | Overijssel | SK03 | Stredné Slovensko |
| BE23 | Prov. Oost-Vlaanderen | DEA4 | Detmold | FR26 | Bourgogne | NL22 | Gelderland | SK04 | Východné Slovensko |
| BE24 | Prov. Vlaams-Brabant | DEA5 | Arnsberg | FR30 | Nord – Pas-de-Calais | NL23 | Flevoland | FI1B | Helsinki-Uusimaa |
| BE25 | Prov. West-Vlaanderen | DEB1 | Koblenz | FR41 | Lorraine | NL31 | Utrecht | FI1C | Etelä-Suomi |
| BE31 | Prov. Brabant Wallon | DEB2 | Trier | FR42 | Alsace | NL32 | Noord-Holland | FI19 | Länsi-Suomi |
| BE32 | Prov. Hainaut | DEB3 | Rheinhessen-Pfalz | FR43 | Franche-Comté | NL33 | Zuid-Holland | FI1D | Pohjois- ja Itä-Suomi |
| BE33 | Prov. Liège | DEC0 | Saarland | FR51 | Pays de la Loire | NL34 | Zeeland | FI20 | Åland |
| BE34 | Prov. Luxembourg (BE) | DED4 | Chemnitz | FR52 | Bretagne | NL41 | Noord-Brabant | SE11 | Stockholm |
| BE35 | Prov. Namur | DED2 | Dresden | FR53 | Poitou-Charentes | NL42 | Limburg (NL) | SE12 | Östra Mellansverige |
| BG31 | Северозападен | DED5 | Leipzig | FR61 | Aquitaine | AT11 | Burgenland (AT) | SE21 | Småland med öarna |
| BG32 | Северен централен | DEE0 | Sachsen-Anhalt | FR62 | Midi-Pyrénées | AT12 | Niederösterreich | SE22 | Sydsverige |
| BG33 | Североизточен | DEF0 | Schleswig-Holstein | FR63 | Limousin | AT13 | Wien | SE23 | Västsverige |
| BG34 | Югоизточен | DEG0 | Thüringen | FR71 | Rhône-Alpes | AT21 | Kärnten | SE31 | Norra Mellansverige |
| BG41 | Югозападен | EE00 | Eesti | FR72 | Auvergne | AT22 | Steiermark | SE32 | Mellersta Norrland |
| BG42 | Южен централен | IE01 | Border, Midland and Western | FR81 | Languedoc-Roussillon | AT31 | Oberösterreich | SE33 | Övre Norrland |
| CZ01 | Praha | IE02 | Southern and Eastern | FR82 | Provence-Alpes-Côte d'Azur | AT32 | Salzburg | UKC1 | Tees Valley and Durham |
| CZ02 | Střední Čechy | EL11 | Ανατολική Μακεδονία, Θράκη | FR83 | Corse | AT33 | Tirol | UKC2 | Northumberland and Tyne and Wear |
| CZ03 | Jihozápad | EL12 | Κεντρική Μακεδονία | ITC1 | Piemonte | AT34 | Vorarlberg | UKD1 | Cumbria |
| CZ04 | Severozápad | EL13 | Δυτική Μακεδονία | ITC2 | Valle d'Aosta/Vallée d'Aoste | PL11 | Łódzkie | UKD6 | Cheshire |

| Code | Region | Code | Region | Code | Region | Code | Region | Code | Region |
|---|---|---|---|---|---|---|---|---|---|
| CZ05 | Severovýchod | EL14 | Θεσσαλία | ITC3 | Liguria | PL12 | Mazowieckie | UKD3 | Greater Manchester |
| CZ06 | Jihovýchod | EL21 | Ήπειρος | ITC4 | Lombardia | PL21 | Małopolskie | UKD4 | Lancashire |
| CZ07 | Střední Morava | EL22 | Ιόνια Νησιά | ITH1 | Provincia Autonoma di Bolzano/Bozen | PL22 | Śląskie | UKD7 | Merseyside |
| CZ08 | Moravskoslezsko | EL23 | Δυτική Ελλάδα | ITH2 | Provincia Autonoma di Trento | PL31 | Lubelskie | UKE1 | East Yorkshire and Northern Lincolnshire |
| DK01 | Hovedstaden | EL24 | Στερεά Ελλάδα | ITH3 | Veneto | PL32 | Podkarpackie | UKE2 | North Yorkshire |
| DK02 | Sjælland | EL25 | Πελοπόννησος | ITH4 | Friuli-Venezia Giulia | PL33 | Świętokrzyskie | UKE3 | South Yorkshire |
| DK03 | Syddanmark | EL30 | Αττική | ITH5 | Emilia-Romagna | PL34 | Podlaskie | UKE4 | West Yorkshire |
| DK04 | Midtjylland | EL41 | Βόρειο Αιγαίο | ITI1 | Toscana | PL41 | Wielkopolskie | UKF1 | Derbyshire and Nottinghamshire |
| DK05 | Nordjylland | EL42 | Νότιο Αιγαίο | ITI2 | Umbria | PL42 | Zachodniopomorskie | UKF2 | Leicestershire, Rutland and Northamptonshire |
| DE11 | Stuttgart | EL43 | Κρήτη | ITI3 | Marche | PL43 | Lubuskie | UKF3 | Lincolnshire |
| DE12 | Karlsruhe | ES11 | Galicia | ITI4 | Lazio | PL51 | Dolnośląskie | UKG1 | Herefordshire, Worcestershire and Warwickshire |
| DE13 | Freiburg | ES12 | Principado de Asturias | ITF1 | Abruzzo | PL52 | Opolskie | UKG2 | Shropshire and Staffordshire |
| DE14 | Tübingen | ES13 | Cantabria | ITF2 | Molise | PL61 | Kujawsko-Pomorskie | UKG3 | West Midlands |
| DE21 | Oberbayern | ES21 | País Vasco | ITF3 | Campania | PL62 | Warmińsko-Mazurskie | UKH1 | East Anglia |
| DE22 | Niederbayern | ES22 | Comunidad Foral de Navarra | ITF4 | Puglia | PL63 | Pomorskie | UKH2 | Bedfordshire and Hertfordshire |
| DE23 | Oberpfalz | ES23 | La Rioja | ITF5 | Basilicata | PT11 | Norte | UKH3 | Essex |
| DE24 | Oberfranken | ES24 | Aragón | ITF6 | Calabria | PT15 | Algarve | UKI1 | Inner London |
| DE25 | Mittelfranken | ES30 | Comunidad de Madrid | ITG1 | Sicilia | PT16 | Centro (PT) | UKI2 | Outer London |

(Continued)

Table A.3 (Continued)

| | | | | | | | | | |
|---|---|---|---|---|---|---|---|---|---|
| DE26 | Unterfranken | ES41 | Castilla y León | ITG2 | Sardegna | PT17 | Lisboa | UKJ1 | Berkshire, Buckinghamshire and Oxfordshire |
| DE27 | Schwaben | ES42 | Castilla-La Mancha | CY00 | Κύπρος | PT18 | Alentejo | UKJ2 | Surrey, East and West Sussex |
| DE30 | Berlin | ES43 | Extremadura | LV00 | Latvija | PT20 | Região Autónoma dos Açores | UKJ3 | Hampshire and Isle of Wight |
| DE40 | Brandenburg | ES51 | Cataluña | LT00 | Lietuva | PT30 | Região Autónoma da Madeira | UKJ4 | Kent |
| DE50 | Bremen | ES52 | Comunidad Valenciana | LU00 | Luxembourg | RO11 | Nord-Vest | UKK1 | Gloucestershire, Wiltshire and Bristol/Bath area |
| DE60 | Hamburg | ES53 | Illes Balears | HU10 | Közép-Magyarország | RO12 | Centru | UKK2 | Dorset and Somerset |
| DE71 | Darmstadt | ES61 | Andalucía | HU21 | Közép-Dunántúl | RO21 | Nord-Est | UKK3 | Cornwall and Isles of Scilly |
| DE72 | Gießen | ES62 | Región de Murcia | HU22 | Nyugat-Dunántúl | RO22 | Sud-Est | UKK4 | Devon |
| DE73 | Kassel | ES63 | Ciudad Autónoma de Ceuta | HU23 | Dél-Dunántúl | RO31 | Sud – Muntenia | UKL1 | West Wales and The Valleys |
| DE80 | Mecklenburg-Vorpommern | ES64 | Ciudad Autónoma de Melilla | HU31 | Észak-Magyarország | RO32 | București – Ilfov | UKL2 | East Wales |
| DE91 | Braunschweig | ES70 | Canarias | HU32 | Észak-Alföld | RO41 | Sud-Vest Oltenia | UKM2 | Eastern Scotland |
| DE92 | Hannover | FR10 | Île de France | HU33 | Dél-Alföld | RO42 | Vest | UKM3 | South Western Scotland |
| DE93 | Lüneburg | FR21 | Champagne-Ardenne | MT00 | Malta | SI01 | Vzhodna Slovenija | UKM5 | North Eastern Scotland |
| DE94 | Weser-Ems | FR22 | Picardie | NL11 | Groningen | SI02 | Zahodna Slovenija | UKM6 | Highlands and Islands |
| | | | | | | | | UKN0 | Northern Ireland |

*Table A.4* List of data and sources used for regional panel

| | DATA | SOURCE |
|---|---|---|
| 1 | Total intramural R&D expenditure (GERD) by sectors of performance and NUTS 2 regions. UNIT: Percentage of GDP | EUROSTAT |
| 2 | Patent applications to the EPO by priority year and NUTS 2 regions.UNIT: Number | EUROSTAT |
| 3 | HRST by sub-groups and NUTS 2 regions. Persons with tertiary education (ISCED) and/or employed in science and technology. UNIT:Thousand | EUROSTAT |
| 4 | Population aged 25–64 with tertiary education attainment by sex and NUTS 2 regions. First and second stage of tertiary. Unit: PERCENTAGE education (levels 5 and 6) | EUROSTAT |
| 5 | Life expectancy by age, sex and NUTS 2 region. AGE: Less than 1 year | EUROSTAT |
| 6 | Population aged 25–64 with upper secondary or tertiary education attainment by sex and NUTS 2 regions. Upper secondary, post-secondary non-tertiary, first and second stage of tertiary education (levels 3–6) | EUROSTAT |
| 7 | Gross domestic product (GDP) at current market prices by NUTS 2 regions. Purchasing Power Standard per inhabitant | EUROSTAT |
| 8 | At-risk-of-poverty rate by NUTS 2 regions. Unit: Percentage of total population | EUROSTAT |
| 9 | Early leavers from education and training by sex and NUTS 2 regions. Percentage. AGEFrom 18 to 24 years. Population on 1 January | EUROSTAT |
| 10 | Population on 1 January by age, sex and NUTS 2 region. Unit:Thousand | EUROSTAT |
| 11 | Economically active population by sex, age and NUTS 2 regions (x 1000) | EUROSTAT |
| 12 | Population aged 25–64 with tertiary education attainment by sex and NUTS 2 regions. UNIT: Percentage. ISCED11 | EUROSTAT |
| 13 | Employment by sex, age and NUTS 2 regions (x 1000) | EUROSTAT |

### a. Human development index

This index was introduced by UNDP in 1990 in its first Human Development Report (HDR). The purpose of this indicator is to measure (however partially) the well-being of communities to complement the GDP indicator, based on three components: life expectancy, education and standard of living.

The first indicator measures *life expectancy at birth*. This indicator is important both for the intrinsic value associated with longevity and for its close relation to other relevant characteristics of human life, such as good health and adequate nutrition. For this reason in particular, given its relationship with these and other indicators to which a high value is assigned, in the absence of full information on people's health and nutrition, life expectancy is often used as one of the most important proxies for human development (for example, Ranis et al., 2000).

From the first issue of the HDR, *education* is measured by the adult literacy rate, aiming at obtaining essential and easily available information on learning and knowledge-building of a person. The second HDR introduced an additional indicator: mean years of schooling (MYS), i.e., the average number of years of education received by people aged 25 and over, converted from education attainment levels using official durations of each level. The 2010 HDR replaced the adult literacy rate with the expected years of schooling (EYS) calculated as the number of years of schooling that a child of school entrance age can expect to receive if prevailing patterns of age-specific enrolment rates persist throughout the child's life. The arithmetic average of MYS and EYS allows us to derive a *combined education index* used to measure the second component of HDI.

The control over resources needed to ensure a *decent living standard* is perhaps the most difficult component to measure, as it requires information on the access and distribution of basic resources such as land, technology, credit, consumer goods, etc. The proxy indicator used in this case is the GNI (Gross National Income) per capita measured in purchasing-power-parity. As income increases, the marginal contribution of one unit of income to the increase in capabilities of a person gradually decreases (Anand and Sen, 2000). To take this characteristic into account, GNI per capita data are expressed in natural logarithms.

HDI is calculated in two steps. The first calculates a standardised index for each dimension based on the following relation:

$$\text{Dimension index} = \frac{(\text{actual value} - \text{minimum value})}{(\text{maximum value} - \text{minimum value})} \tag{1}$$

The maximum and minimum values (goalposts) are chosen so as to transform indicators expressed in different units into indices ranging between 0 and 1. These values become definitive and represent the minimum values as the 'natural zero' and the maximum values as 'aspirational goals'. The minimum and maximum values of the four indicators constituting HDI in the 2014 Human Development Report were as follows.

Dimension Indicator Minimum Maximum

| | |
|---|---|
| Health: | Life expectancy (years) 20–85 |
| Education: | (a) Expected years of schooling 0–18; (b) Mean years of schooling 0–15 |
| Standard of living: | Gross National Income per capita (PPP 2011 $) 100–75,000 |

After applying formula (1) to the two basic indicators of the Combined Education Index, to Life Expectancy and to the natural logarithm of real GNI per capita in PPP, to calculate the HDI it is necessary to compute the geometric mean of the three components.

$$HDI = \left(I_{Health} * I_{Education} * I_{Income}\right)^{1/3}$$

The analyses that follow will use UNDP's standard methodology. In particular, for the countries panel the HDR data provided by its statistical office are directly used. As for the *European regions* panel, the HDI is adapted due to unavailability of detailed data at the regional level. Education will be measured by the percentage of population aged 25–64 with upper secondary or tertiary[2] education attainment. This appears to be the most useful proxy for measuring the level of formal education for the European regions, where the overall completion of the primary and secondary education has been achieved for some time. To identify goalposts, I employed the maximum and minimum values of the period considered (2000–2012), since it was not possible to employ the ones defined by the UNDP for country indices. This method was used in the first issues of HDRs, from inception until 1993. On the other hand, the averages, the intermediate indices and final indicator were developed by using the methodology of the 2015 report (UNDP, 2015), as presented previously.

To avoid false correlations when comparing indices, I employed a type of HDI that I name HDI★, (that excludes the income component). Another benefit of this adaptation is that it allows us to isolate the 'investment in people' component of the index and facilitates the comparison with levels and variations in per capita income.

### b. Innovation capacity index

This index was developed following a methodology defined by Archibugi and Coco (2004), similar to that applied by UNDP in 2001 HDR, as discussed in Chapter 4. It is based on the three main components of technological capabilities:

A  creation of technology;
B  technological infrastructures; and
C  development of human skills.

The authors developed two indicators for the first component, while the second and third each have three. Thus, the eight sub-indices are as follows:

(A1)  patents;
(A2)  scientific articles;
(B1)  internet penetration;
(B2)  telephone penetration;
(B3)  electricity consumption;
(C1)  tertiary science and engineering enrolment;
(C2)  mean years of schooling;
(C3)  literacy rate.

However imperfect (Capriati, 2013), the *number of patent applications* is an important and widely used measure of codified knowledge generation. Unlike Archibugi and Coco's (ArCo) approach, which uses the number of patents registered by the USPO in the United States, the current study uses the number of patents filed under the Patent Co-operation Treaty (PCT). The PCT, an international treaty administered by WIPO, facilitates the acquisition of patent rights in a large number of jurisdictions. The PCT system simplifies the process of multiple national patent filings by reducing the requirements to file a separate application in each jurisdiction. This approach allows to reduce distortions arising from choosing a single national or regional system, which leads to a larger number of requests from that country/region.

The *number of publications* taken into consideration by the study derives from the World Bank database that includes scientific and technical journal articles.

The scholars who developed the index that this study took as a reference (Archibugi and Coco, 2004) do not insert data on *R&D expenditure relative to GDP* due to the scarcity and unreliability of such data with regards to certain developing countries. The decision to build a database with developed or rapidly growing countries allows us to overcome this limitation.[3] Thus, a third subindex, i.e., 'creation of technology', was added to the first dimension, besides patents and publications, as well as the ratio between R&D expenditure and GDP.

With regards to the second dimension, 'technological infrastructures', the data used (source: the World Bank) are the same as those used by the study quoted above. The only difference introduced to the dimension was with regards to sub-index 'telephone penetration', to which the newer technology of the fixed (wired) broadband subscriptions (per 100 people) was added alongside the number of fixed and mobile subscription per 100 inhabitants. Both for the electric power consumption (kWh per capita) and the number of mobile and fixed telephone lines, logarithms were calculated. This was done because in both cases the technologies are well-established in a large number of countries, and the calculation of logarithms allows us to assume that the marginal contribution of an additional unit of these technologies to innovation decreases with an increase in the available infrastructure. With regards to the broadband, it has been added to the indicator without this correction, as it is a relatively new and less widespread technology.

The third dimension in the ArCo index, the 'development of human skills', is based on three indicators: (a) tertiary science and engineering enrolment, (b) mean years of schooling and (c) literacy rate. In the index calculated for countries, the second indicator will be retained, while the third will be replaced with Expected Years of Schooling (EYS) and the first with the School enrolment at tertiary level (% gross). The first replacement allows me to use data more homogeneous with the HDI, which replaced adult literacy rate with EYS in 2010. In the second case, on the other hand, the choice to use participation in overall university courses rather than more specific scientific and engineering disciplines as an indicator resulted from the availability of data, which was particularly limited for some countries for the period the study focused on.

Finally, another alteration concerns the methodology of aggregation: the three indices for each dimension will be aggregated through a geometric, rather than an arithmetic mean. The reason for choosing such strategy is the need to ensure an approach homogeneous to the one employed in building the HDI.

The Innovation Capacity Index at the regional level will only partially follow the technique used for its calculation at the national level, due to lower availability of data, particularly for certain regions and for a sufficiently extended period of time (the study covers the period 2000–2012). The data will not include sub-indices related to technological infrastructure. Eurostat provides data on the use of internet and broadband but the earliest available information dates only to 2006, and even so, the data are largely incomplete.

It was therefore decided to limit the index calculation to two dimensions at the regional level, i.e., to the creation of technology and the development of human skills.

For the first dimension, two indicators will be used: (a) number of patent applications at the EPO per one hundred thousand inhabitants and (b) R&D expenditure as a percentage of GDP.

For the second, the data from the two following sub-indices will be used:

a)  *Human Resources in Science and Technology (HRST)* as a percentage of the labour force[4] that includes graduates and non-graduates who are engaged in scientific and technological activities; this information was considered an adequate way of covering human skills of the highest quality.
b)  *The percentage of population aged 25–64 with completed upper secondary or tertiary[5] education.* This indicator has already been used to build the HDI at the regional level. It increases information on overall education, going beyond the purely scientific and technological activities that are measured by the previous indicator.

### c. Income

To measure income and material well-being in the considered geographical areas, the GNI (Gross National Income) was used for national analysis, and the GDP (Gross Domestic Product) was used at the regional level. In the first case, the data are adjusted for purchasing power parity. At the national level, a more accurate measure of the actual well-being enjoyed by residents of a country was preferred. As we know, the main difference between GNI and GDP is that the first does not include the income of non-residents who were paid in the country, but adds the income of residents outside the country. In particular, this balance is influenced by the profits of multinational companies as well as by financial returns. Normally, these incoming and outgoing income flows compensate each other and consequently, the differences between the two values are not significant, with the exception of those small countries whose tax policy favours the attraction of real and financial investments from abroad. In our sample, a significant difference between GNI and GDP (i.e., over 10%) is observed only in Ireland, the Czech Republic and Luxembourg.

### d. Performance indicators

In addition to the levels of the indices for human development, innovation and growth, we are interested in performance indicators that enable us to evaluate their change over time. In recent years, the problem with a careful selection of performance indicators for a group of countries emerged in particular with reference to the Millennium Development Goals (MDGs) and the need to make a proper assessment of the changes occurred since the signing of commitments by countries participating in the UN initiative. On this, see in particular Fukuda-Parr et al., 2013; Fukuda-Parr and Greenstein, 2010; Gidwitz et al., 2010; Rodriguez-Takeuchi et al., 2015. The progress of economic variables is conventionally measured by either the relative variation rate or the 'shortfall reduction'. As it is known, the relative variation rate refers to the variation of an indicator relative to the initial value, whereas the 'shortfall reduction' is calculated by the percentage reduction of the difference between the values at the beginning and the end of the period and a predetermined[6] maximum level. Since both methods assume linear trajectories in the mapping of variables, they may create distortions in the assessment of the countries' performance. These distortions can favour either developed or developing countries.

In fact, the most widely used measurement, the *percent variation*, inflates variations that occur starting from the low values, compared to those that occur starting from the highest values. Bringing, for example, life expectancy from 50 to 60 years in terms of percent variation means obtaining an improvement of 20%. The same variation in terms of absolute value, when calculated for moving life expectancy from 70 to 80 years, has a percentage value of 14%. However, starting from low values, the level of investment required to ensure acceptable living conditions is relatively low; conversely, efforts to improve an already high indicator are presumably more expensive and the simple percent variation of the index does not give due weight to these differences.

On the contrary, the alternative measure of variations across a time period, the *shortfall reduction*, gives more weight to the efforts made by developed countries: a country that starts at 90 with respect to an indicator that has a maximum value of 100 and progresses in the period of 5, has a variation of 50% when it is calculated following this method; a country that starts at 50 and achieves the same variation of 5, records an increase of 10%.

Another possible measurement of variations in economic variables is the 'deviation from fit', i.e., the deviation of a country from its expected performance given its initial level. This technique solves many of the major drawbacks of the previous two methods: in fact, it takes into account the point of departure of each country and the attained nonlinear progress. Following a more realistic hypothesis – that countries starting at different levels grow at different rates, this way of calculating variations is not fundamentally either in favour or against developing countries (Gidwitz et al., 2010; UNDP, 2010).

Following Rodriguez Takeuchi et al., 2015 of the Overseas Development Institute (ODI), a UK-based think tank, I developed a progress path that a country could expect to follow on the basis of a simple regression that predicts the final level for each indicator, for each country, taking into account its initial level.

Here, in order to account for possible non-linearities encountered along the progress path, I follow a data-driven approach by using fractional polynomials. This allows to select the best-fitting form among an extended family of curves and for each variable to behave in a more flexible way, in order to avoid having to impose any predetermined shape and ensuring a better fit to the data. Then, the deviation from fit for each country is computed as:

$$(I_t - I_{t-s})/(I^\star_t - I_{t-s})$$

Where $I$ is the considered index, $t$ is the final year of the considered time series (in our case 2012), $s$ the number of years that separates the initial and final year of the series (in our case 17 for panel 1 and 12 for panel 2), and the asterisk indicates the estimated value of the index following the method indicated above.

The used index is therefore equal to the ratio between (a) the difference between the actual final value and initial value for numerator, and (b) the difference between the expected final value (derived from the regression) and initial value for denominator. This ratio can be greater than 1 if the actual performance is better than expected, less than one if the performance is worse than expected, or equal to one if the expected and actual performance are equal. In rare cases, it can also have a negative value if within the considered period, the country finds itself worse than the starting level.

### e. Convergence and divergence indicators

Do the three dimensions analysed for the 40 countries and 266 regions tend to converge or to diverge over time? There is a vast literature that analyses convergence with regards to economic growth. Generally, in order to assess whether the gap between countries is shrinking or expanding over a period of time, we use computations which in practice show whether developing countries made more rapid progress than the developed ones. There are two main types of convergence (see Barro and Sala-i-Martin, 1992): the *beta convergence*, i.e., a negative relation between income growth and its initial level (see e.g., Mankiw et al, 1992; Sala-i-Martin, 1996; and Evans and Karras, 1997) and the *sigma convergence*, i.e., a reduced dispersion of the considered variable among countries with the progress of time (see e.g. Young et al., 2008). In the first case, the measure of variation employed is the average annual percentage variation, a strategy which, as discussed above, has many limitations. Because of this, it can be stated that a negative correlation between the initial level of income and its variation for a sample of countries with different levels of income per capita is statistically obvious. Although this measure of convergence is of little interest, it will be calculated for the sake of completeness. The information obtained from calculating the standard deviation, the sigma convergence, in my opinion appears to be more indicative. This measurement is not unduly affected by the initial level and allows us to follow the dispersion values year after year and track the underlying trends. As argued earlier, I chose a method for measuring performance over the time that does not depend on the starting level of the analysed variables, but rather on the distance from an estimated trend (deviation from fit). I am not aware of any method of calculating convergence associated to deviation from fit, so for this type of analysis

I will resort to traditional methods mentioned earlier, the sigma and beta convergence.

## A.3. Tables

*Table A.5* Per capita income, ICI and HDI in 40 countries, year 1995

| RANK | | GNI | | ICI | | HDI* |
|---|---|---|---|---|---|---|
| 1 | LU | 62400 | US | 0.508 | AU | 0.906 |
| 2 | NO | 49490 | SE | 0.506 | NZ | 0.869 |
| 3 | CH | 44318 | CA | 0.496 | US | 0.861 |
| 4 | US | 39079 | FI | 0.483 | CA | 0.859 |
| 5 | DK | 35694 | NO | 0.478 | NL | 0.847 |
| 6 | NL | 33626 | JP | 0.459 | SE | 0.845 |
| 7 | BE | 32810 | AU | 0.457 | NO | 0.845 |
| 8 | DE | 32643 | NZ | 0.443 | BE | 0.839 |
| 9 | AT | 32038 | IL | 0.440 | UK | 0.830 |
| 10 | JP | 31571 | CH | 0.434 | JP | 0.826 |
| 11 | IT | 31073 | NL | 0.417 | IL | 0.824 |
| 12 | FR | 30495 | UK | 0.415 | IS | 0.813 |
| 13 | CA | 30174 | DK | 0.409 | FI | 0.811 |
| 14 | AU | 29242 | IS | 0.389 | CH | 0.808 |
| 15 | SE | 28794 | DE | 0.381 | FR | 0.805 |
| 16 | IS | 27375 | FR | 0.378 | DE | 0.801 |
| 17 | UK | 26306 | BE | 0.375 | DK | 0.801 |
| 18 | FI | 25488 | KR | 0.374 | IE | 0.797 |
| 19 | ES | 25004 | AT | 0.338 | ES | 0.786 |
| 20 | NZ | 23441 | IE | 0.310 | KR | 0.785 |
| 21 | IE | 22819 | SI | 0.296 | AT | 0.781 |
| 22 | EL | 21545 | IT | 0.273 | SI | 0.779 |
| 23 | PT | 20935 | LU | 0.270 | CZ | 0.770 |
| 24 | IL | 20356 | ES | 0.263 | IT | 0.762 |
| 25 | CZ | 17622 | CZ | 0.262 | PL | 0.758 |
| 26 | SI | 16758 | SK | 0.254 | SK | 0.754 |
| 27 | KR | 16549 | RU | 0.232 | EL | 0.752 |
| 28 | HU | 14959 | HU | 0.231 | LU | 0.745 |
| 29 | SK | 13141 | EL | 0.210 | HU | 0.734 |
| 30 | CL | 12380 | PL | 0.208 | PT | 0.732 |
| 31 | RU | 11991 | PT | 0.186 | EE | 0.726 |
| 32 | MX | 11941 | EE | 0.184 | CL | 0.722 |
| 33 | TR | 11372 | ZA | 0.179 | RU | 0.684 |
| 34 | PL | 10725 | CL | 0.144 | MX | 0.645 |
| 35 | BR | 10602 | BR | 0.137 | ZA | 0.637 |
| 36 | EE | 10087 | MX | 0.098 | BR | 0.625 |
| 37 | ZA | 9139 | TR | 0.089 | CN | 0.581 |
| 38 | ID | 5593 | CN | 0.074 | TR | 0.555 |
| 39 | CN | 2460 | IN | 0.014 | ID | 0.545 |
| 40 | IN | 2087 | ID | 0.010 | IN | 0.458 |

*Table A.6* Differences in ranking position for 40 countries between 1995 and 2012

| | DIFF 2012–1995 | | |
|---|---|---|---|
| | *GNI* | *ICI* | *HDI** |
| AU | 3 | 5 | 0 |
| AT | 2 | 2 | −3 |
| BE | −5 | −2 | −15 |
| BR | −1 | −1 | 0 |
| CA | 3 | −11 | −8 |
| CL | −3 | −1 | 3 |
| CN | 1 | 5 | 0 |
| CZ | −2 | 2 | 4 |
| DK | −4 | 8 | 3 |
| EE | 7 | 10 | 5 |
| FI | 5 | 0 | −8 |
| FR | −2 | −5 | −3 |
| DE | 3 | 0 | 9 |
| EL | −3 | 1 | 2 |
| HU | −4 | −1 | −2 |
| IS | −2 | 7 | 6 |
| IN | 0 | 0 | 0 |
| ID | −1 | 0 | 1 |
| IE | 5 | 0 | 14 |
| IL | 1 | −2 | 1 |
| IT | −8 | −4 | 2 |
| JP | −5 | −4 | −6 |
| KR | 5 | 17 | 12 |
| LU | −1 | −2 | 0 |
| MX | −3 | −2 | 0 |
| NL | −2 | −2 | 0 |
| NZ | 0 | −4 | 0 |
| NO | 1 | −4 | 4 |
| PL | 3 | −1 | −2 |
| PT | −5 | 4 | −2 |
| RU | 1 | −3 | 0 |
| SK | 3 | −6 | −4 |
| SI | 2 | 5 | 7 |
| ZA | 0 | −4 | −4 |
| ES | −2 | 0 | −1 |
| SE | 9 | −6 | −11 |
| CH | 0 | 4 | 5 |
| TR | −1 | 3 | 3 |
| UK | 0 | −6 | −4 |
| US | 0 | −2 | −8 |

## A.4. Details about empirical analysis

### *a. Virtuous circles analysis*

The system in (1) Chapter 6 could have not been consistently estimated equation-by-equation using standard Ordinary Least Squares (OLS). Indeed, the disturbance is correlated with the endogenous variables, which violates the assumptions of OLS. Moreover, because some of the explanatory variables are the dependent variables of other equations in the system, the error terms among the equations are expected to be correlated. Rather, the Three-stage Least Squares (3SLS) method chosen uses an instrumental-variables approach to produce consistent estimates and Generalised Least Squares (GLS) to account for the correlation structure in the disturbances across the equations. More in detail, it can be thought as producing estimates from a three-step process:

1. In the first step, which is critical for the consistency of the parameter estimates, the instrumented values for all endogenous variables are developed. These can simply be considered as the predicted values resulting from a regression of each endogenous variable on all exogenous variables in the system;
2. In the second step, a consistent estimate for the covariance matrix of the equation disturbances is obtained, based on the residuals from a 2SLS estimation of each structural equation;
3. In the third step, a GLS-type estimation is performed using the covariance matrix estimated in the second stage and with the instrumented values in place of the right-hand-side endogenous variables.

### *b. Spatial analysis*

When the analysis is carried out at the level of regions (panel 2), the spatial dimension becomes of uttermost importance. Indeed, it becomes harder to justify the assumption that Income, Innovation and Human Development values are independent across regions, since correlation in this case is likely to be present not only between regions in the same country (due to common country-specific shocks), but also between adjacent regions in the same or in different countries (because of trade and spillovers). It follows that, at the regional level, spillovers enhanced by spatial proximity must be taken into account, which requires relying on a spatial approach. In this approach, it is assumed that the structure of cross-sectional correlation is related to the location and proximity among units, which are thus defined according to a pre-specified metric given by a weight matrix characterising the pattern of spatial dependence (Anselin, 1988 and 1999; Pesaran, 2004; Lee and Yu, 2010). Clearly, proximity can be defined not only in terms of physical space, but also with respect to other types of metrics, such as economic, political or social distance (Conley, 1999; Conley and Topa, 2002; Pesaran, Schuermann and Weiner, 2004).

Therefore, the SAR (spatial autoregressive or spatial lag) model has been tested in order to take into account whether Income, Innovation or Human Development performances of a given region can be affected by the values of the same variables in other adjacent regions. To assure the consistency of the results, first alternative specifications have been tested using simple OLS, thus without taking into account spatial effects ($\rho=0$). Then, by using the outlined weighting scheme ($W^{5n}$), the appropriate Moran's I test on OLS residuals has been performed to get preliminary evidence of spatial dependence. Indeed, the Moran's I statistic for residuals is the most commonly employed first-step specification test for spatial autocorrelation: basically, it tests whether the attribute values of features are dependent on those at other locations. Its interpretation is parallel to a correlation coefficient (although its values are not bounded by the -1, +1 interval): a positive and significant value for this test signals a positive spatial dependence, namely the occurrence of similar levels of a variable over nearby regions; on the contrary, a negative value signals negative spatial dependence, that is the joint occurrence of low- and high-attribute values over neighbouring units (Moran, 1950; Anselin, 1999). In addition, since the Moran's I test does not specify which spatial model is more appropriate, the robust and non-robust tests based on the Lagrange Multiplier have been performed for both spatial lag and spatial error dependence in OLS residuals (see results in Table A.7 below).

As expected, the Moran's I test proves that a positive spatial dependence exists: indeed, a p-value lower than 0.01 in all specifications leads to reject the null hypothesis of no spatial autocorrelation in the residuals. This supports that in order to get unbiased and consistent estimates, spatial models should be employed instead of non-spatial OLS estimations.

The LM-SEM tests the null hypothesis of no spatial autocorrelation in the error terms, whereas the LM-SAR tests the null hypothesis of no significant spatial autocorrelation in the dependent variable. As suggested by Florax and

*Table A.7* Spatial diagnostics (computed on OLS residuals)

|  | (1) | (2) | (3) | (4) | (5) | (6) |
|---|---|---|---|---|---|---|
| Moran's I | 403.814 | 339.526 | 212.851 | 175.009 | 81.722 | 296.478 |
|  | (0.000) | (0.000) | (0.000) | (0.000) | (0.000) | (0.000) |
| LM SAR | 205.072 | 258.965 | 35.081 | 2.141 | 56.139 | 5.745 |
|  | (0.000) | (0.000) | (0.000) | (0.143) | (0.000) | (0.017) |
| LM SEM | 467.111 | 330.240 | 129.429 | 87.715 | 19.068 | 252.114 |
|  | (0.000) | (0.000) | (0.000) | (0.000) | (0.000) | (0.000) |
| RLM SAR | 180.337 | 232.337 | 1.879 | 6.513 | 37.174 | 31.034 |
|  | (0.000) | (0.000) | (0.170) | (0.011) | (0.000) | (0.000) |
| RLM SEM | 442.375 | 303.611 | 96.227 | 92.087 | 0.103 | 277.404 |
|  | (0.000) | (0.000) | (0.000) | (0.000) | (0.748) | (0.000) |

p-Value in brackets

Table A.8 OLS estimates results

| Explanatory variables | Dependent variables | | | | | |
| --- | --- | --- | --- | --- | --- | --- |
| | Income | | Innovation | | Human Development | |
| | (1) | (2) | (3) | (4) | (5) | (6) |
| Income$_{t-1}$ | 0.4581*** | | 0.9202*** | | | |
| | (0.0257) | | (0.0183) | | | |
| Innovation$_{t-1}$ | | | | | 0.3781*** | 0.1599*** |
| | | | | | (0.0097) | (0.0039) |
| Human Development$_{t-1}$ | | 0.5831*** | | 1.2316*** | | |
| | | (0.1718) | | (0.3565) | | |
| Poverty | -0.2134*** | -0.4023*** | -0.0668*** | -0.7918*** | 0.0992*** | 0.0062 |
| | (0.0216) | (0.0232) | (0.0215) | (0.0672) | (0.0092) | (0.0092) |
| School Leave | 0.1696*** | 0.2478*** | -0.2288*** | 0.2948*** | -0.2441*** | -0.1316*** |
| | (0.0120) | (0.0340) | (0.0199) | (0.0466) | (0.0116) | (0.0083) |
| Gender Equality | -0.4146*** | -0.0037 | 1.1658*** | 1.4369*** | 0.2272*** | -0.1084*** |
| | (0.0558) | (0.0618) | (0.0651) | (0.1372) | (0.0256) | (0.0273) |
| Fixed Investments$_{t-1}$ | -0.0068 | -0.1787*** | | -0.8386*** | | |
| | (0.0344) | (0.0485) | | (0.0959) | | |
| Constant | 10.8194*** | 11.2402*** | -9.8155*** | 2.1152*** | -3.8082*** | 0.2660*** |
| | (0.1082) | (0.1828) | (0.2070) | (0.3566) | (0.1026) | (0.0244) |
| N Obs. | 3192 | 3192 | 3192 | 3192 | 3192 | 3192 |
| Cross sections | 266 | 266 | 266 | 266 | 266 | 266 |
| R-squared | 0.5346 | 0.3891 | 0.6258 | 0.4437 | 0.6119 | 0.5920 |

Robust standard errors in brackets; * p < 0.1, ** p < 0.05, *** p < 0.01

Table A.9 Variables used in this study (Panel 1)

| Variables | Mean | Standard Deviation | | | Min. | Max. | Obs. | Cross Sections |
|---|---|---|---|---|---|---|---|---|
| | | Total | Between | Within | | | | |
| Income | 28471.75 | 14589.33 | 14382.09 | 3300.73 | 2087.48 | 81441.30 | 720 | 40 |
| Innovation★ | 0.46 | 0.23 | 0.21 | 0.10 | 0.00 | 1.00 | 720 | 40 |
| Innovation | 0.41 | 0.18 | 0.17 | 0.07 | 0.01 | 0.81 | 720 | 40 |
| Human Development★ | 0.81 | 0.10 | 0.09 | 0.03 | 0.46 | 0.97 | 720 | 40 |
| Human Development | 0.81 | 0.09 | 0.09 | 0.03 | 0.46 | 0.94 | 720 | 40 |
| Democracy | 0.71 | 0.19 | 0.18 | 0.06 | 0.00 | 1.00 | 720 | 40 |
| Transparency | 6.43 | 2.23 | 2.20 | 0.46 | 1.70 | 10.00 | 720 | 40 |
| Income Inequality | 0.34 | 0.09 | 0.09 | 0.02 | 0.21 | 0.67 | 720 | 40 |
| Gender Equality | 0.72 | 0.13 | 0.12 | 0.04 | 0.33 | 0.92 | 720 | 40 |
| Employment | 55.80 | 7.31 | 7.11 | 2.01 | 38.60 | 75.10 | 720 | 40 |
| Social Expenditure | 10.42 | 3.10 | 2.97 | 0.99 | 1.70 | 18.50 | 720 | 40 |

Table A.10 Variables used in this study (Panel 2)

| Variables | Mean | Standard Deviation | | | Min. | Max. | Obs. | Cross Sections |
|---|---|---|---|---|---|---|---|---|
| | | Total | Between | Within | | | | |
| Income | 22121.84 | 8846.35 | 8500.89 | 2498.70 | 3400.00 | 85900.00 | 3458 | 266 |
| Innovation | 0.10 | 0.09 | 0.09 | 0.02 | 0.00 | 0.61 | 3458 | 266 |
| Innovation* | 0.21 | 0.12 | 0.12 | 0.02 | 0.00 | 0.63 | 3458 | 266 |
| Human Development | 0.64 | 0.14 | 0.13 | 0.06 | 0.00 | 0.89 | 3458 | 266 |
| Human Development* | 0.63 | 0.13 | 0.12 | 0.05 | 0.00 | 0.92 | 3458 | 266 |
| Poverty | 17.08 | 7.00 | 6.77 | 1.83 | 0.21 | 50.09 | 3458 | 266 |
| School Leave | 15.08 | 8.42 | 7.89 | 2.98 | 1.40 | 58.80 | 3458 | 266 |
| Gender Equality | 0.81 | 0.11 | 0.10 | 0.04 | 0.38 | 1.12 | 3458 | 266 |
| Fixed Investments | 21.08 | 5.08 | 4.11 | 3.00 | 7.94 | 53.45 | 3458 | 266 |

Table A.11 Matrix of correlations (Panel 1)

| Variables | Income | Innovation* | Innovation | Human Development* | Human Development | Democracy | Ttransparency | Income Inequality | Gender Equality | Employment | Social Expenditure |
|---|---|---|---|---|---|---|---|---|---|---|---|
| Income | 1.0000 | | | | | | | | | | |
| Innovation* | 0.7373 | 1.0000 | | | | | | | | | |
| Innovation | 0.7080 | 0.9498 | 1.0000 | | | | | | | | |
| Human Development* | 0.7050 | 0.7942 | 0.8791 | 1.0000 | | | | | | | |
| Human Development | 0.8002 | 0.8111 | 0.8759 | 0.9812 | 1.0000 | | | | | | |
| Democracy | 0.7114 | 0.6969 | 0.6880 | 0.7193 | 0.7602 | 1.0000 | | | | | |
| Transparency | 0.4045 | 0.5984 | 0.6001 | 0.4995 | 0.5261 | 0.4893 | 1.0000 | | | | |
| Income Inequality | -0.5187 | -0.5112 | -0.5107 | -0.5498 | -0.5503 | -0.5248 | -0.1877 | 1.0000 | | | |
| Gender Equality | 0.4071 | 0.6449 | 0.6766 | 0.6073 | 0.5737 | 0.3499 | 0.3298 | -0.3906 | 1.0000 | | |
| Employment | 0.2662 | 0.304 | 0.2821 | 0.1593 | 0.1193 | 0.0679 | 0.206 | -0.1469 | 0.4522 | 1 | |
| Social Expenditure | 0.6985 | 0.7562 | 0.7638 | 0.7388 | 0.777 | 0.7767 | 0.4852 | -0.5044 | 0.6282 | 0.0853 | 1 |

Note: all correlations are significant at 1% level

Table A.12 Matrix of correlations (Panel 2)

| Variables | Income | Innovation★ | Innovation | Human Development★ | Human Development | Poverty | School Leave | Gender Equality | Fixed Investments |
|---|---|---|---|---|---|---|---|---|---|
| Income | 1.0000 | | | | | | | | |
| Innovation★ | 0.5120 | 1.0000 | | | | | | | |
| Innovation | 0.5985 | 0.9577 | 1.0000 | | | | | | |
| Human Development★ | 0.5661 | 0.5462 | 0.6989 | 1.0000 | | | | | |
| Human Development | 0.7455 | 0.5905 | 0.7347 | 0.9576 | 1.0000 | | | | |
| Poverty | −0.3229 | −0.3566 | −0.4142 | −0.3568 | −0.4029 | 1.0000 | | | |
| School Leave | −0.1302 | −0.2464 | −0.3726 | −0.6065 | −0.4837 | 0.3778 | 1.0000 | | |
| Gender Equality | 0.1837 | 0.3312 | 0.4384 | 0.4310 | 0.3537 | −0.3382 | −0.4600 | 1.0000 | |
| Fixed Investments | −0.2057 | −0.2719 | −0.3079 | −0.3021 | −0.2675 | −0.0272 | 0.2140 | −0.2672 | 1.0000 |

Note: all correlations are significant at 1% level

Nijkamp (2003), if both hypotheses can be rejected, one should consider the robust forms of these LM tests (i.e., RLM-SEM and RLM-SAR).[7] It is clear that, only in two specifications (4 and 6) the p-value of the LM test is lower for the spatial error model, thus indicating that this should be the model preferred for estimation; whilst in specification 5 the p-value of the LM robust test is lower for the spatial lag model, and therefore should be more appropriate; in all other specifications, both hypotheses of the spatial autoregressive and spatial error model can be rejected.

Hence, since the primary goal of this analysis is to study spillover effects between close regions, while the SEM does not account for spillovers, a SAR model has been used to test all the specifications. Moreover, it is worth recalling that, as pointed out by the econometric literature, the cost of ignoring spatial dependence in the dependent variable is relatively higher than ignoring spatial dependence in the disturbances (LeSage and Pace, 2009; Elhorst, 2010): indeed, if one or more relevant explanatory variables are omitted from a regression equation, the estimator of the coefficients for the remaining variables is biased and inconsistent (Green, 2002, pp. 133–134); in contrast, ignoring spatial dependence in the disturbances will only cause loss of efficiency.

Table A.8 presents simple OLS results (when spatial effects are not considered, $\rho = 0$) for completeness.

As for the estimation method, the ML procedure has been applied, since it does not require reliable instruments and given that there is no established technique to estimate a dynamic spatial model (see Lee and Yu, 2010; Elhorst, 2010 and Elhorst et al., 2010). Indeed, whilst econometric analysis of dynamic panel models as well as spatial econometrics (for both cross-sections and static panels) are now well developed and documented, econometric analysis of dynamic and spatial models are still at an early stage, since modelling space-time data is quite complex and requires tackling several problems. It is also worth noting that in models including a spatial lag of the dependent variable, the interpretation of the parameter estimates needs to be carried out with caution, considering the direct, indirect and total effects' estimates of the independent variables (LeSage and Pace, 2009).

## A.5. Descriptive statistics

Some descriptive statistics are displayed in Tables A.9 and A.10. Further, Tables A.11 and A.12 also report the correlation matrices between the variables relevant to the regression analysis.

All statistics are computed on the variables taken prior to log transformation. Note that Innovation* means that the education dimension has been excluded from the computation of this index, whereas Human Development* does not include the income component.

As displayed by the above tables, there is quite a high correlation between the variables employed in both panel datasets, especially between the indicators of main interest (i.e., Income, Innovation and Human Development). Obviously, for any interpretative purpose, the reader must refer to the results from the regression analysis above.

## Notes

1 Latvia is missing from the study, as it joined only recently the organisation, thus having no available data for the period considered.
2 Upper secondary, post-secondary non-tertiary, first and second stage of tertiary education (levels 3–6).
3 The data are available in almost all countries and for almost all years. In the case of some countries (Brazil, India, Indonesia, Chile and South Africa), the missing data were estimated using linear interpolations based on available statistics.
4 Persons with tertiary education (ISCED) and/or employed in science and technology. Human Resources in Science and Technology (HRST) are people who fulfil one or other of the following conditions:

   • successfully completed education at the third level in an S&T field of study
   • not formally qualified as above but employed in an S&T occupation where the above qualifications are normally required.

5 Upper secondary, post-secondary non-tertiary, first and second stage of tertiary education (levels 3–6)
6 It is based on the following relationship:

$$[(MAX - y_{t-1}) - (MAX - y_t)]/ (MAX - y_{t-1}) \star 100 \tag{1}$$

After the appropriate changes equation (1) can be simplified to:

$$(y_t - y_{t-1})/(MAX - y_{t-1}) \star 100.$$

Where MAX indicates the maximum final result. To remind ourselves – in our indices, the highest level corresponds to the highest value that a country reaches in the period considered.
7 The RLM-SER and RLM-SAR are indicated as robust because they take into account the potential presence of a spatial lag when testing for the presence of spatially correlated errors or *vice versa*, spatially correlated errors when testing the spatial lag (see Anselin et al, 1996).

## References

Anand, S. and Sen, A. 2000. The Income Component of the Human Development Index, *Journal of Human Development and Capabilities*, 1(1), 83–106.

Anselin, L. 1988. *Spatial Econometrics: Methods and Models*, The Netherlands, Dordrecht, Kluwer Academic Publishers.

Anselin, L. 1999. *Spatial Econometrics*, Dallas, Bruton Center School of Social Sciences University of Texas.

Anselin, L., Bera, A.K., Florax, R. and Yoon, M.J. 1996. Simple Diagnostic Tests for Spatial Dependence, *Regional Science and Urban Economics*, 26, 77–104.

Archibugi, D. and Coco, A. 2004. A New Indicator of Technological Capabilities for Developed and Developing Countries (ArCo), *World Development*, 32(4), 629–654.

Barro, R. and Lee, J. 2013. A New Data Set of Educational Attainment in the World, 1950-2010, *Journal of Development Economics*, 104, 184–98.

Barro, R.J. and Sala-i-Martin, X. 1992. Convergence, *Journal of Political Economy*, 100(2), 223–251.

Capriati, M. 2013. Indicatori di innovazione a livello territoriale (Innovation Indicators at territorial level), *L'industria*, 1, 61–92.

Conley, T.G. 1999. GMM Estimation With Cross Sectional Dependence, *Journal of Econometrics*, 92, 1–45.

Conley, T.G. and Topa, G. 2002. Socio-Economic Distance and Spatial Patterns in Unemployment, *Journal of Applied Econometrics*, 17, 303–327.

Elhorst, J.P. 2010. Applied Spatial Econometrics: Raising the Bar, *Spatial Economic Analysis*, 5(1), 9–28.

Elhorst, J.P., Piras, G. and Arbia, G. 2010. Growth and Convergence in a Multiregional Model With Space – Time Dynamics, *Geographical Analysis*, 42(3), 338–355.

Evans, P. and Karras, G. 1997. International Integration of Capital Markets and the Cross-Country Divergence of Per Capita Consumption, *Journal of International Money and Finance*, 16(5), 681–697.

Florax, R.J. and Nijkamp, P. 2003. *Misspecification in Linear Spatial Regression Models*, Discussion Papers No. 2003–081/3, Tinbergen Institute.

Fukuda-Parr, S. and Greenstein, J. 2010. *How Should MDG Implementation Be Measured: Faster Progress Or Meeting Targets?* International Policy Centre for Inclusive Growth (IPC – IG), Working Paper Number 63.

Fukuda-Parr, S., Greenstein, J. and Stewart, D. 2013, How Should MDG Success and Failure Be Judged: Faster Progress or Achieving the Targets, *World Development*, 41, 19–30.

Gidwitz, Z., Heger, M.P., Pineda, J. and Rodríguez, F. 2010. *Understanding Performance in Human Development: A Cross-National Study*. Human Development Research Paper 42, New York, UNDP.

Green, W.H. 2002. *Econometric Analysis*, 5th edition. Upper Saddle River, NJ, Pearson Prentice Hall.

LaSage, J.P. and Pace, K.R. 2009. *Introduction to Spatial Econometrics*, London, New York, Taylor and Francis.

Lee, L.F. and Yu, J. 2010. Estimation of Spatial Autoregressive Panel Data Models With Fixed Effects, *Journal of Econometrics*, 154(2), 165–185.

Mankiw, N.G., Romer, D. and Weil, D.N. 1992. A Contribution to the Empirics of Economic Growth, *The Quarterly Journal of Economics*, 107(2), 407–437.

Moran, P.A.P. 1950. Notes on Continuous Stochastic Phenomena, *Biometrika*, 37(1), 17–23.

Pemstein, D., Meserve, S.A. and Melton J. 2010. Democratic Compromise: A Latent Variable Analysis of Ten Measures of Regime Type, *Political Analysis Advance*, 18(4), 1–24.

Pesaran, M.H. 2004. *General Diagnostic Tests for Cross Section Dependence in Panels*, CESifo Working Paper Series No. 1229 and IZA Discussion Paper No. 1240.

Pesaran, M.H., Schuermann, T. and Weiner, S. 2004. Modelling Regional Interdependencies Using a Global Error-Correcting Macroeconometric Model, *Journal of Business and Economics Statistics*, 22, 129–162.

Ranis G., Stewart F., Ramirez A. 2000. Economic Growth and Human Development, *World Development*, 28(2), 197–219.

Rodriguez Takeuchi, L., Samman, E. and Steer, L. 2015. *Patterns of Progress on the MDGs and Implications for Target Setting Post-2015*, Overseas Development Institute, Report n. 1.

Sala-i-Martin, X. 1996. Regional Cohesion: Evidence and Theories of Regional Growth and Convergence, *European Economic Review*, 40(6), 1325–1352.

UNDP (United Nations Development Programme) 1990. *Human Development Report 1990*, Oxford, Oxford University Press.

UNDP (United Nations Development Programme) 2010. *Human Development Report 2010: The Real Wealth of Nations: Pathways to Human Development*, New York, UNDP.

UNDP (United Nations Development Programme) 2015. *Human Development Report 2015: Work for Human Development*, Oxford, Oxford University Press.

Young, A. T., Higgins, M. and Levy, D. 2008. Sigma Convergence Versus Beta Convergence: Evidence From U.S. County-Level Data, *Journal of Money, Credit and Banking*, 40(5), 1083–1093.

# Index

Note: Numbers in italics denote figures or tables

For Product Safety Concerns and Information please contact our EU
representative  GPSR@taylorandfrancis.com
Taylor & Francis Verlag GmbH, Kaufingerstraße 24, 80331 München, Germany